AF557823

Journeys with God

Volume 1 of 3

Journeys with God

Belief, Faith
and Trust

Volume 1 of 3

MANOJ NAKRA

RUPA

Published by
Rupa Publications India Pvt. Ltd 2024
7/16, Ansari Road, Daryaganj
New Delhi 110002

Sales centres:
Bengaluru Chennai Hyderabad
Jaipur Kathmandu Kolkata
Mumbai Prayagraj

P-ISBN: 978-93-6156-004-0
E-ISBN: 978-93-6156-480-2

First impression 2024

10 9 8 7 6 5 4 3 2 1

Printed in India

Of Him,
from Him,
by Him,
for Him
and
to Him

CONTENTS

BOOK IS A SELF-TEST

Ramadas had gathered a large number of Palmyra leaves. On each leaf, he had written songs of devotion in his style to Rama. One day, when his eyes fell on the heap, a thought crossed his mind, 'Did I compose these songs for my pleasure or to please Rama?' He wanted to know which of his songs of worship had pleased Rama and decided to throw away the rest. So he flung the whole bundle into the Godavari River, praying that Rama would save the songs He approved of. Almost the entire lot sank to the depths of the river; only 108 floated on the water and were recovered. These 108 songs had arisen from the heart; the rest were tainted by cleverness, artificiality, punditry and pedantry.[1]

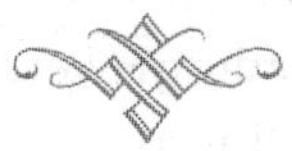

PREFACE

BACKGROUND

I first saw Swami or Sathya Sai Baba[1] in 1972 as a 17-year-old school student. Later, in the mid-seventies, Swami gave me the unique opportunity of spending over four years in His proximity in Brindavan.[2] The 50 years I have spent with Him have been an incredible spiritual journey for me. He has been at the centre of my life. My personality, mindset, motivations, reactions to happenings around me and perspective on life are the inevitable outcomes of my association with Him.

This book is a result of the events that took place over time. They seemed unrelated when they occurred but fit together like a jigsaw puzzle, in retrospect.

I lived in the US from 2001 to 2004, where I learned ethnography[3] as part of my doctoral work. Ethnography is a research method used in social and behavioural sciences to understand how people live, behave, think and interact in the social or work context.

I participated in study circles[4] in the US, listening to people share their experiences with Swami, which allowed me to reflect on the same.

Then, I discovered something meaningful had occurred in my association with Swami. He had been doing what He has always professed, guiding and nudging me on my spiritual journey. I was never alone. He had been accompanying me. The diverse experiences with Swami over the years were connected. Each discrete adventure had been Swami's manifestation at work. The events, their lessons and their meanings appeared engineered. Nothing had been coincidental. Every experience was intentional, like an artist's brushstrokes or the blows of a sculptor's tool before the artwork is ready.

That feeling prompted me to read the narratives of personal

experiences with God. My readings were unplanned. I leafed through material from all religious traditions. I reviewed transcripts of speeches and watched videos featuring individuals sharing their encounters with Swami. Additionally, I interviewed people who had extensive interactions with Swami and recorded these conversations. My next step was to seek approval for the interview transcripts from the interviewees.

I chose passages that deeply resonated with me from the books and transcripts. My selection criteria focused on narratives that conveyed personal, reflective and spontaneous responses to God and were free from the influence of individuals' opinions. The passages had to be grounded in experience; opinions were unacceptable and excluded. If a person narrated a story about another person's experience, I triangulated[5] it with a third person to remove possible exaggeration.

I then organized the extracts into themes. I visualized the many folders with topic labels; each folder had many text files.

WORK THAT RESEMBLES MY METHODOLOGY

Early in my readings, I came across two books whose authors had traversed a similar intellectual journey. William James was an American philosopher, psychologist and physician who worked at Harvard University. He wrote a classic book on religious experiences called *The Varieties of Religious Experience*[6] in 1902. Evelyn Underhill was an English poet and author. In 1911, she authored a groundbreaking work on spirituality called *Mysticism*.[7] In this book, she characterized religion as a 'practical' expression of one's spiritual devotion to God. Both authors substantiated their insights using the personal accounts of spiritual aspirants or seekers.[8] They draw attention to two ideas. First, a devotee's experiences validate and strengthen their relationship with God. Second, this connection with God matures over time. Both books cover significant ground for a lay researcher and can be deemed comprehensive. Furthermore, I believe these concepts are universally applicable and appropriate for individuals of various religious backgrounds and experiences with God. As I read more, I realized their work substantiated and reinforced my emerging observations.

I have detailed the background of the project, outlining the procedures I employed to identify, select, process and analyse information that ultimately shaped this book. This is to demonstrate that the process adheres to a research methodology, enabling you to assess the method's validity and reliability.

In this book, I am not creating new knowledge, but I have recognized a new pattern in existing information. The ideas in *Journeys with God* developed intuitively. The explanation is ex post facto.

SPIRITUAL JOURNEYS WITH GOD

I had started the exercise with an intuition that diverse individual experiences had similarities. I discovered a universality in religious experiences. My initial classification involved three categories: belief, faith and trust. I define the terms as used in the book later. Upon further analysis of the excerpts, I identified more refined sub-categories that suggested a sequential process with a series of steps. For example, below are the categorized narratives related to belief:

- Appearance of belief: labelled as Belief as Awakening
- Beginning the pursuit of God: labelled as Spiritual Quest
- Preparation to meet God: labelled as Being Ready for God
- Experience of meeting God: labelled as Face to Face with God
- Being with God: labelled as Love Beyond Measure
- Humility and acceptance of God: labelled as Acceptance and Action

The sub-categories' labels became the chapter headings for the book.

My reflections on my experiences with Swami have guided the work. They mirrored the diverse spiritual journeys people have undertaken throughout history across various religions, cultures and nations. As the work progressed, I began feeling like we were characters in a spiritual drama scripted and directed by God, who is relentless in pursuing His spiritual purpose—our transformation—irrespective of how much we falter, hesitate, resist, struggle or try to escape. These episodes with Swami are more tangible and animated than those recorded earlier.

Bill Aitken highlights how Swami has made extraordinary spiritual experiences accessible to everyone.

> The student of religion [...] trusting his own experiences of the spirit, no matter how modest that may be [...] calls for a more deeper individual response to the reality of the divine [...] as experienced spontaneously by the heart. The experience is not confined to extra-sensitive souls [...] but is enjoyed by ordinary people who respond to [...] the two Sai Baba figures with a heart full of love.[9]

TRANSFORMATION

Swami identifies the four stages of a devotee's spiritual relationship with God, which begins when a person is attracted to God via inexplicable occurrences or miracles. The attraction becomes an attachment, and the person commits to live a devout and righteous life. God then helps the devotees change or self-transform, inspiring them to see God in everyone and live a selfless life. Finally, they 'recognize and realize' God.

> The Divine must reveal itself largely shaped and modified by the nature of the times, the region and the cultural environment. The signs and wonders I manifest are given names that do not connote the purpose or effect. They can be called *chamathkara*, which leads to *samskara*, which in turn urges one towards *paropakara* and finally results in *sakshathkara*. *Chamathkara* is an act that attracts on account of its inexplicability. Rama's very name means 'He who pleases or causes delight.' Krishna means 'He who draws toward Himself (*Karshathithi-Krishna*).' This attribute of attraction is a characteristic of Divinity.
>
> Why does the Divine attract? It is to transform, reconstruct and reform—a process called *samskara*. What is the purpose of the reconstruction? To make a person useful for society, efface his ego and affirm the unity of all beings in God. The person who has undergone *samskara* becomes a humble servant of those who need help. This stage is *paropakara*. Service of

> this kind done with reverence and selflessness prepares man to realize the One that permeates the many. The last stage is *sakshathkara*. You must know this underlying urge in all as I do.
>
> Let us consider the *chamathkara*, acts that attract and cause wonder. You see a flower. You long to hold it in your hand only when its colour or fragrance is attractive. You enter the market and see heaps of fruits. If the fruits are unattractive, you have no urge to eat and benefit from them. Attraction is the very nature of the Divine.
>
> Once a person draws near, the process of *samskara* starts. Without this, man remains fallow and feeble. He has no dignity or personality. A worthless steel lump is transformed by skilful manipulation and reconstruction into a watch worth several hundred rupees; this results from *samskara*, a peaceful association.[10]

Swami clarifies the role of inexplicable occurrences or miracles in a person's spiritual development. He reveals that miracles are a means for God to attract a person, trigger reflection and encourage the person to ask existential questions. This is the first step in a person's spiritual journey with God. Swami distinguishes between a mere miracle and a transformative miracle, underscoring that an individual's transformation is the real miracle.

> The summer vacation had just ended. Some of the hostel students who had gone home had returned. One of the students, who had returned by train, had a vehement argument about Swami with people traveling on the train in the same compartment.
>
> We were with Swami in the 'safe room' in Brindavan. Swami looked at the boy and enquired about what had transpired on the train. The boy narrated the story of the passengers who had first asked him where he was studying. As soon as they heard that he was studying at Swami's college, they became critical of Swami. The boy added that he had responded to the criticism by defending Swami, citing the many miracles that he had seen.
>
> Swami then asked him, 'What did you tell them?'

The boy replied, 'Swami, I told them about seeing you materializing *vibhuti*,[11] creating rings, curing diseases, etc.'

As I listened to this dialogue, I strongly felt that all the miracles discussed were small, insignificant and not a true reflection of Swami's reality. Swami was beyond this small trivia.

Swami then asked a few other people in the room about his miracles, all of which alluded to different materializations, extraordinary events, cures, etc.

None of the answers were significant. They appeared to be 'diminishing' Swami. They were comparing the sun's brilliance to candlelight. Swami, it appeared, was waiting for the correct answer.

Suddenly, he said, 'You know what my greatest miracle is?' He added, not waiting for an answer, 'You all are my greatest miracle.'

I realized that our transformation is Swami's greatest miracle.[12]

BASIS OF THE BOOK

Journeys with God is not a philosophical treatise. It is my immersive take on the venture with the Divine. I was and am a participant undergoing similar experiences. The book's foundation lies in the evolution of an individual's interaction with God. The words of James succinctly capture the essence of the book.

> (It is a) Record (of) the inner experiences of persons wrestling with (their religious circumstances).[13]

I have attempted to paint a composite portrait of an aspirant's spiritual journey with God.

> A 'composite portrait' (is one) in which all the outstanding characteristics contributed by individual examples are present together.[14]

The diverse spiritual experiences of different people narrate a story of the transformation of man in the company of God. The metaphor that best describes this book is the preparation of a garland of different flowers. Each experience is a flower united by an unseen thread, the thematic classification of the incidents. When Swami's memoirs are compared with the accounts of spiritual experiences documented by seekers throughout history, a remarkable resemblance becomes evident. The excerpt from Underhill's book describes the savoir-faire.

> These experiences exhibit all the variety and spontaneous characteristics of life in its highest manifestations. Together, they constitute phases in a single growth process, involving the movement of consciousness from lower to higher levels of reality and the steady remaking of character.[15]

I recognized patterns in the spiritual experiences of different persons. Forging a coherent narrative requires a re-contextualization of the extracts. I have classified diverse experiences into patterns and avoided giving my opinions to ensure that the material is self-interpretive. Additionally, I have paraphrased some excerpts written in archaic language for easier reading.

> Conceptual processes can class facts, define and interpret them, but they do not produce them, nor can they reproduce their individuality.[16]

James used human experiences to depict and characterize a person's engagement with God and God's influence on the person's transformation. I follow a similar approach. The following excerpt vividly highlights this methodology:

> It brought about a Copernican revolution by looking at religion not as it appeared in the object (God or the universe or revelation) but in the subject (the believing, doubting, praying and experiencing person).[17]

I have shared the background and underpinnings of my work to explain the book's thematic structure. This is a book of narratives of people who have experienced God. All the people quoted in the book are real. The book's meaning lies in how I have structured and presented the experiential anecdotes. I have refrained from analysing the narratives and have taken care not to express my opinions. If my writing inadvertently implies otherwise, please disregard it. I am a spiritual participant rather than a philosopher, with no intention of endorsing any particular viewpoint. My objective is to share observations that caught my eye. The reflective work that became this book was transformative for me.

> Philosophy lives in words, but truth and fact well up into our lives in ways that exceed verbal formulation. There is in the living act of perception always something that glimmers and twinkles and will not be caught, and for which reflection comes too late.[18]

INTRODUCTION

THE STORY OF GOD AND MAN

Journeys with God is a story about God and His devotees. This is a compilation of first-person accounts detailing the experiences of individuals who have forged a connection with God. They were naturally drawn to Him and cultivated a deep and affectionate bond with God.

The story's premise is that a spiritual aspirant and God are like two people who meet, connect, engage and spend time together. An aspirant is an ordinary person who believes, prays and has doubts but may not possess a heightened spiritual sensibility, which develops during their association with God. The 'divine' is essential to their life, which underlies their active devotion to God. I use the word 'active' to distinguish it from a passive acceptance of religion. Religion, for them, is more than procedures and acceptance of prescriptive principles and habits. The words 'faith' and 'religiosity' capture the idea of a conscious and deliberate expression of religion. In a lay understanding of religious belief, individuals are expected to unquestioningly accept fundamental principles and lead morally upright lives. Belief positions a person as a petitioner who, after accepting and believing in God, awaits His grace and benevolence. Religiosity is about religious purpose and piety. This characterization centres on how individuals lead God-fearing lives. Their actions and thoughts are based on their belief as well as their spiritual experiences and contemplations. These factors contribute to their devotedness.

This book is a narration of a close relationship that a person shares with their God. Devotees do not engage with a distant God in their relationship with Him. When they accept God, He becomes real, accessible and their constant and close companion. A devotee engages with an omnipresent and omniscient God. God's continuous presence and the devotee's awareness of this presence bring about joy, vigilance and introspection. These, in turn, shape the individual's thoughts, attitudes and actions.

God's presence demands acceptance and reciprocity.

Devout people actively engage with God. They experience God responding to their prayers, and this engagement becomes a meaningful dialogue. A person's participation with the Divine comprises a series of interconnected experiences. Their every experience with God evokes feelings and triggers contemplation which, on reflection and interpretation, induces spiritual meaning for them. As the experiences with God are appraised over time, they evolve into a spiritual journey of personal development. Thus, the engagement with God is a journey for a person who initially thought God was a distant other but later realized His reality that He is close and accessible. A spiritual journey differs from a physical one in that it does not follow a linear path with milestones. Instead, it's an internal exploration wherein individuals grapple with their inner selves. Throughout this voyage, God remains immutable, whereas a person changes to realize the reality of God.

A person's remaking is a story of their engagement with God, which James characterizes as spiritual participation. When people accept and say yes to God, He becomes an immediate, ever-present reality for them.

> …the essential characteristic of religion […] (is) […] that it […] makes him (man) the actual partaker of […] infinite life. Whether we view religion from the human side or the divine—as the surrender of the soul to God, or as the life of God in the soul—in either aspect […] the Infinite has […] become a present reality. […] Oneness of mind and will with the divine […] is not the […] aim of religion, but its very beginning…[1]

THE BOOK IS ABOUT SATHYA SAI BABA

As I studied and analysed spiritual experiences, I discerned certain themes in people's diverse experiences. Their engagement with God is lively and interactive. God is responsive to the devotion of His devotees, who feel His reciprocity. The idea transformed into a book when I compiled the experiences of seekers/devotees with Sathya Sai Baba. They revealed a universality that James understood over a hundred years ago.[2]

Journeys with God is a construct, a medley of the spiritual experiences of diverse individuals (spanning various religious traditions) with Sathya Sai Baba. These experiences unveil the truth about one's connection with God, emphasizing that every individual can establish a relationship and connect with the divine. This affirms that the supreme being is nearer than one might think.

The similarity of devout experiences across religious traditions reinforces Sai's universality; it underlines the intensity, clarity and vividness of the understanding of His singularity.

The experiences with Sathya Sai Baba form the bedrock of the book. This book is, therefore, the story of Sri Sathya Sai Baba.

Swami describes the engagement of God with a person as a drama in which God plays many roles, such as that of an author, actor and director.

> Sai (Isa, God) [...] is the author, director, actor, witness, and appraiser of the Drama that is ever unfolding. [...] As Rama, Sai instructed, inspired, invigorated, corrected, consoled, and comforted His contemporaries...[3]

God collaborates with each person. The drama of one's connection with God is tailored to their unique spiritual context and state and unfolds within their mind. The drama's script comprises two distinct perspectives: one is the devotee's inner thoughts, emotions and actions in their relationship with God, and the second is their perception of God's response and consequent feelings and reflective thoughts. The script is a compilation of introspective monologues from the depths of an individual's heart. This means that participation with God intertwines these two perspectives.

Swami describes the nature and occurrence of the divine drama. God is the author and screenplay creator who knows the story before it begins. The enactment of the play is a slow revelation of the divine playwright's intent. God orchestrates the play to meet the spiritual needs of a person, and the drama progresses as the person learns to live with God. Every act of the play reflects their inner struggles, reactions and responses to God.

Only the actor understands the story after the drama ends. Swami highlights that the play reaches its conclusion when the devotees recognize their unity with God and understand that their life is, in essence, a divine play.

> When an author writes a play, the entire chronology is in his mind before he sets pen on paper. Take the case of the audience. They grasp the story only after the drama is entirely over. It unfolds itself scene by scene. For the Lord, this Drama, with its three Acts, the Past, the Present, and the Future, is crystal clear because He is Omniscient; His Plan is being worked out, and His Drama is being enacted on the stage of Creation. The entire play must be gone through for the story to reveal itself. Without a clear understanding of the play in which they enact their roles, people cling to the error that they are *Jivis*[4] or *Sadhakas*[5] buffeted by the waves of joy and sorrow. When the play is discovered as mere enactment, the conviction dawns that you are He, and He is you.[6]

This description of the divine drama by Swami is the book's synopsis.

The personal spiritual experiences, including those with Sathya Sai Baba, reveal a universal divine drama. When diverse experiences are collectively classified thematically, they portray God and His engagement with devotees as a universal divine drama. The interactions with Sathya Sai Baba make the divine drama with God unambiguous.

ENGAGEMENT WITH GOD AS A METAPHORICAL JOURNEY

Like a physical journey, a person's spiritual journey has a beginning, an end and milestones that mark progress. Turning toward or meeting God is the start of the spiritual journey after God reveals Himself in spiritual or supernatural self-disclosure. God enables a person's spiritual development under His vigilant watchfulness, protection and love. God accompanies his devotees on their spiritual exploration, but their progress is determined by their spiritual dedication and efforts. The mystic journey is invisible because it begins and ends within a person. Enlightenments are personal and only perceptible to the devotee. The power and influence of spiritual experiences are visible in the changes in the person. Their disposition, thinking and behaviours change. The milestones of a spiritual journey have three characteristics: the experiences, the moments or discernible points when some change happens (milestones) and tangible manifestations of changes in a person (outcomes).

James identified four characteristics of spiritual experiences:[7]

1. Spiritual experiences are intense, cannot be expressed in words and must be personally experienced.
2. Spiritual experiences also have a 'noetic' quality. They are pregnant with meaning and insights. The person undergoing the experience believes that a valuable thing was revealed to them.
3. Spiritual experiences are 'transitory'. They are experienced for a short time but are instantly recognized by the person when they recur.
4. The person having a spiritual experience feels that they are grasped by a great power. The impact of the experience transforms their life. Individuals undergoing a spiritual experience often feel as though they are seized or held by a potent force.

The reflective depictions of the spiritual experiences that I was examining exhibited identical defining traits as outlined by James.

Swami classified the spiritual development of a person into three phases. The first connection happens when they acknowledge and relate to God. The second stage begins when they are attracted to God and exercise earnest spiritual effort to be with Him. The third stage occurs when they realize that God is a perpetual, universal presence.

> In the same way, you can get some idea of what God is by listening to learned people or reading and studying the scriptures. But ultimately, you will not be satisfied with this because you and God remain separate at this stage. Therefore,

> you will attempt to go on to the next step, the deep aspiration to see and experience God directly. How can you get a vision of him? Picturing the form of God you heard described in your heart; continue thinking and contemplating on that form. You must become one with that sacred form, whatever you do, say, see and listen.
>
> The specific form of God you have pictured becomes a thought-form in your mind. The thought-form should then become saturated with the feeling of devotion so that it becomes a feeling-form in your heart. These feelings will gradually deepen and strengthen until one day, you will have a real vision of the Lord. So first, the Lord is heard of and thought of, then he is sought through intense feelings of devotion and yearning, and finally, he reveals himself in a clearly and personally experienced form. In other words, the thought-form becomes a feeling-form, transforming into an authentic experience. That describes the second stage on the path. You get the personal vision of the Lord, whom you have aspired to see, but you also will have the opportunity to converse with him face-to-face.
>
> You gain more satisfaction after seeing the Lord and talking with him directly. But if you are a true devotee, even this golden opportunity will not give you the complete joy you longed for. Now you want to reach God and merge with him. You think, 'I have heard, I have seen; now, I must reach him and be one with him.' In the first stage, when you know that God exists through reading and hearing, you feel that God is separate and you are separate. But in the second stage, you see the Lord and feel that you are part of him. Finally, you move on to the feeling, 'The Lord and I are the same.' Here you think, 'Either I must merge with him, or he must become one with me.' Then there is complete unity.[8]

This book is about these three stages as reflected in the experiences of a spiritual aspirant. There are two ways of looking at the engagement between God and a person. One is from the perspective of God—what He says and does. Two is from the devotee's standpoint, that is, how

God's actions are reflected in their experiences and narratives. This book attempts to present the loving participation of a person with God and God with the person and how God's love for the devotee manifests and is reflected in the person's attitudinal responses.

Incorporating the three components of my previous research, I have classified the three phases of an individual's spiritual journey with God as follows:

- Belief
- Faith
- Trust

Here, the word 'trust' carries a particular context or history.

I first understood and used trust as an operative word in the context of business in my doctoral thesis. Trust implies an unspoken attitude of confidence, acceptance and dependence on another person. Trust was a belief that influenced and defined relationships in an organizational setting.

The word surfaced once in an interview room with Swami. Swami turned around after shutting the door and said, 'Many people have faith in me, but very few trust me.' He distinguished between having faith and trusting God.

Over time, the difference between belief, faith and trust became vivid upon reflection.

I elaborate on the three words below.

BELIEF

A person needs a real and intuitive experience of God to develop belief and faith. People believe in God because they have encountered Him, seen His face, experienced His love and reciprocated His love.[9] The meeting with God is a tangible experience of the transcendent at a personal level. The experience with God is a turning point whereby a person is roused and motivated to seek the divine.

> That decisive event is the awakening of the transcendental consciousness.[10]

Belief in God is not an involuntary response to the spiritual experience. It wells up in a person when they 'resolve' to believe based upon contemplation of the religious experience and reflective intuition.[11] Devotion to God expresses the 'desire' to build a relationship with Him, which is valuable and vital.[12]

The experience of God is a turning point when fundamental changes occur and the person's life acquires new meaning. Underhill emphasizes the scale of the change as a mindset shift; a person's focus shifts from being self-centred to becoming centred on God, thereby transforming how they have lived their lives.

> (A person) is controlled by the deep-seated instincts of self-preservation and self-enlargement. (His world) is organized around his personality as a centre. (Belief) breaks in suddenly and becomes a revelation. The person emerges from a smaller and limited world of existence into a larger world of being. The emergence of intuitions, the consequent remaking, an alteration in the (person's) attitude to the world and the first emergence of (love and desire) for the Absolute constitute this distinctive character in its effect on every department of his life.[13]

FAITH

Faith is beyond belief. Faith manifests in deliberate spiritual endeavour and is not a passive acceptance of God. It changes the believer's life, who now desires a substantive and lasting association with God.

Faith is an expression of belief in action. Belief becomes faith when becoming aware of God transforms into a purposeful yearning to see and be with God. Faith is an active engagement of the entire person with the transcendent. It is not an opinion or compartmentalized intellectual idea.

Belief becomes faith when a person relates to God as someone who is near, accessible and reachable. God is not a remote concept but an integral part of a person's life. The seekers are always living with God and making Him the basis of their life. Faith manifests as love for God. The goal of life is to seek God, and living a spiritual life is the means.

Faith is a lively and enthusiastic attachment to God. James describes faith as passion that afflicts a person.[14] Metaphorically, it is a disease, albeit a good disease. A person who catches this God virus focuses on God using all his faculties.

James Fowler, an American theologian, writes that faith is a verb.[15] It is about having a connection with and building a relationship with God. He distinguishes belief from faith. Belief is about recognizing and accepting God. Faith is the manifestation of a desire to be with God. The passion for God is based on the seeker's spiritual determination, purpose and commitment. Fowler also identifies the comprehensive transformation that faith causes in a person. Outwardly, a person is the same. Faith changes their mindset. They see, feel, think and do things influenced by God.

Swami describes practical devotion. Faith is the first step in a spiritual journey. Practical faith manifests in spiritual activities inspired by a one-pointed desire to lead a spiritual life. Swami uses four keywords—steady, yearning, vigilant and mastery—to describe the working of faith.

> Unshakable faith (*Sraddha*) is the first step. You must yearn to imbibe (my) teachings. You must also be (ever) vigilant and not yield to sloth (spiritual laziness/giving up a spiritual purpose and intensity). Again, it would be best if you did not get entangled with bad company. Mastery over the senses is required to escape (overcome) the influence of such bad company. To do this, a person (has to) strengthen their mind. Do not admit doubt in yourself. The want of faith or steadiness is less destructive than the venom of doubt. (Doubt) is born in *ajnana* (ignorance), and it grows. (This) demon of doubt is destroyed with the sword of self-knowledge.[16]

Thomas á Kempis highlights the acute focus on only God as inherent to faith, the importance of attachment with God and a concurrent detachment from the world on a godly path. He identifies two ways of living a religious life: watchfulness and self-analysis.

> The desire for the knowledge of God, achievable by self-knowledge, depends on rejecting every interest external to the spirit and concentrating on the life within. To attain complete freedom from the world, old desires must be extinguished to make the person independent of natural instincts and emotions. Only by freeing himself from all that could distract him can a man wholeheartedly seek God, which means learning to dispense with the company of other people and not filling the mind with extraneous thoughts. The aspirant must learn to be alone (avoid company) and seek God's company. Progress in spiritual life cannot be made without an effort of the will. The follower (a devotee) must consciously adopt an attitude of continual watchfulness and self-examination.[17]

Swami delineates nine ways through which devotion to God can be expressed and cultivated. When devotees adore God, they see, think about and feel God in everything, thereby relating to God in every way they can through their thoughts, words and deeds and using their emotional energy to connect with God.

> The nine steps in a man's pilgrimage toward God along the path of dedication and surrender are (1.) developing a desire to listen to the glory and grandeur of the handiwork of God and the various awe-inspiring manifestations of divinity. This is the starting point. By hearing about the Lord, we can transform ourselves into divinity again and again. (2.) Singing oneself about the Lord in praise of his magnificence and various exploits. (3.) Dwelling on the Lord in mind and revelling in contemplating his beauty, majesty and compassion. (4.) Entering upon the Lord's worship by honouring the feet or footprints. (5.) This develops into a total propitiation of the Lord and systematic ritualistic worship, in which the aspirant gets inner satisfaction and inspiration. (6.) The aspirant begins to see the favourite form of God, which they like to worship, in all beings and objects, wherever he turns. So, he develops an attitude of Vandana or reverence toward nature and all life. (7.) Established in this bent of mind, he becomes the devoted servant of all,

with no sense of superiority or inferiority. This is a vital step that presages great spiritual success. (8.) This takes the seeker so near the Lord that he feels himself to be the confidant and comrade, the companion and friend, the sharer of God's power and pity, God's triumphs and achievements—his Sakha (friend) as Arjuna had become. (9.) As inferred, this is the prelude to the final step of total surrender or *Atma-nivedanam*: yielding fully to the will of the Lord, which the seeker knows through his purified intuition.[18]

TRUST

Trust is a stage beyond faith. Let us compare trust with belief and faith. The awareness and acknowledgment of God are the bases of belief. Faith is yearning for God. Trusting God is the unquestioned acceptance of and submission to God's will.

Belief is knowledge based on an intuitive perception; a person experiences God and realizes that God is real. Faith has an aspirational quality; a person desires a continuous engagement with God and is motivated and determined to exert spiritual effort to be with the divine.

Underhill highlights the idea that underpins trust and distinguishes it from faith. Faith involves seeking God. The person is with God. The person recognizes God's beauty, attributes and glory and submits himself. Trust involves becoming one with God. In the faith stage, a person desires to be with God. The gopis of Brindavan exemplify this. They enjoyed friendship and companionship with Lord Krishna and loved to be with Him. In the joy of being with God, the separation or distance from God is reinforced because the person who loves God is different from God, who is loved and revered. Experiences with Swami are movingly and inexplicably fascinating. These experiences capture all the attributes of spiritual encounters as identified by James. They evoke an ineffable feeling of deep inner knowing and knowledge. These are accounts of peace, bliss, awe, gratitude, reverence and abundant, unconditional love. They evoke a subjective feeling of being directly connected with the divine. This spiritual high experienced with Him lasts for a while and is sustainable through prayer and meditation but ebbs. Individuals who enjoy His company need to take a spiritual leap, long to always be with Him and want an end to the distance from Him. Eventually, they want to connect permanently and become one with Him.

The desire to be with God is exciting and demanding. It is easy to imagine the joy of being with God because the person has experienced it. It is more challenging to visualize what being with God will entail. Being with God demands that a person surrender unquestioningly to God, have no desires, expectations or self-will or, in other words, abandon oneself to God's will. The act of surrender obliterates a person's ego and self-identity. A leap into a known (God) and unknown (what may come) is based on trusting God, accepting what transpires and trusting that what He does is correct and apt. James alludes to the psychological challenge of taking that leap of faith by trusting God, giving up a personal will and being desireless.

> (In) self-surrender, when the will (is ready, it) bring(s) one close to the complete unification (that is) aspired (with God). (When) self-surrender becomes indispensable, the personal will must be given up until the person ceases to resist or make an effort in the direction he desires to go.[19]

After adoring closeness, separation from God is a phase in the spiritual evolution of a person. God, who was approachable, accessible and responsive becomes inaccessible. Prayers, yearning and anguish have no impact on Him. The person begins feeling abandoned and lonely. With a distant, seemingly indifferent and unresponsive God, the individual must establish a new connection with this elusive God, which requires a pronounced shift in mindset following a personal encounter with God. They must build and strengthen new spiritual capabilities by focusing on the God within. Earlier, personally engaging with God was the goal. It was the basis of detachment, discrimination and motivation towards spiritual goals. Trusting God requires the person to graduate beyond this experience.

The litmus test of trust, when faith transforms into confidence in God, occurs when God is quiet and unresponsive to a person.

Spiritual silence can be emotionally taxing and raise questions about God and one's relationship with Him, but there are no apparent answers from Him. The joy of being with Him recedes and becomes melancholy. Padma Kasturi, who spent her life with Swami, describes her emotions when she experiences His silence. She ascribes a trait of divine detachment to Swami. God showers love and creates an experience of proximity yet remains detached. Even when Swami is silent, she believes that He looks after her. Nevertheless, she wants to re-experience the joy of personal closeness.

> Sometimes, it hurts me because I can say that for the past 25 years, I did not (have a personal meeting) or anything like that. At that time (in earlier years), the (closeness and caring) were so much that I can say that I did not feel the divinity in Him. I considered Him a 'relative.' Now when He is 'dear' to me, I have to find satisfaction in His darshan from a distance. He is 'dear' to my heart and takes care of me. My soul craves for 'nearness,' to hear the sweet voice calling 'Padmamma' the way He used to. Only God has this power of 'detachment' in full measure.[20]

Two metaphors characterize trust: a person undergoing surgery and a baby bird flying out of its nest for the first time. When a person is diagnosed with a medical condition requiring surgery, he does due diligence on the surgeon. He investigates, questions and checks referrals to develop confidence in the surgeon. The test of trust in his decision is his willingness to submit to the doctor in an anaesthetized and supine state. He must allow the doctor to proceed with the surgery. When a person offers himself to the surgeon, his faith changes to trust. Surgery is an example of unquestioning, trustful submission.

Trusting God is taking the leap of faith, like a baby chick taking its first flight. God brings individuals to the crossroads of their spiritual life. After giving them tangible experiences of His reality, He withdraws and becomes unreachable. Before becoming inaccessible, God shares the knowledge of His truth and the know-how to reach Him. God helps them develop spiritual strength, like a bird's parents bringing it food. Trust, akin to a chick taking its first flight, signifies a decisive spiritual moment for a person. Their faith in God, rooted in tangible experiences, is challenged by spiritual ambiguity and uncertainty. Religious choices are made after careful contemplation, similar to a chick preparing to fly.

A person engaged with an unresponsive God must take the next spiritual step by trusting God. This means relying on Him, believing His words and giving up questioning, evaluating and judging Him, even if things do not turn out as expected. A person has to submit to the will of God without any expectation. By giving up their ego, selfishness and interests, they accept God's will in the new relationship. Trust is a natural outcome of the experience of God's love. Brennan Manning highlights this in his book when he says that trust in God manifests in the unconditional surrender of self-will, a commitment with no ifs and buts.[21]

Manning's story illustrates that trusting God means accepting the good and bad in life as His will and love.

> The German mystic John Tauler prayed that God sends a person who could teach him the way to perfection. One day, he heard a voice. It told him to go outside the church to meet his mentor. On the steps was a barefoot ragamuffin.
>
> Tauler said to the man, 'May God give you a good day and grant you a happy life.' The ragamuffin replied, 'Sir, I do not remember ever having a bad day.'
>
> Tauler was surprised and asked, 'Sorrow and grief are part of the human condition. How is that possible?' The beggar explained, 'Whether my stomach is full or hungry, I praise God equally. Even when I am rebuffed and despised, I still thank God. My trust in God's providence and plan for my life is absolute. So, I don't ever have a bad day.' He continued, 'You also wished me a happy life. I am always happy. It would be untruthful if I stated otherwise. My experience with God has taught me that whatever He does is good. Everything I receive—whether prosperity or adversity, sweet or bitter—is a sign of his favour. My resolution every morning is to attach myself to only the will of God. I have learned that the will of

> God is the love of God. By His grace, I have merged my will with His will. Therefore, I am always happy.'[22]

Trust in God requires a person to be devoid of desire or expectations.[23] When a vessel is empty, it receives the most water. God can fill a person to the brim with His love only when their mind is blank, like an empty vessel.

THE BOOK

This book consists of 24 chapters organized in 3 volumes. Belief is the thematic focus of the first volume, and faith and trust are the focus in the second and third volumes, respectively.

CHALLENGES OF WRITING ABOUT GOD

I wish to admit at the outset that it is not easy to write about religious experiences and God. Swami likens it to attempting to grasp the ocean's vastness. The sea is symbolic of the infinitude and boundlessness of God. Humans are limited. Their imagination and experience cap their understanding of God.

> No one can visualize the boundless, limitless expanse of God. God's glory is the shoreless ocean. When one starts describing it, it begins for him; when he finishes it, it is the end so far as he is concerned. But His glory is beyond space and time. The stage on which He plays has no boundaries.[24]

A spiritual experience is a person's encounter with the Divine. The nature and structure of the incident are unique and influence how God is understood and described. There are only two participants: the person and God. The person is a touchstone who vouchsafes for the experience. This is the challenge of writing about spiritual experiences. The knowledge about God is inferred from the written or verbal descriptions of the persons who have experienced God. Swami exemplifies the limitations of human faculties in understanding God. He says that listening differs from participating and seeing differs from knowing.

> Baba used to say: 'Are you able to see a song? You can only hear a song. How can you see a song or hear light? You can only see the light. Miracles are like that; you can only experience them.' [25]

St John of the Cross, a Spanish Catholic priest and mystic, highlights the difficulty of describing the experiences with God. A devotee understands, feels and recognizes God through an interplay of all their faculties—logic and reasoning, emotive responses and intuition. A spiritual experience is intense, palpable and unmistakable. Identifying and describing when the experience begins and ends and its significance is not easy.

> (It) can find no suitable way by which it may be able to describe such lofty understanding and delicate spiritual feeling. (The) inward wisdom is so simple, general and spiritual that it (does) not (become) understanding enwrapped or cloaked in any form or image. It follows that sense and imagination cannot account for or imagine it to say anything concerning it, although it is experiencing and partaking in that rare and delectable wisdom. The language of God is very intimate and spiritual. It transcends every sense and (makes) outward and inward feelings. Evelyn Underhill highlights the difficulty in believing and learning from others' experiences. Spiritual experiences are inherently inexplicable; those who have the experience believe unreservedly. Those who do not have the experience cannot remotely experience or comprehend others' knowledge and feelings.
>
> Those who have seen are convinced; those who have not can never be told. There is no certainty to equal the mystic's certitude, no impotence more complete than that which falls on those trying to communicate it.[26]

Another challenge to writing about God is the impact of the subject matter, God, on the author. While writing, an author must concentrate, ponder and distil ideas about God and spiritual issues. They cannot escape being captivated by God's grandeur. When confronted with God's magnificence, thoughts and ideas about the writing may cease to matter. A tidal flood that overruns everything in its flow symbolizes the overwhelming nature and power of thinking about God and a person's engagement with God. John Trevor expresses this idea in his book.

> Religion is not an opinion. It is neither based on faith nor from knowing facts or learnings from a book. It is an awareness, a consciousness and an evoked intuitive understanding. The state of awareness, or being, becomes firm and intense. It grows. And I find it difficult to describe the experience. It overwhelms my faculties as I try to understand it. And I cannot describe it.[27]

Loving God humbles a person. In the following quotation, Ramakrishna Paramahansa employs four metaphors to highlight the merging of the ego and self-identity with God.

> Think of *Brahman*, Existence–Knowledge–Bliss Absolute, as a shoreless ocean. Through the cooling influence of a bhakta's love, the water freezes at places into blocks of ice. God assumes various forms for His devotees and reveals Himself as a person. With the rising sun of knowledge, the blocks of ice melt. Then one does not feel God is a person or see God's forms. What He is cannot be described. Who will describe Him? He who would do so disappears. He cannot find his 'I' anymore.
>
> If a person analyses, they will not find anything as 'I'. Take an onion. First, peel off the red outer skin; then, you will find thick white skin. Peel these off one after the other, and you will not find anything inside. In that state, a man no longer finds the existence of his ego. Who is there left to seek it? Who can describe how he feels in that state—in his pure consciousness—about the real nature of Brahman? Once, a salt doll went to measure the depth of the ocean. No sooner was it in the water than it melted. Now, who was to tell the depth?
>
> There is a sign of perfect knowledge. A person becomes silent when that state is attained. Then the 'I', like a salt doll, melts in the ocean of Existence–Knowledge–Bliss Absolute

> and becomes one with It. Not the slightest trace of distinction is left.
>
> As long as his self-analysis is not complete, a person will argue with much ado. But he becomes silent when he completes it. When an empty pitcher is filled with water, the water inside the pitcher becomes one with the lake's water outside and no more sound is heard. Sound comes from the pitcher as long as the pitcher is not filled with water.[28]

Ramakrishna Paramahansa uses a story to highlight that silence is the language of a person who has experienced God.

> A man had two sons. The father sent them to a preceptor to learn the knowledge of Brahman. After a few years, they returned from their preceptor's house and bowed low before their father. Wanting to measure the depth of their knowledge of Brahman, he first questioned the older boy. 'My child,' he said, 'you have studied all the scriptures. Now tell me, what is the nature of Brahman?' The boy began to explain Brahman by reciting various texts from the Vedas. The father did not say anything. Then he asked the younger son the same question. But the boy remained silent and stood with eyes cast down. No word escaped his lips. The father was pleased and said, 'My child, you have understood a little of Brahman. What it is cannot be expressed in words.'
>
> In *samadhi*, one attains the Knowledge of Brahman, one realizes Brahman. In that state, reasoning stops altogether and man becomes mute. He has no power to describe the nature of Brahman.[29]

If silence is the language of awareness, the reverse is also true; those who speak may not know. The following quote is by Lao Tzu:

> Those who know do not speak. Those who speak do not know.[30]

I have written this book to recount, reflect and relive the blessing of spending time with Swami. Aitken highlights the idea of 'watching' the divine work from the 'ringside'. Being with Swami makes a person experience the divine presence, unconditional love and the power to attract, captivate and engross.

> A student of grace has been gifted with an opportunity to watch the divine at work from the ringside. The observer has witnessed the unfolding of the extraordinary ordinariness of life's spiritual dimension operating in the daily routine of Sathya Sai. Before your eyes, you can experience divinity, explore its wonders and relive the invigorating impact Buddha, Christ and Shirdi Sai have had on their followers. Here, you feel you are in touch with love's reality as you experience the exhilaration of being in the presence of a person who radiates the bliss of the spirit.[31]

The following story, narrated by Swami, expressively portrays how a devotee can capture God in his heart. An artist repeatedly fails to paint a portrait of Krishna. On each attempt, when he feels confident that he has captured the likeness of Krishna, he discovers that the picture is dissimilar and does not do justice to Krishna's essence. Finally, Narada guides the artist. Krishna is an actor who plays multiple roles in a drama written and directed by Him. A clean, polished mirror is the best way of capturing the Lord's likeness, a metaphor for spiritually cleansing the heart to reflect and capture His image. The portrait of Swami that develops in this book is like the artist's painting. It is a partial and minuscule view of Swami.

> There was once a world-famous artist. He had an extraordinary talent for figure and portrait painting. He came to Krishna and wanted to paint Krishna's portrait. With a beaming smile, Krishna said, 'Well, if you want to paint my image, you can certainly do so. Tell me what I should do.' The artist requested, 'Swami, if you would kindly just sit still for an hour in the same place, I will draw an outline, and then later, I will fill in the details.' Krishna sat down for the artist and remained without moving. The artist made some preliminary sketches. After a while, he prostrated at Krishna's feet and said, 'Swami, I have finished my work now.' Smiling, Krishna asked, 'When

will you show the picture?' The artist answered, 'Swami, I should have it completed by tomorrow.'

Throughout the night, he worked untiringly to accurately paint the Lord's likeness on canvas. The artist was highly pleased with his work. The picture was completed the following morning. He covered the painting with a beautiful cloth and brought it to Krishna. When the fabric covering the painting was removed, it was seen that the form of Krishna had undergone a remarkable change in the intervening twenty-four hours. The artist put the portrait directly alongside Krishna. He looked at the picture and then looked at Krishna. He realized that there was minimal resemblance between the two. Krishna also looked at the painting and pointed out, 'My dear fellow, there seem to be several defects.' The artist said, 'Please forgive me, Swami. Please give me another chance. Let me try again, and I will do better.' It went on like this for ten days.

The artist repeatedly did his work each day, but it was impossible to get an accurate picture. The artist began to feel ashamed. He decided it would be best to disappear from there, so he hurriedly left the city. On the way, Sage Narada met the artist departing from the city. Narada asked the artist, 'You seem quite disturbed. Tell me what is making you so unhappy.' The artist explained to him all that had happened. Narada said to the artist, 'Well, Krishna is a master actor and a master director. He is enacting this whole drama. Using your methods, you will never be able to get a true likeness of him. But if you want to succeed, listen to my words and follow them implicitly.'

The artist agreed to do what Narada instructed. He returned to Dwaraka and went to Krishna the next day, carrying a picture covered with a fine cloth. He told Krishna, 'Swami, I have finally been able to bring you your exact picture. Please have a look. This will always give the correct likeness of you. Whatever changes come into your expression and form, the image here faithfully shows these changes.' Then he got ready

> to remove the covering cloth and said, 'Please accept this as my best picture of you.'
>
> When the cloth came away, it revealed a clean mirror. If you want to paint a permanent portrait of the Lord with temporary materials like brushes, paint, etc., you will not be able to succeed. In the physical universe, everything is temporary. All forms are constantly changing. Such transient forms cannot give a proper vision of the permanent Lord. If you want a clean and unchanging vision of the Lord, you can obtain it only on a pure, clean mirror, which is your pure heart.[32]

This book reflects my limitations as an author writing about the enigmatic. The following excerpt highlights the limits of all forms of expression—words, actions and music—when describing God.

> Neither the intuitive intensity of poetry nor the intellectual eloquence of prose can capture a glimpse of His True Nature within their finite expressions. The resonant symphony of sublime music cannot adequately sing His Divine Glory. Words beat a fast retreat, frustrated in their attempts to fathom His infinite might and majesty. Thus, the scriptures chose to denote Him through negations and denials; the enlightened preferred to designate Him as 'the inscrutable' and 'the inexplicable'.[33]

When I started writing about Swami, I believed I would be transformed. I did not know that I would be remade. Writing has been like a prayer.

CAVEAT EMPTOR

In this book, I have taken care to be gender-neutral. I may have inadvertently referred to a spiritual aspirant using the masculine form. God does not see any difference between men and women. In the snippet below, Swami categorically states that men and women have equal rights and chances to attain Godhead. When I use the word 'man' in the book, it illustrates a person's relationship with God and God with the person. It should be read and understood in a gender-neutral manner.

> *Bhadhram* referred to women as having devotion, spiritual wisdom and detachment equal to men. Still, many are worried when they hear women reciting the *Pranava* (OM) during the auspicious time before sunrise *(brahma-muhurtham)* daily at the Nilayam. They forget that sound is fundamentally Pranava, that all breath has *Pranava* inherent in it. Can women avoid or keep away from OM, which is ever-present in the ether *(akasa)* and whose breath is reciting every moment?
>
> The feminine principle (nature, *Prakriti*) comes first, and the masculine principle (God, *Purusha*) comes second. You say Sita–Rama, Lakshmi–Narayana and Gauri–Sankara; you are not putting the names of Sita, Lakshmi and Gauri in the second place. Women have equal chances and equal rights to attain Godhead.[34]

I have avoided explaining and interpreting Swami in the book, in my attempt to comprehend His intentions. If I have unintendedly erred, please ignore those portions.

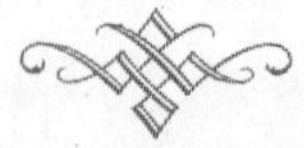

1

BELIEF AS AWAKENING

Belief in God becomes momentous when one recognizes God's role and lives with this awareness. Belief often stems from unusual and seemingly unrelated events and experiences which, upon reflection, are perceived as interconnected and meaningful. There is no evidence that one event led to or caused the other. Their logical harmony reveals and reinforces that God, unknown to them, has been actively participating in their lives. Belief develops through experiences that strengthen the intuitive sense of a deeper connection with God. The substantive understanding of belief is that God is the foundation of life. He is the centre of life, and life and God are not compartmentalized. Fowler, in his book, highlights that belief in God is a person's response to the realization that God and his relationship with God is the central purpose of his life.[1]

The formation of belief is a turning point in people's lives when they establish a connection with God, thereby setting the stage for their transformation. It shifts their perspective on life, thus altering their mindset, including their goals, motivations, thinking patterns and ultimately lifestyle. What stimulates the formation of this transforming belief?

BEFORE BELIEF

Seekers acquire their religion and religious identity from their family at birth. They grow up accepting their inherited religion as a label given by the family and accepted by society. How they practice their religion depends on their disposition, mindset and inclinations. As individuals grow up, they feel free to choose or reject religion or commit to living with the religious ideals they accept.

For some, God becomes a purpose in life. For others, it is a momentary philosophical burden to be ignored.

BELIEF AS AN AWAKENING

The arousal of belief in God is a pronounced personal event. Spiritual understanding arises from deep within the person. Howard Gardner highlights the momentous nature of the evocation of religious belief.

> Changes in faith are intensely personal experiences. [...] Changes of mind in the religious sphere are of enormous moment.[2]

The evocation of belief is a pivotal moment for Underhill.

> ...that decisive event, the awakening of the transcendental consciousness.[3]

BELIEF AND ACCEPTANCE

'Belief' in God is different from the 'acceptance' of God. A landmark change occurs when a person begins believing. It impacts the way they live, and their life gets a new purpose and meaning. The acceptance of God is a recognition and acknowledgment of God. It may be passive and not produce any change in the person who may continue living as usual. Underhill details that awakening to God shifts the focus from self-interest to God.

> This awakening appears to be an intense phenomenon. This phenomenon disrupts the equilibrium of the self, causing a shift in the field of consciousness from lower to higher levels. Therefore, the centre of focus transitions from the subject to an object that has now come into view. However, religious conversion must not be confused or identified as ordinarily understood: the sudden and emotional acceptance of theological beliefs, dwelling upon the margin of consciousness and having no meaning for her actual life.[4]

EXPRESSION OF BELIEF

The belief-forming experience of God is spontaneous. It occurs unexpectedly, is a shock and surprise and shakes up the person. An intense affection and love for God fills their heart and stills their mind. The love changes to conviction and a spiritual commitment to God. A person believes because God shows His face, not because He offers proof.[5]

The direct engagement between God and a person is a way to nurture belief in God. Samuel Sandweiss writes that love and faith are complicated ideas for a person not well-versed in the ways of the religious world. However, Swami is a living manifestation and expression of God. Every person who comes in contact with Him has a dramatic story of their experience of God's love. There is compelling evidence of the evocation of self-transforming belief and devotion.

> Faith in this love, faith in divinity, proves (an overwhelming) stumbling block. So, it is (hugely) fortunate if one has a direct experience of this love; like nothing else, it deepens one's faith in its reality. Sai Baba (has) his most significant impact here, for I am convinced that he is the most compelling evidence of universal consciousness. Sai Baba's universal consciousness, compassion and love are experienced so clearly, dramatically, convincingly and poignantly that he can awaken another's love instantly and turn one to a life of devotion.[6]

The encounter with God is a tangible divine experience substantiating belief in God. God, experienced as accessible, is still distant. The experience affirms a potential reality to be aspired for and realized. Feeling a newfound belief and joy in spirituality can inspire one to become more spiritual.

OUTCOME OF BELIEF

Belief remakes a person. It manifests in how they live and act, which is now inspired by a new awareness of God, omnipotence and omniscience. Belief in God becomes a desire for God, an intention that requires concerted attention and effort to seek a lasting relationship with God.

> Belief arises from the effort to translate experiences of and relating to transcendence.[7]

Swami highlights this in the following excerpt. The statement 'God is nowhere' can be modified to 'God is now here.' *Prahlada* is an asura king known for his devotion to Lord Vishnu. He appears in the narrative of *Narasimha*, Vishnu's man–lion avatar who slays Hiranyakasipu, Prahlada's evil father. Hiranyakasipu and Prahlada lived their lives based on their different beliefs. Hiranyakasipu's life was devoid of a relationship with God, whereas Prahlada believed in the immanence of God. Their ideas influenced their actions and different responses to God.

> Hiranyakasipu sought God in all things and concluded that He was nowhere. Prahlada, on the other hand, believed that He could be found wherever He is sought, so God appeared from the impenetrably hard iron pillar itself![8]

2

SPIRITUAL QUEST

SWAMI AND BELIEF

This chapter is a collection of reflective experiences of spiritual seekers as they turn towards God and discover belief. The experiences establish the basis for recognizing the influence and authority of Swami in affecting each person who connected with Him and whom He touched. The devotees acknowledge God, belief and the need for spiritual practice to spiritualize their life and to intuit the potential to be with God. This is not very different from the seekers quoted in the Introduction.

Imagine the motivation to be religious by experiencing the 'end' of the spiritual journey—God—at the start itself.

Swami does this every day, incessantly.

TURNING TOWARDS GOD

There are moments in a person's life when they introspect and seek answers to existential questions about life's purpose and meaning. The questions are an inkling of a deeper purpose in life. They have no answers, only an intuition of something hidden. A person may have a gut feeling or sixth sense about God, a feeling that intensifies and motivates them to reach out and connect with God.

As the seekers take steps towards God, He also enables them in return. He prepares them to meet Him and receive what He wants. God arranges for the person to seek Him, allowing their desire for God to sharpen before responding. The feeling of extreme anxiety, hopelessness and despair experienced before God answers is God preparing them for an encounter with Him. God is 'emptying' them of attachments and 'demolishing' their ego before He spiritually 'reconstructs' them. The person learns this in hindsight.

When people take steps to connect with God, their concept of God is still conjecture because they lack a direct personal encounter with Him. Instead, they envision their engagement with God as a meeting between two individuals. Devotees attribute conventional qualities such as power, goodness and grace to Him. They also hold specific expectations regarding how God should respond to their material and spiritual needs and wants.

They will learn that an engagement with God, unlike social engagement, is spiritual. To strengthen this connection, they must eliminate selfishness, discipline their ego and become humble and ready to receive God.

In two excerpts from the Bible, Jesus Christ underscores the need for a person to give up their ego or 'leave the self behind' to be with Him, for which he uses the metaphor of 'taking up the cross'.

> Anyone who wishes to be a follower of mine must leave (the) self behind; he must take up his cross and come with me (Mark 8:34).
>
> What does a man gain by winning the whole world at the cost of his true self? What can he give to buy that self back? (Mark 8:36)

Swami describes how devotees can become selfless (egoless) by merging their will with the will of God, symbolic of submitting to God. Swami's discourse makes the message of Jesus Christ practical.

> Who are you when you say, 'This is my body,' who are you? To whom are you referring? The expression 'my body' connotes that you are separate from the body. When you say, 'This is my mind,' the mind is different from you. Similarly, when you say, 'This is my *Buddhi* (intellect),' it means the *Buddhi* is separate from you. In all these expressions, what is that 'my'? That

'my' is 'I.' This 'I' is what was referred to by Jesus Christ as the ego that must be cut. That is the real significance of the cross. You cut the ego.

When you remove the veil of ego and attachment that covers your innate divinity, you will realize the truth [...] this attitude offering of the self (*Atma-arpana*). Still, the *Atma* is He Himself, so what do you mean by offering Him to Himself? What you would offer at His Feet is your egoism! Offer all the pride, all the separateness, all the delusion, all the attachment that the egoism has proliferated into! That is the worship you must do. Bring Me all the evil in you, leave it here, and take from Me what I have, viz. love (*Prema*). Develop the capacity to see all as 'moved and motivated by the One Supreme Reality or Self'. Examine every day what you do and with what motive; then, you can pronounce judgment on your progress. Select only pure motives and pure deeds. You forgot that you are the Atma, and now you remember that you are the Atma. That is all the progress you must achieve; it all looks easy, but it is one of the most challenging assignments. The ear is so near to the eye, but it can never see it!

You say one moment, '*Baba* does everything; I am but the instrument,' and the next moment, the same tongue talks, 'I did this; I did that. Swami did not do this for me.'

What is needed is the conquest of the ego. In its egoistic pride, the bullock shouts, 'Hum hai, hum hai (I am, I am).' So, when it is just a few days old, you tie it to a post away from its mother; you work it to skin and bones, but the animal does not learn the lesson of humility. Even its skin, when drawn tightly across a drum, resounds egoistically, '*Ham Ham Ham.*' So, the skin has to be cut into thin strings, and then when the strings are pulled, the bullock reveals that it has benefitted by all the punishment it has undergone; it murmurs *thum thum thum* (you, you, you), and its ego is gone.

Once, when I asked several people what they would like to be in the hands of God, I got various answers, but no one

> mentioned the flute. I would advise you to become the flute, for then the Lord will come to you, pick you up, put you to His lips and breathe through you. Out of the hollowness of your heart due to the utter absence of egoism that you have developed, He will create captivating music for all creation to enjoy. Be straight, without any will of your own. Merge your will with the will of God.[1]

Swami uses the metaphor of an empty vessel to explain the need to clean the mind and make it empty—egoless—to receive His blessings. A person must get rid of all their desires and expectations to connect with Him and receive His blessings and grace.

> Swami once looked at me and asked, 'Your name is Anil. What does it mean?'
>
> I replied, '*Nilkadu*, meaning that which is "not nil" or is not empty or is full.'
>
> Swami replied, 'If a tumbler is full, I cannot fill it. First, empty the tumbler, and then I will fill it with what I have come to fill.'[2]

A person has to receive, understand and use the spiritual knowledge that God imparts. Swami used two metaphors to elucidate this in a letter He wrote to the students of Brindavan: an inverted pot and a basket, symbolic of the mind. A container has to be empty and facing upwards to receive; an inverted pot can neither receive nor hold anything. When meeting God, a devotee should be humble, devoid of expectations and ready to receive what God wants to give. When God blesses them with benedictions, they must collect and use them, ensuring that nothing is lost.

> Churning the mind with self-inquiry gives the cream of knowledge. Without this the spiritual knowledge will not enter the 'mind-pot,' just as water cannot be collected in an inverted pot. [...] Water does not stay in a basket and wisdom does not stay in the passionate mind.[3]

START OF THE SPIRITUAL JOURNEY

A person's journey to God is an individual and internal process that unfolds within the depths of one's own mind.

It begins tentatively as intuition.

A person may start from an intellectual position of not prioritizing religion and God. When people turn to God, it can be due to curiosity, unanswered questions, personal spiritual insights or the need to address compelling issues.

I share the experiences of individuals seeking God, including those of Leo Tolstoy, to exemplify the formation of belief. His reflections, written nearly 150 years ago, are detailed and identify challenges on the journey of developing belief that will resonate with the experiences of spiritual seekers quoted in this book.

In his spiritual autobiography, Thomas Merton, an American mystic and theologian, describes his religious beginnings.[4] He initially goes with the flow with reflexive acceptance of God and prayer. Merton realizes his need to connect with a benevolent, all-knowing and all-powerful God after he experiences sorrow and fear upon his father's demise. He identifies the dependency upon God as a fundamental need of humans, indeed a part of our nature. Merton writes that religious inclinations are a necessity and an essence of human life.

FLICKERING BELIEF

The seed of religion that a person receives as a family legacy creates a lingering feeling of belief in God. For it to take root, grow and become ardent requires spiritual experiences and the deliberate nurturing of belief. Tolstoy articulates the challenge of living a religious life based on inherited beliefs. He uses the metaphor of inherited belief as 'ice that gradually thaws'; the solid, metaphorically strong ice melts away.

> ...religious doctrine, accepted on trust and supported by external pressure, thaws away gradually under the influence of knowledge and life experiences that conflict with it. A man very often lives on, imagining that he still holds the religious

> doctrine intact imparted to him in childhood. (The reality is otherwise.) Not a trace of it remains.[5]

In his brief autobiographical story, Tolstoy describes his struggle with nascent belief.[6] At the age of 16, Tolstoy gives up his religious faith and inheritance from the family. He is ambivalent about God but lacks the strength to deny God.

> When I was sixteen, I stopped saying my prayers and attending church. I did not believe what had been taught in childhood, but I believed in something. What I believed, I could not at all have said. I believed in a God, or rather, I did not deny God but I could not have said what sort of God. Neither did I deny Christ and his teaching, but I again could not have said what his teaching consisted of.[7]

Tolstoy emphasizes an important point that impedes the strengthening of belief. He does not experience the positive impact of religious beliefs and values. His 'break' from belief happens because of a 'secular' perception that religion and spiritual values must be isolated from life, whereas religion must be the basis of life.

> My lapse from faith occurred among people at our level of education [...] I think it happens thus: a man lives like everybody else, based on principles [...] religious doctrine does not play a part in life; in interaction with others, it is never encountered, and in a man's life, he never has to reckon with it. Religious doctrine is professed far away from life and independently of it [...] it is only an external phenomenon disconnected from life.[8]

DIVISION BETWEEN BELIEF AND LIFE

Tolstoy describes how his goals and values evolved as he searched for meaning in life. The pursuit of worldly fame became the goal, displacing underlying spiritual purpose and meaning. He lost sight of why he was doing what he was doing. Then, his ego took control, thereby intensifying his desire to be famous and wealthy.

> Looking back on that time, I now see that my faith was a belief in perfecting myself. I could not have said what this perfecting consisted of and what its object was. I tried to perfect myself mentally. I studied everything I could, anything life threw in my way; I tried to perfect my will. I drew up rules I tried to follow; I perfected myself physically, cultivating my strength and agility with all sorts of exercises and accustoming myself to endurance and patience through all kinds of deprivations. All this I considered to be the pursuit of perfection. The beginning of it all was moral perfection, which was soon replaced by perfection in general: the desire to be better, not in my own eyes or those of God but in other people's eyes. Very soon, this effort again changed into a desire to be stronger than others: to be more famous, important and richer.[9]

Tolstoy recognizes the pursuit of excellence as progress but fails to acknowledge its spiritual purpose. His natural impulse is that progress must be spiritually centred and directed. A meaningless drifting through life is not progress. He does not want to say, 'I don't know where I am going, but as long as I am going somewhere, it is okay.'

> I went abroad and confirmed my faith in striving after perfection (what perfection means to) educated people, expressed by the word 'progress'. It then appeared to me that this word meant something. I did not yet understand that tormented by how to live, I could not answer, 'Live in conformity with progress.' I was like a man in a boat who, when carried along by wind and waves, should reply to what for him is the chief and only question, 'Whither to steer?' by saying, 'We are being carried somewhere.'[10]

BELIEF AND SOCIAL INFLUENCE

Tolstoy identifies another challenge in his spiritual life. Profoundly religious persons are considered outliers in social settings, comprising family, peers and friends. Subtle social influence has the potential to deflect the emerging sacred intentions of a person who is working on his belief.

> I also remember that when my elder brother, who was then at the university, suddenly, in the passionate way natural to him, devoted himself to religion and began to attend all the Church services, fast and lead a pure and moral life, we all—even our elders—unceasingly held him up to ridicule [...] I (drew) the conclusion that though it is necessary to receive religious instruction and go to church, one must not take such things too seriously.
>
> Tolstoy recognizes how societal pressures hindered his ability to lead a virtuous life.
>
> I wished to be good with all my soul, but I was young, passionate and entirely alone. Every time I tried to be morally good, I met with contempt and ridicule, but as soon as I yielded to low passions, I was praised and encouraged. Ambition, love of power, covetousness, lust, pride, anger and revenge were all respected.[11]

A person working on belief must constantly be watchful.

> (A person) told me how he ceased to believe when he was twenty-six. He once kneeled in the evening to pray—a habit retained from childhood. When S. had finished and settled for the night, his brother said, 'So you still do that?' They said nothing more to one another. But from that day, S. ceased to pray or go to church. His brother's words were like the push of a finger on a wall ready to fall by its weight.[12]

BELIEF AND FAMILY RESPONSIBILITY

Tolstoy explains how, after his marriage and with the added responsibilities of family life, he shifted his focus to earning more money. He redirected his efforts towards enhancing his life through the acquisition of wealth, which was different from pursuing perfection as the ultimate aim of all his actions. Tolstoy laments the duties of family life. He became preoccupied, which prevented him from stepping back and asking deep questions about life and its meaning. Tolstoy is an archetype of a typical person, of how spiritual concerns take a back seat when a person accepts responsibilities.

> I was married. Family life completely diverted me from all searches for the general meaning of life. My whole life became centred on my family, wife and children and increasing our means of livelihood. My striving after self-perfection, which I had substituted for striving for perfection in progress, was replaced by the effort to secure the best possible conditions for myself and my family.
>
> Fifteen years passed. Even though I now regarded authorship as of no importance—the temptation of immense monetary rewards and applause for my insignificant work—I devoted myself to it as a means of improving my material position and of stifling in my soul all questions as to the meaning of my own life or life in general.[13]

THE NEED FOR MEANING

Tolstoy manifested increasing despair as he reflected on the spiritual meaning of life. He ignored the questions, believing that seeking answers to philosophical questions could be attended to later. However, the frequency of the evocation of spiritual questions intensified. He realized the importance of the issue. His efforts to forget the questions by distracting himself with life's routine did not help. Tolstoy was unable to compartmentalize his daily life from spiritual growth. The need for answers and consequent unhappiness overwhelmed him. He compared his spiritual discontentment to inner death, making it difficult for him to focus on work and family. The intensity of wanting answers became very loud, making living impossible. Tolstoy describes a slow strengthening of his spiritual need and its escalation to a point where it becomes a restlessness, longing, yearning and eventually a crisis to resolve. His experience typifies the inner experiences of many seekers of God.

So, I lived, but something strange happened to me five years ago. At first, I experienced moments of perplexity, and though I did not know what to do or how to live, I felt lost and discouraged. But this passed, and I went on living as before. Then these moments of perplexity began to recur frequently and always in the same form. They are expressed in the form of questions: what is it for? What does it lead to?

At first, it seemed to me that these were aimless and irrelevant questions. I thought it was all well-known. I had no time for it, but when I wanted to, I should be able to find the answer. However, the questions began to repeat themselves frequently and demanded replies more and more insistently.

Then what occurred happens to everyone. At first, trivial signs of indisposition appear to which the sick man pays no attention. These signs reappear more often and merge into one uninterrupted period of suffering. The suffering increases, and before the sick man can look around, what he took for a mere indisposition has already become more important to him than anything else in the world. It is death!

That is what happened to me. I understood that it was no casual indisposition but something very important and that the questions needed to be answered. And I tried to answer them. The questions seemed simple, childish ones. Still, as soon as I touched them and tried to solve them, I was convinced, first, that they are not childish but the most important and profound of life's questions, and secondly, that occupying myself with my [...] estate, the education of my son or the writing of a book, I had to know why I was doing it. As long as I did not understand why I could do nothing and could not live [...] And I could find no reply at all. The questions would not wait, they must be answered at once, and if I did not answer them, it was impossible to live.

I felt that what I had been standing on had collapsed, and nothing was left under my feet. What I had lived on no longer existed, and nothing was left.[14]

EXTREME HELPLESSNESS: A TIPPING POINT

The spiritual tipping point is that moment in life when a person feels powerless in 'controlling' life and reaches out to God. The closest metaphor for this is a person standing at the edge of a precipice.[15] It is foggy, and he cannot see ahead. He can neither step forward nor turn back. The only recourse is to reach out to God as a rescuer. The 'darkness' describes a situation wherein a person cannot see God and must unquestioningly trust and reach out to Him.

Elaine Pagels is a Professor of Religion at Princeton University. In *Beyond Belief,* she uses the same metaphor—standing at the edge of a precipice—to describe a personal experience of feeling helpless and not knowing what to do.[16] She visits a church in a vulnerable state out of a need to deal with an uncontrollable situation. Her reflections depict that being in church in the presence of God is a way to deal with her helplessness. Pagels uses the word hope to describe her emotional experience. She highlights that her feeling in the church was not about accepting doctrinal beliefs[17] but a deeper engagement[18] with God. The degree of change is palpable when she writes that she must build a bridge to cross the abyss. Two different authors have used the same metaphor. One author describes it as exemplifying helplessness or a dead end, and the other depicts God as a bridge across the abyss, a means to move ahead.

> A team of doctors performed a routine checkup on our son a year and six months after his open-heart surgery. The physicians (found) evidence of rare lung disease and called us in to say that (he) had pulmonary hypertension—(a) fatal disease. The church was a place to deal with what we could not control or imagine. I often returned to that church. I gathered new energy and resolved to face whatever awaited us. When people say, 'Your faith must be of great help to you,' I wonder: what do they mean? What is faith? I was aware that we met, driven by need and desire. Yet I know what matters in religious experience involves much more than what we believe. The drama (that) played out 'spoke to my condition'. [...] it simultaneously acknowledges the reality of fear, grief and death while nurturing

> hope. When our son suddenly died, the church offered some shelter to bridge an abyss that had seemed impassable.[19]

Father Mazzoleni describes his experiences with an incurable disease. He uses the same metaphor and likens his experience to reaching 'the edge of the cliff'. When he becomes aware of the disease, anxiety and grief overcome him. The first reflective question is, 'Why me?' With time, he recognizes the underlying spiritual purpose of the disease as God's 'greatest blessing'. The condition serves a spiritual purpose. Father Mazzoleni turns towards God with determination, acceptance and submission. He attempts to seek God in a desperate situation; a helpless person reaching out to God while sinking in quicksand shows how a person suspends thinking and reaches out to God.

> It is said that not all ills come to harm us. And the sickness turned up at the right moment, even if it was no fun initially. I am grateful to the Lord for having programmed it at the right moment. I consider my getting sick one of the greatest blessings of my life.
>
> A serious illness also has the merit of taking away every material security. Without the body, our material projects go up in smoke. This discovery benefits anyone about to put himself on a spiritual path. Significantly, when they have not yet acquired enough strength, they will not fall away from it.
>
> To surrender to God at a moment when your material resources are on their way to depletion is undoubtedly not an act of heroism.[20]

Sharon Salzberg writes that suffering prepares a person to receive God. Unhappiness, unanswered religious questions and inexplicable, intense pain can activate a search for God. When suffering becomes unbearable, helplessness makes a person more willing to reach out to God.

> Extreme helplessness is evoked when a person confronts intractable problems that produce pain or despair and need to be managed, from which they can't retreat. These steer a person to believe, a willingness to take chances, even momentary loss of personal control (accepting and waiting for God). The

'moment' of belief, when a person accepts the possibility and becomes willing to 'see' what will happen requires courage to discover the unfamiliar...[21]

Father Mazzoleni writes that pain is a blessing as it signals cure. Pain is a spiritual wake-up call, an alarm bell to nudge a person to seek deeper meaning in life.

> Physically, pain is a blessing because it often signals the ailment in time for a cure. And it is also a blessing in a figurative sense because in this world where people do not want to listen to the silent voice that speaks from inside, it is precisely suffering, sometimes very intense, which wakes them from their torpor. Suffering demands to be understood, not avoided.[22]

Swami identifies pain as His instrument to evoke reflective thinking. Pain helps nudge a person towards God. The experience of pain, coupled with the inability to manage it, allows a person to detach from the world and give up false identification with the body and ego.

> This conversation between a devotee and Sai Baba occurred in Prasanthi Nilayam many years ago. It was first published in Sanathana Sarathi.
>
> Devotee: Swami! The world is very cruel to me.
>
> Swami: That is its nature. The purpose of the world is frustration; it has to engender need. When the need is strong enough, the individual seeks fulfilment.
>
> D.: And fails!
>
> S.: Only when he seeks fulfilment outside himself! If he searches within, he can get it. Within a person, it is always accessible; it is ever responsible. There is pain only so long as an attachment for outer forms remains. Ultimate relief from pain can come only with the loss of ego, the neutralization of that which reacts to something like pain and something else as pleasure, whose memory, whose conditioning, helps recognize the dualities of joy and grief.

D.: But the world, Swami?

S.: The world is pain. Expect nothing from the world but that. I willed the totality of your conditioned existence to be pain to draw you to me.[23]

FEAR OF DEATH: ANOTHER TIPPING POINT

Similar to helplessness, a fear of death also prompts a person to connect with God.

Ramana Maharshi describes how a spiritual seeker uses reflections evoked by a fear of death. This fear has a positive outcome; a person deliberately reaches out to God to alleviate his anxiety. Every person will die. However, a person does not think and worry about it, lest the thought of death overrides their day-to-day work. Death is the disappearance of the body. It is feared because a person identifies with their body. The true self is beyond the body. Ramana Maharshi pinpoints that devout submission to God without expectations is a way to overcome that fear.

> All know they must die sometimes, but they do not think deeply about it. All have a fear of death; such fear is momentary. Why fear death? Because of the 'I-am-the-body' idea. All are fully aware of the death of the body and its cremation. That the body is lost in death is well-known. Owing to the I-am-the-body notion, death is feared as being the loss of oneself. Birth and death pertain to the body only, but they are superimposed on the self, giving rise to the delusion that birth and death relate to the self.
>
> To overcome birth and death, a man looks up to the Supreme Being to save him. Thus are born faith and devotion to the Lord. How to worship Him? The creature is powerless, and the creator is all-powerful. How to approach Him? To entrust oneself to His care is the only thing left for him; total surrender is the only way. Therefore, he surrenders himself to God. Surrender consists in giving up oneself and one's possessions to the Lord

of mercy. Then what is left over for the man? Nothing—neither himself nor his possessions. The man need no longer worry about the body liable to be born and to die having been made over to the Lord. Then, birth and death cannot strike terror. The cause of fear was the body; it is no longer his. Why should he fear now? Or where is the identity of the individual to be frightened?[24]

In the excerpt below, Fowler's fear of death stimulates contemplation. Intense philosophical inquiries spotlight the heightened focus when confronting the fear of death. This prompts re-evaluating one's connections to the world, including relationships with family and friends, and a critical self-examination of life's motives and ambitions.

Four A.M., in the darkness of morning, suddenly, I am fully and frighteningly awake. I see it clearly: I am going to die. This body, mind, lived and living myth and husband, father, teacher, son, a friend will cease to exist. The tide of life that propels me with such force will end, and I, taking this so much for granted, will no longer walk this earth. A strange feeling of remoteness creeps over me. My wife, beside me in bed, seems entirely out of reach. My daughters, asleep in other parts of the house, seem in this moment like vague memories of people I had once known. My work, professional associates, ambitions, dreams and absorbing projects feel like fiction. 'Real life' suddenly feels like a transient dream. In the strange aloneness of this moment, defined by the certainty of death, I awake to the facts of life.

In that moment of unprecedented aloneness experienced in my thirty-third year, I stared into the mystery surrounding our lives. As never before, I found myself asking, 'When all these persons, relations and projects that shape and fill my life are removed, who or what is left? When this biological embodiment of me ceases to function, will there be any I? When the I that is me steps into the darkness, will there be this centre of consciousness, this I am, or not? And if so, by whom will I be met? What continuities will there be between

> these full, fleeting days and years I now taste and savour and any enlargement of time I may experience?'
>
> I looked at it as one might look at an overcoat hanging on the far side of a room, a soul without a body, raiment, relationships or roles alone with—with what? With whom?[25]

QUESTIONS TO CONNECT WITH GOD

The spiritual turning point is a profound and meaningful juncture in a person's life when they choose to lead a life with God. This decision is the culmination of personal experiences that have intensified their quest for meaning. They may turn to God when experiencing fear, pain, sorrow and helplessness. The defining moment is a period of reflection and search for meaning. The spiritual questions still need resolution. The person continues to ask questions and searching for God, who is unknown and unseen. To find answers to religious matters, a person must commit to searching for meaning. They have to face God to ask Him about their relationship. Because of the profundity of spiritual questions and lack of easy answers, they experience spiritual anxiety. With no answers from external sources, they become sensitive and discover spiritual insights.

Questions arise when the spiritual journey starts. Father Mazzoleni expresses dissatisfaction with his past studies into truth. He underlines the imperativeness of sustaining spiritual inquiry and not giving up on the search using the alibi of belief. Spiritual questions get resolved by a commitment to and practice of religion. Religious beliefs cannot be a starting point of the spiritual journey and a milestone to be achieved.

> I have always been relatively rational in my investigations, yet even with the theological knowledge I acquired through my studies, I was not satisfied with my past inquiries into truth. The answers offered by official doctrine left some unknowns for me to fill in. When I would put the same questions in turn to other priests, they would say, 'It's faith that tells you that.' This is one of the most senseless answers I have heard because the power of faith is such that if I have it, I have

> already resolved all doubts. So, what need would I have of religion if I have already arrived at the destination of faith? [...] if religion is a means that is supposed to lead me to faith, why does it answer me by referring me to precisely what I am looking for?[26]

Tolstoy describes his struggle to resolve reason and belief.

> Rational knowledge presented by the learned and wise denies the meaning of life [...] the whole of humanity receives that meaning in irrational knowledge. And that irrational knowledge is faith, that very thing which I could not but reject. It is God, One in Three, the creation in six days, the devils and angels and all the rest that I cannot accept as long as I retain my reason.
>
> My position was terrible [...] By faith, it appears that to understand the meaning of life, I must renounce my reason, the very thing for which meaning is required.[27]

Tolstoy resolves the conflict between faith and reason by bringing God into perspective. He redefines the question he was asking. He realizes that reason alone does not give answers to spiritual questions, but every religious question or doubt connects him with God.

> I understood that it was impossible to seek rational knowledge for a reply to my question [...] a different statement of the question can obtain an answer only when the relation of the finite to the infinite is in the question. And I understood that however irrational and distorted the replies given by faith might be, they have the advantage of introducing a relation between the finite and the infinite into every answer, without which there can be no solution. Whatever I stated in the question, that relation appeared in the answer.[28]

Tolstoy reveals how God gently comes back into his life through his reflections. It is not an outcome of deep thinking. One day, a question became an insight and then acceptance. His story portrays that a person can get an intuitive insight into their relationship with God as they search for a meaningful life and connection with God. The turning point happens when Tolstoy realizes he must live for God. This awareness energizes him. He can live a life focused on God because he knows the purpose of life.

> 'I remember,' he says, 'one day in early spring, I was alone in the forest, listening to its mysterious noises. I listened, and my thought went back to what, for these three years, it always was busy with: the quest for God. But the idea of him,' I said, 'how did I ever come by the idea?'
>
> And again, there arose in me, with this thought, glad aspirations towards life. Everything in me awoke and received meaning [...] Why do I look further? A voice within me asked. He is there: he, without whom one cannot live. To acknowledge God and to live in the same thing. God is what life is. Well, I live, seek God, and there will be no life without him...
>
> After this, things cleared up within and about me better than ever, and the light has never wholly died away. I was saved from suicide. Just how or when the change took place, I cannot tell. But as insensibly and gradually as the force of life had been annulled within me, and I had reached my moral deathbed, life's energy came back gradually and imperceptibly. And what was strange was that this energy that came back was nothing new. It was my ancient juvenile force of faith, the belief that the sole purpose of my life was to be better. I gave up the life of the conventional world, recognizing it to be no life, but a parody of life, which its superfluities keep us from comprehending.[29]

Merton shares how spontaneous feelings led him to love and seek God, even without answers to spiritual questions. He believes that searching for spiritual answers strengthens and deepens a person's love for God and that God's presence is constant, even when He may seem unresponsive.

> I read the Gospels, and my love developed [...] I belong to the church because of the inner peace I experienced in them. I was filled with a need and a deep desire that I would find

happiness with God. Jesus was attracting me to the Church, pulling me, helping me get rid of the chains that anchored me.[30]

MEANING OF LIFE IN LIFE

Tolstoy reflects on life, family and work, envisaging the emptiness of social identity and external factors. He realizes that nothing matters after death. He identifies engaging with the world as an adornment: tangible, external, pleasurable, attractive and yet meaningless. He differentiates between seeking the 'meaning of life' and seeking 'meaning in life'.

> The two drops of honey that diverted my eyes from the [...] truth longer than the rest, my love of family and writing—art, as I called it—were no longer sweet to me. 'Family,' [...] I said to myself. But my family—wife and children—are also human. They are in the same boat as I am: they must either live in a lie or see the terrible truth. Why should they live? Why should I love them, guard them, bring them up or watch them?
>
> 'Art, poetry?' [...] Under the influence of success and the praise of men, I had long assured myself that this was a thing one could do though death was drawing near—death, which destroys all things, including my work and its remembrance; but soon I saw that too was a fraud. It was plain to me that art is an adornment of life, an allurement to life. But life had lost its attraction for me, so how could I attract others? As long as I was not living my own life but was borne on the waves of some other life—as long as I believed that life had a meaning, though one I could not express—the reflection of life in poetry and art of all kinds afforded me pleasure: it was pleasant to look at life in the mirror of art. But when I began to seek the meaning of life and felt the necessity of living my own life, that mirror became unnecessary, superfluous, ridiculous or painful for me. I could no longer soothe myself with what I now saw in the mirror, namely, that my position was stupid and desperate.[31]

POTENTIAL OF BELIEF

Tolstoy embodies the archetype of a religious person who sees belief as essential knowledge, which gives life profound meaning and purpose.

> ...besides rational knowledge, which had seemed to be the only knowledge, I was forced to acknowledge that [...] humanity has another knowledge—faith [...] Faith remained to me as irrational as it was before, but I could not admit that it alone gives humanity a reply to the questions of life and that, consequently, it makes life possible.[32]

He highlights that faith gives meaning to life and endows a person with unlimited potential, capacity and the possibility of becoming something more significant and grander. Tolstoy describes faith's influence, supremacy and comprehensive role in a person's life. He writes that faith is not the basis of God. Instead, faith comes before God; it is the strength of a person whose life centres on God.

> Whatever the faith may be and whatever answers it may give and to whomsoever it gives them, every such answer gives the finite existence of man an infinite meaning [...] This means that only in faith can we find meaning and possibility for life. What, then, is this faith? I understood that faith is not merely 'the evidence of things not seen' and is not a revelation (that defines only one of the indications of faith), is not the relation of man to God (one has first to define faith and then God, not define faith through God) [...] Faith is the strength of life. If a man lives, he believes in something [...] If he does not see and recognize the illusory nature of the finite, he believes in the finite; if he understands the illusory nature of the finite, he must believe in the infinite...[33]

SPIRITUAL ACTION

The reflective narratives of this chapter reveal the nature of the struggle to develop belief. Swami describes the role of the mind in discovering the truth. His description markedly encapsulates the experiences.

> The *Antahkarana* (inner-psyche) has four names based on differences in behaviour. When it is concerned with thoughts, it is called *manas* (mind). It is called *chiththa* (consciousness) when it is restless and wavering. It is called *buddhi* (intellect) when concerned with inquiry and understanding. When it is associated with the sense of 'mine' (possessiveness), it is called *ahamkara* (egoism). Why are four different names and attributes given to the same entity (the *Antahkarana*)? The mind is preoccupied with distinctions and differences.
>
> The urge in the mind that animates the senses is stronger than the sense organs themselves. The eyes, for instance, are merely instruments for seeing, but seeing itself is a power superior to them. Similarly, hearing ability is higher than the mere ear. The mind is superior to the sense organs and superior to the mind is '*buddhi*' (intellect), the power of discrimination. Above the *buddhi* is the animating life principle, the *Jeeva*. Above the *Jeevaathma* (the individual soul) is the *Paramatma* (supreme soul).
>
> An attractive deluding veil exists between the individual and the divine, *Maya* (illusory power). When this veil falls, the *Jeeva* and the *Paramatma* become one. When the mind turns away from the senses to the *Buddhi* for enlightenment, *Ananda* (divine bliss) starts to flow and the glory of '*Atma*' (divine soul) is revealed. *Buddhi* promotes the search inward. While the sense organs—the eye, the ear, the nose, the tongue and the skin—open out toward external objects, true *sadhana* (spiritual discipline) turns the vision inwards. It is seldom realized how near is the goal of self-realization once the sense organs turn inwards.[34]

Swami uses the revelation of the Bhagavad Gita to Arjuna to show the momentousness of spiritual resolve and action. Most sensitive and reflective persons experience some anxiety about the meaning and purpose of their lives, but few take resolute action to discover answers. Some people accept the discomfort or anguish that these questions raise and carry on with life as if this mental condition is normal. The keys to spiritual life are foresight and a determination to act to find meaning.

> You may wonder why the Gita was taught to Arjuna. Among the Pandavas, the oldest brother, Dharmaraja, who was the pillar of virtue, might be considered better spiritually qualified than Arjuna. Why was the sacred Gita not taught to Dharmaraja, who was known for his outstanding moral strength? Or, if you were to consider physical prowess, then Bhima, the most powerful among the brothers, would have qualified for the teachings. Krishna could have given the Gita to Bhima, but he did not. Why not? Why did he give it only to Arjuna? Dharmaraja was the embodiment of righteousness, but he did not have foresight. He did not think about the future consequences of his actions. He thought about their effects only after events and felt sorry for his actions. He had hindsight but not foresight. If you take Bhima, he had great physical strength but little intelligence. He could uproot a tree, but he lacked in discrimination. Arjuna, on the other hand, had foresight. For example, Arjuna told Krishna, 'I would rather be dead than fight against these people. Even if we win the war, it will mean so much suffering later on.' In contrast to Arjuna's anguish about all the suffering that the war would wreak, Dharmaraja was pulled into a royal game of dice, in which he lost everything, including his wealth, kingdom and even his wife. He was anguished and remorseful afterward.[35]

3

BEING READY FOR GOD

DIVINE PLAN, HE CAN WAIT

God orchestrates a unique plan for every individual by taking on the roles of a producer, director and even an actor in the drama of their life. However, individuals often remain unaware that their life follows a script penned by God, leading them to seek answers and guidance through prayer and hoping for divine responses.

God solemnly promises the seekers that they will return to Him. He decides the timing of a person's return to Him. He works on a spiritual scale and is not hurried by the needs and emotions of the actors. The person has to believe in His promise and be patient. The drama of life is a person's struggle to recognize and believe the promise of God and be spiritually determined and patient.

In the forthcoming passage, Swami elaborates on this concept and delineates His conduct.

> I know everything that happened to everybody in the past, present and future, so I'm not so quick to give people the mercy they implore of me. I know why a person is suffering in this life and what will happen to him in the next, so I cannot act the way people want me to. They call me cold-hearted one time and soft-hearted the next. Why don't I do this? Why don't I do that?[1]

> You may be seeing me today for the first time, but you are all old acquaintances of mine. I know you through and through.[2]

THE PERSON STRUGGLES

The struggle in one's relationship with God is recognizing experiences as God's handiwork, forging a connection and grasping His spiritual purpose. The following dialogue between Arnold Schulman, the author, and Dr Gokak represents the nature of such a grind. The author wishes to write a book on Swami.

> 'What I don't understand,' the writer finally said, 'is why Baba told me to write the book, and then after I had signed the contract with the publisher and gone to all the expense and trouble of coming halfway around the world, why would he tell me now I can't write it? If he didn't want me to write the book, all he had to do was say so initially.'
>
> Gokak hesitated, clearly trying to find the most delicate way of saying it. 'I think he's afraid. He's indicated to me that he's a little concerned that you may not be at a level of spiritual development...'
>
> 'I didn't pretend to be on any level spiritually,' the writer said.
>
> 'Yes, yes, I know,' Gokak said, 'but he thinks perhaps it is impossible to write about him until you have developed your spiritual self further. He told Kasturi, I think it was in 1948, that he could write a book about him, but he didn't permit him to actually do it until 1961.'
>
> 'That's a little long for me to wait,' the writer said. 'And, anyway, if he's God, didn't he know how undeveloped I was spiritually when he agreed to let me write the book in the first place? Why should he put me through all this, leaving me like that after he promised I could go on tour with him and now suddenly not let me write the book?'
>
> 'It is very difficult to understand,' Gokak said.
>
> 'I think you ought to tell him how I feel about it,' the writer said, 'and to point out to him that if we wait until I have developed [...] am evolved as Baba would like me to be, the book will come out like Kasturi's, so full of adoration nobody in America would believe it.'

'Well,' Gokak ventured tentatively, 'I think Baba also feels, he said this, he will be busy the next few weeks with all the people coming to the *Shivarathri* festival. He won't have any time to give you any special attention.'

'I don't want any special attention,' the writer said. 'All I want is to be invisible, just to watch him quietly without interfering, just to be an observer.'[3]

ACCEPTANCE

God's primary interest in each person is regarding their spiritual destiny. Simultaneously, earthly concerns can drive a person's connection with God. Due to this dichotomy between God's purpose and an individual's practical considerations, a person may take time to fathom the intent behind God's actions. They often understand His reasons only after experiencing the consequences of His deeds. People struggle to engage with God because they need time to realize that divine logic differs significantly from how humans think.

Father Mazzoleni describes how God envelopes people in His gentle care when they reach out to Him. They begin to experience that circumstances magically change for the better.

> I have discovered that when the Lord takes a person to heart because the individual has invoked Him in his moment of need and asked Him for spiritual blessings, everything proceeds as if by a magical and perfect plan. Even now, I continue to have experiences of how protective this Divine Mother is who, to defend Her beloved children, turns all events to Her children's advantage in unfathomable ways—or, I should say, to the benefit of their spiritual evolution. I underline this last clarification because what we believe to be good for us rarely is in the eyes of Him, who guides our destiny and knows its most important and profound turns. The son cannot always detect benefits in the events by which he seems to be dragged, often without his even realizing it. Still, in the course of life, sometime later—months or years—those events will reveal themselves to

have been providential. Human logic is not compatible with divine reason.[4]

Sunder Iyer, an alumnus of Swami's college, recognizes his gentle preparation and development before meeting Swami. It begins innocuously with colouring Swami's photos. Then, his interest is piqued, and he begins asking questions about Him, finally opting to study in His college in Brindavan. All this without any family connection with Swami or ostensible personal inclination.

I was a school student in Bombay (now Mumbai) when I met Mr Sai Datta, a photographer. Sai Datta took black and white photographs of Baba and then coloured them. Sai Datta was willing to teach me the technique of colouring B&W photos, and I saw pictures of Sai Baba for the first time.

I started adding colour to Swami's pictures. It didn't occur to ask me who he was. I focused on colouring the images. I ventured to ask him about Sai Baba. My curiosity was aroused because I saw more and more pictures of Sai Baba. He explained that this was Sai Baba, the reincarnation of the Sai Baba of Shirdi.

The first book I read was *Summer Showers in Brindavan* in 1972. I found Swami's speeches to be down to earth. He was simplifying esoteric truths. I was starting to get attracted. In retrospect, I now realize that when the time is right, the master will search for a disciple and vice versa. Something started to arise within that was beyond me, which I didn't understand, but it seemed to make sense with Sai Baba. I didn't look upon him as God. I began to go back to Sai Datta for more pictures to paint.

Sai Datta first told me about Swami's college. He advised me to look at the college as an option after school.

I wrote a letter to my father trying to sell the idea of a college with a spiritual atmosphere and with no distractions. Father immediately agreed, happy that I was beginning to focus on my studies, and allowed me to explore the possibility of Swami's college.

I also wanted to explore this choice before making a final decision. Sai Datta suggested that to resolve my questions about the college, I could consider attending a summer course. I got the date of the Maharashtra state entrance exam for the summer course. I needed to prepare for the exam. Unfortunately, the examination day coincided with my last school board exam. I was unable to take the state entrance for the summer course. I could not convince the president of Maharashtra's Sai organization of the need for a second examination.

The summer course was crucial, both for my dad and I. Without this option, I could not plan a trip to Parthi. I couldn't have gone alone. I needed to be in a group. This sense of futility and disappointment was my first lesson in prayer. For the first time in my life, I decided to pray, but I didn't know how to pray. How does God listen to my prayers? I asked my uncle if there was a way to make a wish happen. My uncle advised me to chant the Soundarya Lahiri. I did the prayer continuously for twelve days. Nothing happened. I again asked my uncle about what I needed to do. He advised me to wait patiently. I turned to Baba and threw a challenge, 'If this has to work, you better do something.'

After two weeks, a Seva Dal member came to the house to inform me of the second entrance exam for the summer course. I wrote the exam and was selected; this was my first encounter with Swami.

My first darshan was nothing spectacular. Swami is simple. I was not fascinated by his creations. I was a member of a group that Swami had called for an interview after the summer course ended. The participants of the group asked spiritual questions. I had been curious about what He talks about in interviews. Swami was straightforward, soft-spoken and spontaneous.

I decided to join Swami's Institute.[5]

SPIRITUAL PATIENCE

A relationship with God develops gradually. Ramana Maharshi specifies why some people respond quickly to God. He uses the metaphor of coal, charcoal and gunpowder to illustrate the idea.

> ...a piece of coal takes longer to ignite; charcoal is comparatively easier to ignite and takes a little less time. In contrast, gunpowder ignites instantly, with different grades of people coming in contact with Mahatmas.[6]

Spiritual patience is an instrumental trait.

Swami uses an example of a devotee prepared to take 50 lifetimes to be and become one with God. Reaching a spiritual objective cannot be accelerated by coveting it. A devotee's progress towards God is a growth of faith, disposition, devotion, effort and longing.

> Baba once narrated a story. We were all craving something and appearing impatient.
>
> Swami said, 'You don't even understand the value of being with me. Two days ago, one devotee asked to become one with me. I told him it would take fifty lifetimes to become one with Swami. He started crying. I asked him why he was crying. He replied, "Baba, these are tears of joy because I know I will come to you after fifty lifetimes. I am so happy. Thank you, Swami." This is true devotion. But you want everything tomorrow. Swami, come to the hostel today. Swami, do this today.'[7]

Every person can afford to be patient. They must believe in God's promise that everyone will realize their oneness with God.

Swami uses the life story of a raindrop to explain spiritual patience and untiring perseverance with God. A raindrop engages in a never-ending cycle of striving; it rises from the sea, becomes a raindrop and returns to the ocean as a river.

> The raindrop has come from the sea. Wherever it falls, it yearns to reach the sea, its source. When it falls on some solid

(impermeable) ground and gets lost, it again evaporates and becomes a raindrop. It has no 'peace' (flows and flows) until it merges with the sea. It is happy when it joins a stream or a river that flows towards the sea. Man is the raindrop. The urge to reach the source, namely, the Lord, is in everyone. Some achieve that Goal quickly, some late. But all must reach it.[8]

NO ONE ESCAPES FROM GOD

In God's creation, there are no failures. Swami reinforces God's promise that each person will reach God.

Every being in the universe has the potential to transcend the senses. Even the little worm will one day rise above their feelings and senses (e.g., Eyes – Sight, Ears – Hearing, Tongue – Taste, Nose – Smell, Skin – Touch, etc.) to reach God. No life will be a failure. There is no such thing as failure in the universe. A hundred times a man will hurt himself, a thousand times he will tumble, but in the end, he will realize that he is God.[9]

Swami underscores that a person's goal is to reach God. No one escapes the return to God.

I will tell you, there is no escaping it; all creatures have to reach God someday by the long or short route.[10]

It is futile for a spiritual aspirant to understand the avatar. Instead, they must learn to enjoy being engaged with God. Swami emphasizes the importance of unwavering spiritual determination and utilizing each moment for absorption in God. This is achieved through spiritual practices and seeking His grace.

You may ask me to speak about my mystery. It is not easy to understand it. When you have the chance, gather all the joy you can. There is no use in bolting the door after the thieves have robbed and fled. Seize the chance, and do not repent later that you missed the opportunity. Remember, you must come to me at least within ten more births, if not in this birth! Strive

> to acquire grace; grace is the reward for spiritual practice; the highest spiritual discipline is to follow the instructions of the master.[11]

GOD RELENTLESSLY PURSUES AND CAPTURES DEVOTEES

Sandweiss quotes Swami to highlight reciprocity in a person–God engagement. God searches for devotees just as spiritual aspirants search for God.

For many years after that first trip, I maintained a deep and continuous search for God, trying to find Him [...] yearning to have faith [...] Never did it occur to me that God could be searching for me! I quote Swami:

> 'I am searching; I am searching; still searching. I searched in the past, and I search and search now for the man that knows and observes his true *dharma* [righteous action].'[12]

The parable of the prodigal son in the Bible is a story of a father's love for his errant son. It illustrates God's warm reception of a devotee who reaches out to Him and exemplifies the enthusiasm with which God seeks His devotees.

> In the gospel of Luke, Jesus tells the well-known parable of the prodigal son. A son asks his father for his inheritance, then squanders it as he lives a life of indulgence. With nothing left of his fortune, he is forced to work as a hired hand for a pig farmer. He is so destitute that he longs to eat the food of the pigs. Realizing that his father's servants have better working conditions, he resolves to return to his father, beg forgiveness and ask to be his servant. (Luke 15:20–24)

However, he is welcomed with loving arms upon arriving at his father's house. His father is overwhelmed with joy at his son's return and holds a feast in his honour.

> So, he got up and went back to his father. While he was still a long way off, his father caught sight of him and was filled

> with compassion. He ran to his son, embraced him and kissed him. His son said, 'Father, I have sinned against heaven and against you; I no longer deserve to be called your son.' But his father ordered his servants, 'Quickly bring the finest robe and put it on him; put a ring on his finger and sandals on his feet. Take the fattened calf and slaughter it. Then let us celebrate with a feast because this son of mine was dead and has come to life again; he was lost and is found.' Then the celebration began. (Luke 15:20–24)

Swami identifies the devotees' role and obligation, which are their first step, to experience God's love and reciprocity, which are His hundred steps.

> Come one step forward, and I shall take a hundred toward you. Shed just one tear, and I shall wipe a hundred from your eyes [...] When the night grows chill, you draw the rug tighter around you, is it not? So, too, when grief assails you, draw the warmth of the name of the Lord closer around your mind. Out of all the hundreds of thousands [...] you alone have gained this contact through your good luck. Let at least the desire to be saved sprout in you, and I shall see that it grows and gives fruit, provided you yearn and try. To pour the nectar of grace, the vessel must be cleaned. Clean it and demand the nectar; do not grieve later that you missed the chance since it has come within reach. You will not know Me in a trice or even in days. It is something that has to be realized in stages, in due course, through discrimination, non-attachment and clear-sightedness.[13]

Aitken amplifies God 'searching' for devotees into God's 'pursuit' of devotees. He suggests that God takes radical steps to catch a devotee's attention, attracting and pulling them closer and helping them disengage from the world.

> How a teacher can dog the footsteps of a likely devotee and hook him with drastic intervention.[14]

The central idea of the poem *The Hound of Heaven* by Francis Thompson (1859–1907) is that God is an integral part of humanity.[15] He is not separate or distant from people. The poetic expression of this principle is the 'pursuit' of a person by God; God is like a hunter after His prey. People may 'run away' from God if they are distracted and motivated by desires and attachments, captivated and entangled in unimportant things and neglecting spiritual truths. God tracks them and enables their return to Him with acceptance and submission. He targets each person.

The poem begins with a person admitting that they fled to hide from God. Their remoteness from God is an intellectual gap, a difference triggered by their thoughts and ideas.

> I fled Him, down the nights and down the days;
> I fled Him, down the arches of the years;
> I fled Him, down the labyrinthine ways
> Of my own mind; and in the mist of tears
> I hid from Him...[16]

The poem emphasizes that God is relentless in the pursuit of devotees.

> And the Great Huntsman is remorseless in his determination to win the soul [...] The poem [...] keeps up the chase in the most vividly dramatic realism.[17]

The spiritual aspirant will experience God's relentlessness like a hound snapping at their heels at every moment.

> The footfall of the Hound is heard in all the pauses of the poem [...] you hear the patter of the little feet padding after the soul...[18]

Father Mazzoleni vividly demonstrates the concept of God seeking a devotee through his encounter with Swami. He senses a compelling force leading him to Swami. In that experience, he realizes that once God decides to pull a person towards Himself, it is impossible to escape. He feels that God has grasped him and illustrates the idea with a metaphor.

> A real miracle was taking place, given that, in a sense, I was already kidnapped, and I had no possibility of undoing my decision. The road was the one that was to bring me with no chance of delay into an Abode of the Highest Peace. It was no longer my responsibility to do anything to bring myself back to my true home.
>
> There was someone who was watching over me and planning my return. No matter how much I struggled to escape that grip, it would have been fatal to me to loosen it, and He to whom I had entrusted my salvation could no longer allow it. A mother's love is great, even when she chases her child because he refuses to take his medicine and grips him firmly in her arm to make him take it![19]

Schulman writes that nothing hinders a person's repossession by God. He highlights that God's spiritual timing, when He decides to capture a devotee, is everything. When the time is right, everything magically falls into place with strange coincidences of synchronicity. God's pull is all-powerful. No one can resist Him.

> A man may search the entire world for his Master, a sage had written, but not until the time was right could he find Him. But when the pupil was ready, the Teacher would do the calling, and nothing the student could do could prevent his Master from drawing him to his spiritual home; distance, lack of money, business and family ties would be resolved seemingly logically and effortlessly.[20]

Father Mazzoleni describes his feelings when he reaches *Puttaparthi* and is waiting for *darshan*. He is apprehensive about what will happen, so he uses a quote from the Bible to manage his anxiety. God captures a person. He chooses the moment to engage and relate with a devotee. His presence in *Parthi* is symptomatic of Swami having chosen him.

> The moment of a close encounter was drawing near. I was full of misgivings because I had read that it is not easy to meet and sometimes even see Him.

> No. This could not happen. I was not going to see Him; He was coming to me to draw me to Himself.
>
> 'You did not choose me. No, I chose you.'[21]

IMPLORE GOD FOR HELP

In the following passage, Father Mazzoleni is praying to God to intervene and help him in his moment of uncertainty and grief.

> O God, how far away You feel! But if it is true that You are so close to us in our moment of trial, reach out Your hand and free me. I don't know what to do; I'm confused; I don't understand. Intervene, I beg You. Find a remedy, whatever it may be: sacrifice whatever You wish. I shall accept anything from Your hands, even those cures which make me suffer. But I beg You, don't leave me like this, alone in this affliction.[22]

Tolstoy uses the metaphor of a baby bird falling from a nest to explain his spiritual helplessness and restlessness. He believes that whatever his current predicament, he belongs to God, is a part of His scheme and God knows his situation.

> But again and again [...] I returned to the same conclusion that I could not have come into the world without any cause, reason or meaning; I could not be [...] a fledgling fallen from its nest as I felt myself to be. Or, granting that I am such, lying on my back crying in the high grass, I cry because I know that a mother has borne me within her, has hatched, warmed, fed and loved me. Where is she—that mother? If I am deserted, who has abandoned me? [...] Who was that someone? [...] 'God'? He knows and sees my searching, my despair and my struggle.[23]

YOU SEE HIM, AND THEN YOU DO NOT

Tolstoy describes how he reasoned and searched for God, recognizing Him as the cause and basis of creation. He believes that he is an expression of the power that is God. Nevertheless, he cannot accept the traditional religious descriptions of God and His relationship with His creation—man. This unresolved question fills him with unhappiness. As his despair increases, he implores God for clarity.

> I sought God, hoped that I should find Him, and [...] addressed prayers to that which I sought but had not found [...] If I exist, there must be some cause for it and a cause of causes. And that first cause is what men have called 'God'. And I paused on that thought and tried [...] to recognize the presence of that cause. And as soon as I acknowledged that there is a force in whose power I am, I at once felt that I could live. But I asked myself: What is that cause, that force? How am I to think of it? What are my relations to that which I call 'God'? And only the familiar replies occurred to me: 'He is the Creator and Preserver.' This reply did not satisfy me [...] I became terrified and began to pray to Him whom I sought [...] But the more I prayed, the more apparent it became that He did not hear me [...] And with despair in my heart [...] I said: 'Lord, have mercy, save me! Lord, teach me!'[24]

Tolstoy describes his emotions as he accepts the reality of God and seeks to discover a relationship with Him but fails to find the connection. He feels that God is detached from him. The initial belief and acceptance of God that occurred with the emotional experience ebbed away, making him unhappy and worried.

> 'He exists,' said I to myself. And I had only for an instant to admit that, and at once, life rose within me, and I felt the possibility and joy of being. But again, from the admission of the existence of a God, I went on to seek my relation with Him [...] and again, that God, detached from the world and me, melted like a block of ice, melted before my eyes, and again nothing remained. Again, the spring of life dried up within me, and I despaired.[25]

Swami uses the story of Gajendra to illustrate how God responds when a person turns towards Him, reaches out, accepts Him and surrenders to His will.

> There is a good story of Gajendra, the elephant, which conveys the meaning of bondage well. In the thick forest of life, a wild elephant, man's mind, will be roaming. This mind becomes thirsty for sensual pleasures. To quench that thirst, it begins to drink in the lake of worldly activities. The moment the elephant puts its foot in the lake, the crocodile of attachment catches hold of its leg. The elephant cannot free itself. With this attachment, the elephant struggles until it becomes weak. When it becomes weak, it prays to be saved by God. When such a prayer, in desperation, is made to God, the grace of God will descend on the person. When the elephant's vision turns toward God, God's vision also turns toward the elephant. This is what is called *Sudarshana,* or holy vision. When you turn toward God, God will turn toward you.[26]

TIMING OF GOD AS READINESS TO RECEIVE

God engaging with a person is a unique moment. He times His revelation to have a spiritual impact. A person's readiness is their preparedness to understand, value and imbibe His message in the disclosure.

According to Paul Tillich, a person receives God's grace when they are filled with anxiety and restlessness in their pursuit.

> The grace of God blesses a person when they are emotionally feeling low, distressed, agitated and helpless. God reaches out when a person thinks their life is meaningless and going nowhere. It strikes when the person feels distant from God.[27]

Aitken reinforces how God times His entry into the life of a spiritual aspirant. There is nothing random or accidental in His work. He creates conditions for the spark of devotion to be lit, and His timing is right. Aitken mentions spiritual anxiety as a condition for God to evoke love for God in a person's heart.

> Grace can strike us from any direction [...] it would be wrong to assume it is as random as lightning. One must be at the right place and time for the flame to ignite [...] Usually, decisions

> have led us there, and more often than not, the decisions have been hard, involving much wrestling with the soul even though the situation may have seemed trivial at the time.[28]

Sandweiss reflects on his experience with Swami; Swami responds to him when he is profoundly depressed, desperate and mentally prepared to accept Him.

> I don't know why it should happen now; perhaps his approaching me the other day in my deepest despair was the turning point. I am beginning to feel incredibly blessed. Perhaps there is something to the story that God waits and tests, allowing specific experiences only when one is ready.[29]

Swami uses the metaphor of a bud blossoming into a flower to explain the timing of His engagement with devotees. He explains that like waiting for a bud to bloom, He must also wait for the right spiritual moment to act. Swami affirms that He will engage with everyone and does not discriminate amongst people; everyone will get an opportunity with Him.

> One day, Swami called me and showed me a couple of letters the students had written. He said the students were jealous because he talked and showed attention to one particular student. He added that the boys need to realize that there are 650 boys in the hostel, and it is physically impossible to speak to everyone. He then added, 'None of you understand. Everything is time; everything is time. This boy was in the school and studied from the first standard to the twelfth. I am only speaking to him now. Why did I not speak to him all these years? Because it is a question of time. Understand that for the bud to become a flower takes time. One can neither hasten it nor slow it down. It will take its prescribed time to flower. In the same way, tell the boys and everybody that everything is time, and when their time comes, Swami will speak to them.'[30]

Swami uses three metaphors to explain the timing of His engagement with devotees: the removal of a mature cataract from the eyes, natural falling of a scab from a wound and ripening of fruit.

> After my parents settled in Prasanthi Nilayam, I regularly visited the ashram with my family. During my first interview with Swami in 1984, I asked Him why He made me wait all these years, although I had been worshipping Shirdi Sai since childhood and had my first darshan of Parthi Sai in 1950. Swami replied, 'My child, everything has its proper time, and this is the right time for you. For example, when we have a cataract, the doctor operates on it only when it is mature; otherwise, the eye gets damaged. Also, if you have a wound on your body and remove the scab before it heals completely, there will be bleeding; when the wound heals naturally, the crust will fall off.
>
> Further, if there is a fruit in the tree, and when it is ripe and falls, it is very sweet. But if you pluck it when it is unripe, you are wasting the fruit because it will not be sweet. Thus, for everything, the time has to be correct. So, this is the right time for you.'[31]

Ramakrishna Paramahansa exemplifies the timing of God's action using the metaphor of draining an abscess only when it is ready to burst.

> He said to Rakhal, 'You were angry with me, weren't you? Do you know why I made you angry? There was a reason. Only then would the medicine work. The surgeon first brings an abscess to the head. Only then does he apply an herb so that it may burst and dry.'[32]

The *Bhagavad Gita* illustrates the magnitude of the right moment for God to impart knowledge to a person. God's idea of the right time is implicit in Krishna giving the *Bhagavad Gita* to Arjuna on the battlefield. Krishna allows Arjuna's grief to intensify. Finally, Arjuna refuses to fight unless Krishna solves his dilemmas. Swami explains this in the following excerpt.

> Krishna, acting, allows the despondency to deepen and darken. When Arjuna finally threw down his bow and refused to fight, confessed that he had lost all sense of right and wrong and prayed that Krishna should teach him how to solve his problems best, only then did Krishna come forward.[33]

> At the very beginning of the Gita, Krishna could have taught the principle of devotion and commitment to duty and selfless action. But Krishna chose not to do so. He started speaking only after listening to Arjuna's weeping and lamentations for a long time. While Arjuna was carrying on, Krishna did not interfere at all. He patiently waited while Arjuna verbalized his confused state. Finally, Krishna asked, 'Arjuna, are you done? Have you vented all your feelings?' It was only at this point that Krishna started teaching.[34]

In this incident, Ramana Rao experiences Swami and His omniscience. He first sees Swami while stuck on a roadside amongst milling crowds. The incident is unplanned; it happens by chance. The nature of the experience and the author's instinctive obeisance to Swami from a distance becomes a nostalgic memory. Swami recalls the incident in their subsequent meeting, even though the author only saw Him from a distance. The story suggests that however insignificant, every experience of a person with God has a purpose. The person may take time to recognize God's handiwork. The author is amazed by Swami's ability to use a minor detail for tremendous impact.

> Once in Hyderabad, I stopped and parked my scooter by the road outside the compound where Swami was visiting. The street was full of people. On inquiry, I learned that Sai Baba of Puttaparthi was in (the) house and was about to leave. I tried to retreat in vain. By then, more two-wheelers had gathered. Inside the compound was a shamiana where bhajan was in full swing with devotees. With the crowd pushing me inside, I stood with my back to the compound wall, eagerly waiting for Swami to go out to make way for me to get out. Baba came out into the *pandal*. All faces lit up with joy as he walked as though floating in the air, reaching out for their letters, blessing them, talking to some, restraining them from touching his feet. For the first time, I looked at him. He was short in stature. Even though I was five or six rows away, his bright orange-coloured attire, the crown of his hair and his radiant face with a sweet and compassionate smile were

visible to me. As he got into the waiting car, people started chanting the Indian version of hallelujah, 'Bhagawan Sri Sathya Sai Baba Ki Jai'. After the car sped away, I noticed my hands inadvertently joined in obeisance. I smiled to myself about his stunning charisma.

I didn't mention this incident to anyone and forgot all about it. I never thought I would see Baba again.

And when I did see Swami, my friend told Him, 'This is the first time for him to see Swami....' Baba interrupted and said, 'Not the first time. This is the second time. He has already seen me in Hyderabad at Boorgula Ramakrishnarao's place.' He looked at me and added, 'Didn't you?' I was dumbfounded.[35]

TIME IS NOTHING FOR GOD

In a letter, Swami explains how a person learns that the world is temporary, becomes thoughtful and starts seeking God. The time this takes may appear prolonged. He cautions that God's timescale is different from that of humans. From God's perspective, the time it takes for God to respond and engage with a person is insignificant.

> The time will come when the whole of this dream will vanish. To everyone, there must come a time when the whole universe will be found to have been a mere dream, when we shall find that the soul is infinitely better than its surroundings. In this struggle through what we call environments, there will come a time when we shall find that these environments were almost zero compared to the power of the soul. It is only a question of time; time is nothing in the infinite. It is a drop in the ocean. We can afford to wait and be calm.[36]

PREPARATION TO MEET GOD

God creates the context and emotionally and intellectually prepares a devotee to receive what He wants to give them. The 'meeting' with God serves a spiritual purpose. In the upcoming passage, Dr Bhagvantham cites Dr Radhakrishnan, India's second president, to explain the psychological context of extreme helplessness driving individuals to seek a connection with God. Dr Bhagvantham broadens this perspective, underscoring people's uncertainty, unease and anxiety when meeting Swami. Feeling helpless makes meeting God even more memorable and transformative. Swami prepares people to meet Him.

> For every individual, there comes an hour, sometimes or other, for nature is not in a hurry, when everything that he can do for himself fails, when he sinks into the gulf of utter blackness, an hour when he would give all that he has for one gleam of light, for one sign of the Divine. When he is assailed by doubt, denial, hatred of life and black despair, he can escape them only if God lays His hand on him.—Dr Radhakrishnan
>
> Such mental state generally precedes a man's preparedness to face divinity in all its splendour [...] many a visitor to Prasanthi Nilayam and many a devotee of Baba [...] have had their own experiences akin [...] It often results in total surrender to the Supreme. Any ego by which one still has one's capacity, either of intelligence or wealth, to help one pull himself out of the mess around him impedes reaching a state of total surrender.[37]

Underhill describes the experience of the encounter with God. According to her, a new 'consciousness' can unexpectedly begin after someone has been spiritually restless. She emphasizes that the unique experience is triggered externally and does not hatch from internal reflections. The inner disquiet was a preparation for the experience.

> The onset of this new consciousness seems to the self so sudden, so clearly imposed from without rather than developed from within, as to have a supernatural character [...] (even) [...] the abrupt conversion is really [...] the sequel and the result of a long period of restlessness [...] The deeper mind stirs uneasily in its prison, and its emergence is the last of many efforts to escape. The subject's temperament, surroundings, the vague but persistent apprehensions of a super-sensual reality he could not find yet could not forget; all these have prepared him for it.[38]

In the forthcoming excerpt, Father Mazzoleni describes his meeting with Swami. He uses a mother's relationship with her child as a metaphor to express the underlying warmth and compassion he experienced during the meeting. He characterizes the nature of the meeting as a benediction: God giving Himself to the devotee.

> A completely new experience had slipped in, a personage who was to take my entire life, not immediately but gradually, with the ability of a God who skilfully lures his own after allowing them to use up all their cartridges. The Master of Masters was waiting for me at the pass, but he was entering my life, not in a dominant way, but gently, so that His power would not frighten me, and His heat would not burn me. It was He who [...] was presenting Himself with the resolute sweetness of a mother who wants to give back to her son what the son, through distraction, had himself misplaced.[39]

Rupak Changkakoti describes his gradual movement into Swami's orbit in the following narrative. He spent many years with Swami. He recollects his emotions, and a desire to be near Swami that becomes intense and is expressed through singing bhajans with an ulterior motive. He wanted Swami to notice him, but when he sang, he sang to God and experienced something unique each time. He calls it a different kind of 'awareness'.

> My earliest recollection is of our family being invited to a Sai Bhajan. We assumed the *bhajan* would be like a traditional *kirtan*, where guests can walk in anytime. We arrived late after the bhajan was nearly over. As a consolation, the organizer gave us a small photograph of Swami, which we placed on the altar at home.
>
> The relationship developed as a natural process. I had no questions. We started attending bhajans, and I learned a few Sai bhajans. I distinctly remember the first Sai bhajan I sang, *Govind Hare Gopal Hare*, a song Swami sings often. I felt transported to a different dimension when I first sang this song. I find the experience difficult to describe. It was a beautiful

experience, feeling free, joyful and fulfilled. When the bhajan was over, the organizer started crying. He came and hugged me and said that my song had emotionally touched him, and he had felt as if he was in Swami's presence.

Whenever I sing, I feel immersed in the bhajan of losing or forgetting myself. The bhajan is flowing, and the words are coming, but I am not concentrating. It is like a different level of awareness. It still happens sometimes.

I visited Parthi in 1972 as a Seva Dal member. Poorna Chandra Auditorium was under construction. I did not meet Swami, but he was always around. Each time Swami came close, I felt excitement within. I even lack the words to say what I felt. It was not awe but a diversity of emotions. Swami would often pass by and ask, 'Where have you come from?' and 'What is your name?' and my heart would be fluttering with a multitude of emotions.

The next trip was to the 1973 Summer Course in Brindavan. Swami often asked me the same questions, 'Where have you come from?' and 'What is your name?' One day I got an opportunity to sing the bhajan *Bhaja Govindam Bhaja Gopalam Keshava Madhava*. I had the same experience of losing myself in the bhajan before Swami. Swami would often come, we would sit around him, and he would ask me to sing the same bhajan. The bhajan has a crescendo where we sing '*Keshav Madhav deen dayalam deen dayalam deen dayalam*' and then pick up speed until it ends. It was like a burst of bliss. I had the same feeling each time I sang in his presence. I sang this song in front of him five or six times.

The following year I joined Brindavan College.

A slow transformation was occurring inside me. I had a desire to be physically closer to Swami. It was a desire. I didn't make any effort. I didn't try. It was just an intensity to be with him. Bhajan was a way to be visible to him. Every time I sang, it was the same remarkable experience. When singing in front of Swami, one is trying to appeal to the Divine, not the physical Swami in front, but appealing to God, that indescribable God.[40]

TAKING THE FIRST STEP

Preparing for an encounter with God requires deliberate effort by a seeker. Seeking and meeting God is unlike any other endeavour that a person has undertaken. They must develop a seriousness of purpose, focus their energies and diligently perform tasks to pursue this goal.

Fulton Sheen highlights the importance of the spiritual purpose of a devotee.

> What men ask about Divinity is never as important as why they ask it.[41]

The saying, '*Yad Bhavam Tad Bhavathi*' (as are the feelings, so are the results), emphasizes the quality and purity of the thoughts and intentions that precede action. What one believes and the focus and goal are important, not what one says or does. Swami elaborates:

> Suppose you wear a particular dress and stand before a mirror. You will find the exact reflection in the mirror. Similarly, your thoughts and feelings reflect in the outside world. Everything that transpires is a reaction, reflection and resound of your true intention and mindset.[42]

God creates situations to help people clarify and refine their motivations in seeking God. God is an active participant in helping a person improve their motives to engage with God.

A person may not always get an immediate response from God as they try to find Him. Seeking God and getting a response from Him may involve a long wait. The wait for God to respond to prayers is a spiritual process of preparing the aspirant to meet Him. During this process, the seekers concentrate on God and intensify their desire for Him. An apt metaphor is a magnifying glass that focuses the sun's rays igniting a fire. Waiting strengthens concentration, devotion and love for God.

Ramakrishna Paramahansa mentions that the first step must be of the devotee and about the role of spiritual perseverance.

> Everything depends upon the will of the Lord. Perseverance is necessary for God-vision. If you merely sit on the shore

of a lake and say, 'There are fish in this lake,' will you get any fish? Go and get the things necessary for fishing; get a rod, line and bait, and throw some food into the water to entice them. Then, from the deep water, the fish will rise and come near when you can see and hook them. You wish me to show you God while you sit quietly by without making the slightest effort! You want me to set the curd, to churn the butter and hold it to your mouth. You ask me to catch the fish and put it in your hands. How unreasonable is your demand?[43]

HUMILITY

Ramakrishna Paramahansa used to say that a person must be guileless to develop faith in God quickly.[44] The intelligence to manage worldly activities can create doubts and forms of pride, such as pride in learning and wealth, which can impede a spiritual journey. Sheen suggests that seekers of God must harbour humility, self-awareness, a readiness to learn and openness to new ideas.[45] He writes that God relates easily with simple and humble persons. God also connects with highly educated people who know their knowledge is insignificant and understand what they do not know.

Ramana Maharshi emphasizes that to meet God, aspirants must give up their ego, cultivate humility and accept and surrender to God.

> Many visitors saluted Sri Bhagavan (Ramana Maharshi) with the prayer, 'Make me a bhakta. Give me moksha'. After they left, Sri Bhagavan thought aloud: they all want bhakti and moksha. If I tell them, 'Give yourself to me,' they will not. How, then, can they get what they want?[46]

> The life of Jesus also illustrates that a person should be respectful and humble to meet God. Jesus was born in a cave to a simple family of modest means. His glory remained hidden from everyone at birth. To see Jesus, everyone had to enter a cave. To enter the cave that had a low ceiling, each person had to bow, a gesture symbolizing submission before seeing God.

> Seekers of God who 'bend' are humble and submit to and see God, whereas others may miss Him altogether.[47]

INITIAL EMOTIONAL PRESENTIMENTS

The path to God starts with self-doubt and involves experiences that create strong emotions, which begin affecting daily life. The following reflective excerpts reveal the evocation of spiritual feelings and reflect how God influences seekers. The narratives, one of a Christian mystic, another from the Ramayana and the third with Swami, are similar. The awareness or knowledge is based on tangible personal experience and intuition. The emotional trigger can be a book, God's teachings or an unexpected mystical experience. God has no limitations. He influences a person in many ways.

Merton writes about the mystical experience that started his spiritual journey. It occurred unexpectedly when he was not even a spiritual seeker. He did things that he had never done before. It was an enlightening and emotional experience whereby he gained insight into his spiritual condition. He began praying, thanking God for helping him. He went into a church and kneeled, something he had not done before. As he prayed, he experienced a quiet, heartfelt joy. He realized that his life would improve and described it as a rebirth. The author felt that God had pulled him close; God made the first move, and he responded to the overture from God. The emotions and understanding evoked in him were a premonition of significant changes expected in the future.

> Abruptly intense feelings and faith were evoked, filling me with profound insight and creating a spiritual urgency. The experience was unlike anything I had encountered before. The nature of my prayers changed. I began to pray intensely, with all my being, thinking and heart.
>
> I went to the Church and had a very substantial spiritual experience. I surrendered. My acceptance and submission were a struggle.
>
> I had never walked into a church to pray. I began doing this with the sole purpose of engaging with God.

> Sometimes, I walked out of the Church into the open street, feeling that I had been reborn. I sat outside, meditating on the joy of my inner peace. I knew my life was now going to change and how I would become better.[48]

In the following quotation, Swami narrates the story of *Vibhishana*, *Ravana's* brother. It occurs at a time when *Vibhishana* has not met Lord Rama. As he listens to Rama's story, intense emotions arise within him. From then on, he continuously thinks about Rama and desires to be in His presence.

> Vibhishana listened to the story with joy and tears in his eyes. He installed those divinely charming figures in the temple of his heart and yearned deeply to be in their presence and fall at their feet. 'Will they receive me? Can I be saved? Do I deserve to be blessed by them?' he asked himself [...] He offered in his mind all that he had and was; he began living in the constant meditation of their glory from that very moment.[49]

Dr Sandweiss is apprehensive about his first meeting with Swami. In the forthcoming experience, he feels mysteriously revitalized when discussing Swami with another devotee.

> I don't know what kind of a strange situation I'm getting into—I'll have to wait and see.
>
> It's strange that when my spirits become low and I begin to feel I'm chasing some meaningless dream if I talk to a devotee of Baba, my spirits are lifted [...] something genuine and electrifying comes across and uplifts me.[50]

INEXPLICABLE ATTRACTION, CONFIDENCE AND INTENSIFYING URGENCY

Phyllis Krystal writes about her experience with Swami before she met Him. It begins when her eyes are drawn to Swami's piercing eyes on a book cover, and she is compellingly and mysteriously drawn to him. Her experience is similar to Vibhishana's emotional reaction when he hears about Lord Rama and is yet to see Him.

> I first heard about Baba in April of 1972 [...] As I reached a high shelf to pull down a book, another book fell at the same time [...] I [...] was immediately impressed by the picture of the most striking-looking man on the cover [...] I scarcely noticed [...] his features as my attention was riveted on his eyes, which seemed to penetrate my very core.
>
> I leafed through it [...] I paused to study more carefully several other pictures of Baba [...] those extraordinary eyes seemed to dominate everything. As I studied each photo, I began to feel very strongly drawn to him and wanted to know more about him [...] the attraction was so compelling that I started to read it as soon as I reached home. Once started, I found it impossible to put down [...] I was fascinated by [...] Sai Baba, but even more by the strange way he seemed to speak to me from the pages of the book [...] I was developing an extremely strong desire to meet him in person as soon as possible![51]

Suzie Parvati Reeves is moved by a magazine article on Swami and strongly desires to travel to India to meet Him. She first ignores the news report but takes it home and rereads it. She is affected by the words Swami uses to address humanity as 'embodiments of true love'. She describes the appellation used by Swami by employing a metaphor. It was like a key opening a lock, a sentence that opened her mind and gave her intuitive insight.

> (The) magazines had arrived and were piled high. As I looked, I was caught by a small black and white photograph of a handsome man with a crown of Afro hair. Sathya Sai Baba was written below the picture. It was about a guru in India. I dismissed the attraction. Yet something was radiating from that face [...] I took the magazine home.
>
> [...] I began to read the article about the magnetic man in the picture. The author was an Englishman writing about his recent visit to India, Prasanthi Nilayam (The Abode of

> the Highest Peace), and the Ashram of Sathya Sai Baba. The place was in South India in a small village called Puttaparthi.
>
> He wrote about his experiences. It was another world, like something in a dream, yet I could see it before my mind's eye. It fascinated me that such a place existed. The magic entered when the author described the personal interview Sai Baba had granted him after four months of waiting. When they were finally alone in the tiny interview room, he saw the 'Embodiment of Pure Love' before him. This sentence was so powerful; it went straight to my heart. I cannot forget the impact I felt at that moment, like a key turning in an old lock. If pure love exists in this world, I have to see it with my own eyes, even if it means going all the way to India.[52]

Krystal narrates experiences that intensified her desire to travel to see Swami. She noticed Swami in a photograph and was irresistibly attracted to Him. When she saw a movie of Swami walking amongst devotees, her desire to meet Swami further intensified.

> I began to feel very strange in participating [...] in a group worshipping the figure of Baba as if he were God [...] Sai Baba possessed a human body, though a distinctive-looking one. But despite my doubts, I felt irresistibly drawn to him, especially to one picture of him in the centre of the altar, which depicted his radiantly smiling face framed in its halo of black hair.
>
> The meeting ended with the showing of a film [...] It depicted Baba moving among the crowds [...] I was fascinated by this first sight of him slowly walking in and out among the adoring visitors [...] I soon became aware of an electric quality emanating from him throughout the film. I was reminded of the similar sensation I had felt while reading the two books about him. The more I watched his slight orange-clad form glide gracefully here and there among the crowd, [...] my original desire to fly to see him increased. I knew with a profound inner certainty that I would not be satisfied until I could have first-hand experience with him.[53]

Reeves recounts an event that deepens her longing to meet Swami; it clarifies her lingering questions and resolves ambiguities and uncertainties.

> I arrived at the flat [...] about fifteen people gathered for meditation [...] everyone sat in a meditating posture. I was new to this, never having stayed motionless in one place for long. Every part of me was aching. I thought, what a price to pay for information on a strange guru.
>
> I noticed a black-and-white picture of Sai Baba on the wall. His eyes were intense and powerful. When I sat with closed eyes, trying to meditate, I saw Sai Baba appear as if he was before me. He looked familiar, like someone I had known for a long time.
>
> It was midnight when Dasaratha turned to me. I told him about the intriguing guru named Sathya Sai Baba. Dasaratha immediately assured me that Sai Baba was a great Holy Man, genuine and respected.
>
> 'Suzie, do you read spiritual magazines?' No. 'You're a fashion designer, and Sai Baba has had to appear in a fashion magazine to call you. You must go to India. He has called you.' It sounded like a command, but he only repeated words my heart had been declaring all along. This was precisely the prompting I needed.[54]

Fortuitous occurrences continued happening with Reeves. She attended a religious symposium straight out of a hospital after a surgery for the screening of a film on Swami. She became emotional and used the appellation 'my guru' for Swami. All her experiences fell into a pattern, apparently related but without a causal connection, and increased her desire to meet Swami.

> I received an invitation to a Spiritual Symposium [...] The program had indicated a film. No title was (given) [...] in the auditorium was a sign: A Film on Sathya Sai Baba. I sat there with tears of gratitude filling my eyes, watching this fascinating film about the life of my 'guru'.

> The movie showed Sai Baba as a boy, later a young man, in the village of Puttaparthi where he was born. He was a beautiful, divine being. The images seemed to come to life. The best surprise was the closing photograph, a large coloured photo of Sai Baba wearing a yellow robe, and my prayer picture. That evening, I became aware of a presence in my room. I felt Sai Baba was with me, yet my mind doubted, calling it imagination.[55]

Schulman shares an overwhelming urge to write a book about Swami, a desire he unsuccessfully attempts to conquer. He resists accepting that Swami may have triggered the desire to write the book.

> One day, for no reason he could discover, he realized that he had somehow developed a compulsion of his own. He tried to deny it, suppress it and finally rationalize it, but it wouldn't leave him. He had to face it. Something inside of him (he refused to accept the possibility that it might be something outside of him) demanded that he write a book about Sai Baba.[56]

WAITING FOR GOD

Preparing to meet God is a process enabled by God to remake a person. To develop their relationship with God, the seekers reflect, examine their beliefs and seek new knowledge. The process is not prosaic and mechanical. God is recognized as silently participating. The person discovers God's magnificence and accessibility, and spiritual emotions are evoked when preparing to meet God, which is a devotional and transformational process. At night, a person with a torch can see everyone he casts light upon, but no one can see him until he turns the light on himself. Similarly, God sees everyone, but no one can see Him until He reveals Himself.

The following reflections of a devotee illustrate how the spiritual wait for a response from God is preparation for meeting God.

> Life is seemingly an eternal wait for Swami to acknowledge, recognize and respond. As I wait, I realize that the mind gets

> centred on Him. As I wait, I can choose to meditate, look inward and learn something. If I learn to be humble, that is a great lesson. Time ceases to count in Prasanthi Nilayam. The world outside no longer matters. All attachments and relationships with family and friends are on hiatus. I only think of Sai Baba. He fills my mind. It has been ten days.[57]

Father Mazzoleni describes the evolution of his thinking as he developed confidence and conviction in Swami by trying to understand who He is and what He embodies. Father Mazzoleni was an ordained priest. For him, the formation of belief was a knowledge-acquisition process. His thirst for discovery and understanding surpassed his Christian beliefs, allowing him to embrace new knowledge that could complete and complement his current perspective. The search for new knowledge is an extreme adventure because it heightens uncertainty and fear. Father Mazzoleni is aware that new knowledge might demolish his past theories and beliefs and require him to reconstruct new ideas, a psychologically unsettling experience. He likens this process to tearing down a building to construct a new tower on a new foundation, but he intends to overcome his fears and doubts by reading and learning about Swami. As he experiences Swami through His words, he has a lively, emotional and spiritual experience. He perceives divine authority and certainty in Swami's words.

> If I wanted a decisive answer on Sai Baba, the cowardly cautions of those who fear the unknown or believe they have already absorbed the truth available to the human mind would be no help. If I wanted an answer this time, I would have to loosen my moorings, go out into the open water and dive deep.
>
> Now, my search was beginning to seem like an adventure; it was the most inspiring adventure of my life. I followed two methods, one destructive and the other constructive. The first consisted of making a clean sweep of certain theological preconceptions while promising to salvage them later if necessary.
>
> I pretended, so to speak, to be a theologian who had forgotten everything he had learned, all his dogmas and beliefs.

I became a blank slate, with nothing to defend and nothing to affirm that wasn't a product of common sense.

I asked myself, 'Can God, to whom every religion attributes all power, wisdom and love, be reduced by mankind to the limits of a single incarnation?' I found myself in a dilemma that I could not escape. If I say God can incarnate more than once, I collide with the Church and its doctrine. Suppose I maintain that God could not have had other incarnations besides Jesus Christ. In that case, I rub against the Truth—that is, against God Himself—by implying that God is incapable of doing anything more than humans can figure out.

This was the destructive method. To rebuild, you have to tear down the old building.

Here began the constructive method. I had to obtain everything possible from Sai Baba's discourses and writings. Only in this way would I be able to dissolve doubt. Looking inside him, at his thoughts and habits, studying his movements and sayings, I would at least know more about his nature. By interrogating him about who Jesus was for him, I would discover who he was.

I was in a state of great mental excitement. My heart told me I was standing on a diamond mine, and every move I made to scratch the soil filled me with trepidation and emotion. It was as if I were afraid to discover that all that treasure was real and available to me, that it was right there under my feet.

When my eyes rested on His words, I felt an instant thrill that transported me mysteriously into a divine atmosphere. I could not tell anymore if the things I was reading were taken from the gospel or if they came from some heavenly book unknown to most people. I was struck by a flash of certainty that what I was reading had to have a divine origin. Above all, I was struck by the authority and magnificence of His declarations.[58]

Father Mazzoleni describes his thoughts and feelings when he begins following Swami. Swami gently evokes acceptance and awareness of who He is in the author. The author experiences peace with a stilled mind based on intuited knowledge about Swami. He experiences his transformation. It is a complete renewal. He uses a metaphor of old and new clothes; he has shed old ideas of God and religion and accepted Swami.

> The Director of my life wanted to bring me to that solitude that would allow Him to reign undisturbed in my heart. Thus, He induced me not to place my hope in institutional support to give me security that only He can provide. He does not want old clothes worn when He invites people to His wedding. And by now, I was almost undressed, waiting for a new wedding garment.[59]

Father Mazzoleni writes about his experience of waiting for Swami, and his reflections reveal the spiritual potency of darshan, the beholding of Swami. He discovers that getting to know Swami was not a sequential process of studying Him, learning about Him and understanding Him. Intuitive knowledge is evoked within him when he sees Swami. Patiently waiting for darshan is experienced as a time of personal communication between a master and devotee. The spiritual blessing is delivered silently and reflected in learning elicited in the devotee by being in the master's presence.

> (For me) Studying Sai Baba meant seeing Him first, investigating His activity and understanding His thoughts and message. Although I expected to take these steps individually, I soon discovered they were not separable. Sai Baba began to be a message from the moment I first saw Him. Because of this, someone who sees Him has already received an enormous gift. I don't say this rhetorically because the things you understand upon meeting Him may be enough to revolutionize your life. However, they are only a tiny part of what you did not know then and will gradually discover in subsequent events.[60]

PERSONAL REFLECTIONS WHEREBY THE RELATIONSHIP DEVELOPS

A person must be patient in one's engagement with God. Aspirants want God to respond to them immediately. God meets His devotees when the time is right for His engagement with them.

Swami does not respond to the expectations of Diana Baskin. She was expecting Swami to recognize and talk to her immediately. He did not notice her, much less speak to her. She felt humiliated and got angry. The incident illustrates that God does not respond to a seeker's expectations. He waits and prepares the person to become ready to receive Him and His spiritual gifts.

> My mother urged me to join the Ratanlals and go without her. There was a large crowd when we arrived, and I could see Sai Baba only from a great distance. I sat very uncomfortably cross-legged on the ground among masses of people throughout long, tedious talks in Indian languages. While all the time, I was burning with the desire to meet Sai Baba and thought this was not what I had expected of our first meeting.
>
> When the talks and celebrations were over, I followed the Ratanlals to the college courtyard area, where only a few people could enter.
>
> Finally, Sai Baba appeared! I held my breath and felt my heart pounding in anticipation of that great moment when He would greet me with a smile of recognition and say something like, 'You have come; I have been waiting for you, my beloved disciple.'
>
> He walked directly towards me and smiled as He greeted Mrs Ratanlal on my right and Mr Ratanlal on my left; He ignored me completely. Sai Baba made me feel invisible, small, and humiliated. I felt such deep pain and rejection on the ride back to Bangalore that all my pent-up emotions turned to anger. I chain-smoked the entire four hours. When we reached the hotel, my boiling anger had turned into a high temperature![61]

The following experience with Swami reveals that the time a person spends waiting for God is preparation to receive God. He blesses two sisters and leaves the third sister, Rani, alone. When He is queried about His unusual behaviour, He reveals a deep understanding of Rani's psyche.

> Swami came in the morning and spoke to both of my sisters. Then He looked at me, turned around and left without asking me anything. The next day, He came and did the same thing—He talked to them, looked at me but said no word. Then, I think it was on the third day that my elder sister felt sorry for me and told me, 'We feel He has been talking to both of us, but He is not talking to you; we are feeling sad about it. Today, I will ask Swami why He is doing this!'
>
> So, when Swami came, she asked, 'Swami, why are You ignoring my other sister? You haven't even asked who she is! Why are You doing this?'
>
> He said, 'I have a reason. I know her feelings and thoughts. She is uncomfortable here, in this atmosphere, or with My form. She thinks, "His Hair, His Robe! I have not seen anybody like this!" She feels a little strange. So, I am giving her time. I am not ignoring her but giving her time to settle down and feel at home. Everything is so strange to her; she is confused and can't understand. So, at this stage, I cannot tell her anything.'
>
> I felt He was giving me His Grace to settle my mind. After a few days, He called me for an interview.[62]

Ramana Rao narrates his experience of his visit to Prasanthi Nilayam, Swami's ashram. He was motivated to study, learn and understand Swami. Ramana first enquires from the devotees in the ashram about money offerings and gets a rebuttal. He feels a little out of place amongst the people who all appear to be devoted. He also fears Swami would persuade him to adopt the spiritual path, but when Swami avoids him, he feels His action was deliberate. Ramana's perspective evolves as he concentrates on the ashram's positive aspects and Swami's benevolent actions.

The passage exemplifies Swami's way of working. People often come to Him with presumptions and expectations. Swami creates experiential learning situations before He talks to them. In the following narrative, the protagonist has notions and biases. Ramana Rao's experiences gradually eliminate all his reservations and doubts. Swami allows Ramana to test and evaluate Him. Preparing individuals to be more open to accepting Swami involves crafting circumstances and contexts that promote receptivity.

> I inquired about the nature and result of their interviews with Baba. I asked them discreetly whether Baba had accepted any offering of money from them. They sneered at me with their denial.
>
> In the afternoon, around two hundred men and women sat before the Mandir. The whole atmosphere was pulsating with devotion, and I suddenly felt out of place there, devoid of any spiritual aspirations. I was frightened that Baba might call me and ask for a promise to give up this and that and take up bhajans. I was in a dilemma about whether to sit or get out, escaping the possible unpleasantness and embarrassment. Just then, the door of the verandah opened. With his face aglow with a soft, sweet smile, Baba came out. He entered the lines like a breeze of bliss, ambling, methodically looking at the faces and collecting letters from the devotees, simultaneously indicating and signalling some of them to go to the verandah and join the group chosen for the interview. Baba called in the person beside us but did not glance toward us. I thanked God. But I was deeply distressed by my friend's disappointment. I would have been pleased if he had been called for an interview, leaving me out. With all our strategic moves failing to attract Baba's attention, I was sure that Baba was deliberately avoiding us.
>
> I interviewed more people whom Baba had called for an interview. It was the same story with everyone. Before they opened their mouths, Baba himself would give an account of their problems and assure them, 'Don't worry.' Hearing them, I

wondered if I was in some mythological age witnessing miracles. Considering their education, social background and sincere tone, it was ridiculous to believe and unreasonable to disbelieve.

There were no priests, no tickets for darshan and no donation boxes. There was no intermediary between a devotee and Baba. This impressed me. Whatever the nature of Baba's miracles, one thing had to be admitted: everyone who came here would return happier. Whether Baba could ultimately grant salvation to his devotees, he was relieving their anxieties and bestowing upon them mental peace. It is great. Baba was extraordinary and engaged in excellent humanitarian service with his supernatural powers. All his devotees worship him as God incarnate. I could not find any other person worthy of such worship and devotion.

I wished to show him my veneration if only he would look at me. He did not allow either of us to express our reverence.

I met four of the first batch of interviewees. One man who saw me came to me and asked, 'Will Baba call me again?' Baba had granted (him an) interview. His soiled dhoti, vest, four-day-old unshaven beard and pungent odour all spoke of his poverty. I enquired about the reason for his coming. He was preparing for his daughter's marriage. A fortnight before the wedding, there was a burglary in his house. Twelve hundred rupees cash, the silk saree for the bride and silk clothes for the bridegroom and the sacred *mangalsutra* made of gold were all stolen. I asked him why he came here instead of going to the police. I saw Baba two years back at Rajahmundry, and since then, I have been worshipping him. I remembered Baba and came here for his help. 'Did you tell all this to Baba in the interview room?' I asked. 'When I saw Baba, I broke down and fell on his feet, and with my voice choked, I couldn't say a word.' He looked pitiful with tears. My recollection of Baba giving a gold ring to the affluent businessman who did not need it and driving away this poor man enraged me against Baba's indiscretion and partiality towards the rich.

> I explained to my friend about the miserable plight of this man. He pulled out his wallet and counted fifty rupees, to which I added my share of fifty rupees to be given to him. Just then, a man around fifty called, 'Jagannath! Who is Jagannath who just now came out of the interview room?' Our man went forward. After ascertaining he was the right man, he beckoned the student who accompanied him with a tray from which he took out a silk saree, silk dhoti pair and an envelope and gave them to Jagannath and said, 'Take this *prasadam* from Swami. Go home at once and perform the marriage of your daughter happily.'
>
> I stood by Jagannath. He was so euphoric that we did not dare offer him the trivial amount.[63]

Sathyajit Salian's experience is split into four segments for easier understanding. The expressive memories depict his growing desire for a closer connection with Swami and reveal Swami's silent involvement over five years. The story depicts how waiting for Swami to respond is emotionally exhausting. It focuses the mind, refines the desire and makes him pine for Swami, for God.

In the first incident, Swami cleverly signals recognition, even though He says nothing.

> I (did not have) interactions with Swami (during) the first five years of my stay. The first five years were a very different experience. I remember we used to have this ceremony where one person would go with a gown and another would go with a robe. Sanjay Singh and I had adjacent roll numbers. He and I went to Swami. He had the gown, and I had the robe. Swami was talking to Sanjay Singh. Sitting next to Sanjay, I thought, let me at least take *padanamaskar*. I was holding Swami's feet. Slowly, I put my fingers under his toe. (I think) Swami decided (to) do some sculpting. He pressed my finger with his toe, and I tried to keep a straight face with all my finger's agony. This was one experience and interaction I had during the first five years of my stay.[64]

The narrator calculates and plans an engagement with Swami. The attempt is futile.

> A desire to 'be close to him' was evoked. I had hardly put any effort into being close to him. I was (more) calculating. I thought that I would work for the annual sports meet. I will do well, and Swami will put a medal around my neck. Ego had come to the fore. It was enough to 'show off' in front of Swami. The sports meet occurred. Swami returned after the sports day, and we asked him, 'How was the sports day?' He replied, 'Good.' And I reverted to chattering.[65]

In the following story, Sathyajit Salian becomes emotional. He writes about the increasing pain triggered by Swami, who does not appear to notice him. He feels that Swami is consciously avoiding him. This realization prompts deeper reflection and yearning for God.

> He slowly made me go deeper.
>
> I was sitting for darshan. Swami was walking amongst the students and looked at the person beside me. Then his eyes look upwards and away. He missed contact with me and walked away.
>
> I kept reflecting on the experience of Swami not looking at me. I thought, 'What had really happened?' Slowly, the pain of being distant from him increased. 'When such an incident occurs, a person cannot cry. Swami is squeezing my heart. I have to be strong. I am a Mumbai boy. I can't appear weak.' So, what does one do? I would run to the hostel and up the hill near the Hanuman statue. Far away from everybody, I could cry to my heart's content. I would be thinking, 'He came close. He didn't look at me. I wonder why.' And then, I would put up a brave face and return to the hostel.
>
> That was how he made me yearn.[66]

A desire to serve Swami is evoked and intensified. In the following excerpt, Salian makes eye contact with Swami for the first time. This moment is heartrending, devoid of any spoken words. He feels and experiences an exchange of love, Swami's love.

> The desire wells up to serve Swami. I still recall the first-ever experience of touching Swami's feet. It was in my second year of college. I used to sit right in front of the interview room. Swami used to finish the interviews and step out. He would stand on the upper step of the *mandir*, his hands held behind his back, looking at the boys. The boys were disciplined.
>
> First, the birthday boys came forward, and then everyone started clambering.
>
> I was sitting right in front. Swami called me and beckoned me to come. Swami was standing and talking to someone. I found myself at his feet, lost in contemplation. The tray I held, made of metal, accidentally bumped into Swami's foot. I quickly withdrew the tray, worried it might have caused him discomfort as it had touched his feet. Unaware that Swami had ceased speaking, I raised my gaze only to find him looking directly at me. I will never forget that moment. Swami had not spoken to me for two years. I vividly recall that exchange even now when I go to the mandir. I saw Swami standing, and I was sitting, and the exchange of love happened. The experience created a yearning for more. I wanted more (of Swami).[67]

In her reflections, Reeves recounts the roller-coaster journey of her connection with Swami. She describes the otherworldly bliss she experiences when Swami interacts with her. In contrast, a deep sadness and self-doubt creeps in during Swami's moments of silence or apparent disengagement. These emotional downturns nudge her to introspect and seek answers to her inner questions. Her experience is symptomatic of a person who wants Swami to react and respond to her every hope, fear and need. For Swami, a person is a spiritual work-in-progress, something the person may not know. Swami only responds to the person in a religious context for a spiritual end goal.

> There are moments of delight and assurance when Baba stops, looks into my eyes, smiles lovingly and I feel a connection. And there are periods of rejection when He doesn't notice me. The insecurities return. I lose confidence, the fear of not being loved, not being worthy of love.[68]

EXTREME INTERVENTION

Manning suggests that God motivates and induces a person on their spiritual journey.

> When life is quiet, relationships intact, finances secure and physical health flourishing, complacency, self-sufficiency and a feeling of personal command of one's destiny deludes and lulls us. It is an illusion of control. The reality of God is that He always shatters every delusion. As we lose power, confidence deserts us and we become vulnerable and open to new ideas. God makes possible the realization that we are incomplete and have received our life and being from another. This decision reaches our roots, transforms us and demands the renunciation of belonging to that self. Through this fundamental act of dispossession, we acknowledge the illusion of control, which becomes an option to connect to the reality of God.[69]

Schulman arrives in Brindavan to join Swami on a trip, only to discover that Swami has already departed. However, his experiences and contemplations imply that Swami's absence was part of a divine plan to guide him towards a deeper connection with Swami and steer him towards a more enlightened spiritual journey, which gradually unfolds through his reflections. Swami pushes him to the limits of his tolerance, making him amenable to receiving new knowledge. Schulman's patience is tested as he encounters an experience that starkly differs from his initial expectations. He transcends through complete unpredictability, unsure of what lies ahead. Amidst this fog of uncertainty, Swami appears when Schulman is on the verge of breaking down. It dawns on him that Swami operates in diverse and unpredictable ways, defying conventional human reasoning. Swami's primary interest lies in an individual's pursuit of God.

> The next night, when they (Prof. Gokak and Arnold Schulman) arrived at Whitefield, they discovered that Baba had left at about three o'clock that afternoon. Gokak was baffled. He was explicitly told to be there at seven to introduce the writer

and discuss some urgent business concerning the college Baba wanted to begin in Bangalore.

'Did he say anything?' Gokak asked the caretaker, a mild and beaming little man in his seventies. 'He just said, "Let us go. We're leaving."' the caretaker reported. 'You know how he does. And they left.'

'At three o'clock?'

'Two, three o'clock,' the caretaker said. Gokak and the caretaker laughed. They were used to Baba's inexplicable behaviour and enjoyed it.

'You never know what he's going to do,' Gokak said.

'I came ten thousand miles just to go on this tour with him,' the writer said.

'When you see him,' Gokak said, 'he will tell you everything. Even about this conversation.'

'You never know what he's going to do,' the caretaker said.[70]

The author falls seriously ill after dinner at Dr Gokak's house. The illness takes a severe toll on him, making him realize he is ill-prepared for the upcoming three-week trip with Swami through the Indian countryside. He eventually falls asleep and has a dream involving Swami. Upon awakening, the fever has subsided, leaving the author baffled. Struggling to make sense of this inexplicable experience, he attempts to dismiss it as mere coincidence.

The night before, at about midnight, he began vomiting, having diarrhoea simultaneously and shivering uncontrollably. He took his temperature and discovered with great alarm that it was a hundred and four. Every few minutes, he took the pills he had brought along for such emergencies, but each time, he vomited them up again immediately after swallowing them.

There was no possible way he could survive a two- or three-week tour through villages, he decided. If eating the food prepared at Dr Gokak's house could make him sick, how could his body cope with the food in the villages?

He put on the clothes he had with him, including an overcoat, and crawled under all the blankets he could find.

His teeth were chattering. The back of his head was throbbing with stupefying pain.

Finally, at about four o'clock in the morning, he dozed off. In a dream, or what seemed to be a dream, he saw Baba standing at the foot of the bed. The writer was startled. He sat up. Baba just stood there looking stern and disapproving, then disappeared.

The writer could hardly breathe. Nothing like this had ever happened to him before. He had no idea whether he had just awakened or if he had been sleeping at all. He didn't know if he saw a dream or a hallucination. Then, to his surprise, he noticed that he was no longer shivering. His nausea had gone, and, taking his temperature, he noticed that so had his fever.

Earlier in the evening, before he got sick, he had been reading about Baba in the book Gokak had given him. Several cases had been reported in which Baba had appeared to his devotees in dreams, often to solve desperate problems. Baba could leave his body and travel through astral time and space.

The cases were fascinating to read, but none of them seemed credible. He reasoned that having read the book caused him to have the dream. The fact that he no longer felt ill was coincidental.[71]

FORTITUDE: THE ELEVENTH-HOUR INTERVENTION

In the following piece, which occurs later in Schulman's association with Swami, he reaches a breaking point in his patience. Despite spending considerable time with Swami, his research for writing a book has made no progress. Initially motivated to write the book to convincingly prove Swami wrong, he has been unable to gather any material for his project. Frustration and despair dominate his emotions, and beneath the surface, there is a simmering sense of anger. This narrative depicts his emotional turmoil and desire to distance himself from the ashram.

Finally, the writer decided enough was enough. There was no hope of his being able to document anything about Baba

> with scientific accuracy. He had devised the idea of irrefutably disproving many of the claims he had heard about Baba. Now, he didn't know what to write. He had seen enough and heard enough to realize the only thing he knew with any certainty was that he had to escape Puttaparthi. If he had to wait for Baba, he would wait at what passed for a luxury hotel in the relative comfort and sanity of a city. If Baba didn't show up in three or four days, hell with the book.[72]

Father Mazzoleni finds himself in extreme discomfort in this contemplative passage, likening his experience to the depths of hell. Drawing upon his knowledge of scriptures, he discerns that Swami, much like God, is testing the boundaries of a devotee's patience and endurance.

> I could not take it anymore. On the verge of desperation, I asked myself, 'What made me come here into this hell? What an idiotic idea to have had!'
>
> It was the moment of the test. The time had come to determine how much I would suffer from having the most significant thing possible. Even mythological tales often relate that fierce animals and poisonous snakes protect the great treasures hidden in the crypts of mysterious ruins. Only the daring adventurer can access those riches after overcoming all the obstacles.[73]

The following example deals with a mundane request. Swami waits until the very last moment before responding. The protagonist is upset and angry and challenges Swami. In His subsequent dialogue, Swami explains the need for a person to wait patiently for God's grace to manifest.

He pushes us to the edge before he responds.

> The announcement schedule of my school results made me ineligible for Bangalore College. The principal advised me to attempt a seat at the new Parthi College starting a month later. I went from Bangalore to Parthi. I didn't want to go back. I had decided to be a part of the place. The principal

of Parthi College asked me to fill out the form, reiterating the need for school grades of at least 60 per cent and above. I was apprehensive. Everything fitted in except the exam results. I had scored 48 per cent to 49 per cent and just managed to scrape through. I prepared the application, gave it to the office and awaited the formal interview. The principal saw my marks and expressed his inability to waive the strict academic standards established by Swami. My begging for a seat was of no avail. He advised me, 'Only Baba can help you. You should have thought about this before. I can think of accommodating you in BA, not BCom.'

This was a huge stumbling block. I had two weeks to decide whether to stay or return to Bombay. I couldn't afford to lose an academic year. The BA option was not an option. My father was explicit. No BA. I started sitting for darshan, holding letters for Swami. I made sure I was sitting in the first line. I was asking and praying to Swami. Sometimes, he would take the letters.

I had the final one or two days left. I had booked the tickets to return via Dharmavaram. I was distraught with Baba. I wrote a powerful letter to Baba, an angry letter. I recollect some thoughts, 'As a young boy, I was against God and rituals. No one explained them to me. When I read your teachings, I thought they made sense. I started accepting you as a teacher. Now, I want to be a part of your college. This is the only opportunity I need to sanctify my life and understand you by being in your college. I have two days left, and college has started. But it looks as if you are not interested in having me. In this case, this is goodbye. The moment you take this letter, your and my relationship is over. I am going away. If I don't get admission, I may never believe in your divinity.'

I went and sat in the front row for darshan. I was sitting with a letter held in my folded palms. The anger had built up. I thought I would look into His eyes and give the letter. It was an unforgettable moment.

He came for darshan. He came very close, opened his second and third fingers like a scissor, held the letter and asked, 'What is it?' This was the first time he was talking to me. I exclaimed, 'Baba! Baba! BCom! BCom!' He gently replied, 'What? BCom? Be Calm. You want BCom, Be Calm.' Swami looked at the principal sitting on the verandah from the darshan line, pointed to me and nodded. He opened his finger's scissors grip, released the letter and walked away.

The moment the darshan got over, the principal beckoned me. I was excited and said, 'Did you see, sir? Swami spoke to me.' The principal replied, 'Your prayers have been answered. Come see me tomorrow.' I was still uncertain and asked, 'Will I get BCom?' He replied, 'I will give you whatever you want.'[74]

Sandweiss was pushed to the limits of his patience on his first trip. He broke down in acute despair. He gave up hope of finding answers to his questions after traveling to Swami. Swami's discourses were challenging his professional knowledge and belief systems. Sandweiss questioned himself and labelled the journey to Swami as foolishness. This vulnerable moment became the moment for Swami to intervene, nudge and turn him Godward.

What am I doing here? I was exhausted. A primitive ceiling fan revolved, not stirring my sluggish, dejected spirits.

I hope you're happy now, I thought miserably. This Sai Baba hasn't given you a second glance. He doesn't know you exist. After ten days in his presence, I remained doubtful.

Baba had just delivered a ninety-minute discourse that was unsettling to me. What he had said was not just contrary to contemporary psychiatric thought; it seemed years behind the times and psychologically unsophisticated. His uninformed challenge to my system of beliefs was the last straw. How could I even for a moment consider this foolishness?

Trained in the most advanced country in the world, in the best schools, and exposed to the leading theories and the latest techniques in psychiatry, how could I expect to find anything here? I know more about the mind and emotions, the way

> to inner peace, than anyone in this primitive, underdeveloped country. [sic] Sai Baba teach me anything about the way to inner peace? The whole trip was an exercise in self-torment!
>
> My trip had been a failure. I had come seeking the meaning of life and had found confusion. I was one of the thousands unrecognized by Sai Baba. I was a fool, and it was time to go home.[75]

In the next reflective excerpt, Schulman realizes the need to focus on the original goal of writing the book on Swami. He acknowledges that Swami has been subtly shaping his spiritual receptivity all along, while he has primarily reacted to Swami's actions with feelings of annoyance, hurt and unhappiness. Schulman's reactions mirror the struggles of a seeker attempting to comprehend the deeper spiritual currents beneath his surface responses to various situations.

> Meanwhile, the writer fought his impatience. He knew his time had not been wasted but resented being left behind. His anger stemmed more from his psychological issues than the actual circumstances. Acknowledging this truth, he grappled with the challenge of setting aside his wounded pride and focusing on the task he had arrived to accomplish.[76]

Ramakrishna Paramahansa uses an analogy to explain that God always responds at the right time and is never in a hurry to respond.

> However, until the right time comes, God remains just a three-letter word to many who remain impervious to spiritual teachings. God is in no great hurry to direct our minds to Him. The mother cooks, and the child remains happy playing with toys. When the child no longer wants the toys, throws them away and cries for its mother, she comes running, takes it on her lap and begins to nurse it. Similarly, when we yearn for God, the source of supreme Bliss, He quickly responds to our prayer.[77]

God's delay is strategic and based on the assimilative spiritual capacity of a devotee. Ramakrishna Paramhamsa explains the idea of 'green' devotion.

Devotion to God may be said to be 'green' so long as it doesn't grow into a love of God, but it becomes 'ripe' when it has grown into such love. A man with 'green' bhakti cannot assimilate spiritual talk and instruction, but one with 'ripe' bhakti can. The image on a photographic plate[78] covered with the film is retained. On the other hand, thousands of photos may reflect on bare glass, but not one is retained. As the object moves away, the glass becomes the same as it was before. When one is ready to assimilate spiritual instruction, He responds.

The mother bird does not break the shell of the egg until the right time arrives.[79]

4

FACE TO FACE WITH GOD

MYSTICAL UNDERCURRENTS IN THE EXPERIENCE

The accounts of encounters with Swami, as narrated by devotees, and the experiences of other God seekers share many similarities but also exhibit some striking contrasts. Spiritual experiences are usually described as unusual, dramatic, vivid, intense, intuitive and unambiguous. The engagement with Swami has some differences. A person who engages with Swami can talk to and even touch Him. Even though He is tangible, Swami is elusive. He is palpable and abstract, accessible yet challenging to understand. With Swami, a person constantly juggles the dichotomy of being engaged with infinity in a finite sense. In the presence of Swami, they do not need explanations, do not need to reason or use their faculties to try to understand Him. They can enjoy being with Him, where their mind is calm like a perennial river. They feel enveloped in God's love.

EXPERIENCE OF GOD

Underhill describes the substance of religion or spirituality as a person 'in love with the Absolute', trying to 'set up a direct relationship with the Absolute'.[1]

People develop a deep-rooted bond with God when they relate to God as being close and accessible. This belief becomes a certainty when a person has a definite, unambiguous and indisputable experience of God. James highlights:

> Every religious person has the recollection in which a direct vision of the truth, a direct perception, perhaps of a living God's existence, swept in and overwhelmed the languor of the more ordinary belief.[2]

Merton experiences a truth beyond the comprehension of his mental faculties. He feels profoundly conscious and filled with God's love. For him, God comes to life. This relationship with God is based on a 'belongingness'; he belongs to God, and God belongs to him. Merton knows that the realizations are a gift from God, and not the consequence of his efforts.

> Suddenly, an awareness, understanding and realization formed that God belonged to me. The awareness was intense, profound and intangible. This was when faith was evoked and deepened. I felt the nearness of God, His immediate presence. An overwhelming experience. This was not my imagination at work. I felt it deep in my heart. Akin to a tangible experience of Truth, a feeling of love.
>
> The first thought that came to my mind was, 'Heaven is right here in front of me!'
>
> The experience filled me with joy, peace and happiness, an experience I have never forgotten. I have been able to reconstruct the experience with faith and love.
>
> Faith makes God real and apparent, a blessing from God, not something that springs from within.[3]

Prof. Christian Moevs describes his introduction to Sathya Sai Baba and his spontaneous feelings and insights.

> Swami stealthily inched his way into my life.
>
> I remember first seeing his image and hearing his name when my sister invited me to dinner at her apartment in New York. She gave me a book to read by Dr Samuel Sandweiss, *The Holy Man and the Psychiatrist*. I opened Samuel Sandweiss' book. I got to page three.
>
> When I first read his words, I recognized something in me, and I could do nothing about that. It is just a fact. It's

> not a belief. It's part of the reality. It is a recognition. It is a much deeper experience. Something that Saint Augustine says: whatever the evidence for or against, something in you says this is true.
>
> My own life, my whole spiritual life, started with my contact with Sai Baba. I was born, raised and baptized a Catholic. I managed to go very nicely through 30 years as a Catholic without a real spiritual life. My encounter with Sai Baba awoke me to the reality of Christ. One can write off all the things you read in the Gospels. Knowing Sai Baba made me recognize that all the stories in the Bible are not just fanciful. It was shocking to realize that all the stories of the Bible are true.
>
> I had to go to India and encounter Sai Baba to awaken to the reality of my faith. I arrived in India and went to the first darshan that evening. I was sort of out of it at that moment. But then Swami appeared. Just seeing him was another one of the enormous shocks. I remember just dissolving into tears watching Swami go by and watching a lady reach out to touch the hem of his robe. I realized that nothing in this life could account for that connection that I saw and felt. There's nothing but God. The spiritual path makes every other path seem very bland. If you take one step on this path, the most extraordinary things happen and joys come that cannot be described.[4]

Underhill summarizes a person's experience of God. Her description is rooted in a setting where a person is face-to-face with a personified God. She describes it as an encounter between a lover and beloved. God is concrete, accessible and someone who exemplifies the divine qualities of truth, goodness and beauty. The aspirants feel very close to God, and devotion is aroused. They know that they belong to God and that God, in turn, loves them. A desire to lose their sense of separateness from God and merge with Him evokes.

> Evoked emotions separate into two. (First) The Contemplation of Transcendence, the ineffable greatness of the Absolute

> Godhead which (is) perceived and in which he desires to lose himself. God is the Perfect-Goodness, Truth, Beauty, Light, Life and Love. (And second) The Contemplation of Immanence is a predominating sense of nearness, intimacy and sweetness rather than transcendence. The dominant emotion is intimate affection, emphasizing the personal experience as an adorable friendship. Reality is a Person, from the subject's point of view, a personal encounter of Lover and Beloved.[5]

Underhill explains the characteristics of a spiritual journey, which is vivid, intense and may last only for a brief duration. The occurrence makes one aware of an underlying reality. The seekers feel the omnipresence of God and are saturated with wisdom and insights.

> Mystic conversion is a single and abrupt experience. It usually involves a sudden and acute realization of splendour and adorable reality in the world never perceived. In so far as I am acquainted with the resources of language, there are no words by which this realization can be described. It is of so actual a nature that, compared to the ordinary world, seems but twilit at best. Consciousness suddenly changes its rhythm, and a new aspect of the universe rushes in. The teasing mists are swept away and reveal, if only for an instant, the sharp outline of the Everlasting Hills.[6]

EXPERIENCE OF GOD IS IMMERSIVE

Underhill highlights the unique nature of the experience.

> Contemplation is accompanied by a feeling of an exalted kind. The total experience transcends mere feeling, just as it transcends mere intellect. It is a complete act of perception inexpressible. The experience involves the whole person, the indivisible personality whose powers and nature are only partially hinted at in such words as Love, Thought or Will.[7]

EXPERIENCE OF GOD IS LIKE AN EARTHQUAKE

Manning refers to God's tremendous, transformational power as an earthquake in which the aspirant is awestruck.

> God is described as 'a divine and terrible radiance'. He uses the word terrible to indicate an experience of unbearable intensity from an old Jewish epigram that says, 'God is not a kindly old uncle; he is an earthquake.'[8]

EXPERIENCE OF GOD IS LIKE THE IMPACT OF A HAMMER

Sandweiss uses the metaphor of a hammer hitting and shattering a rock to describe the swift, unexpected and radically transforming nature of his experience with Swami. He highlights the change of mindset that occurs.

> Almost immediately, as if a hammer had struck and shattered solid rock, I underwent a sudden cataclysmic change inside myself, a shift in my mental perspective of reality that is far easier to label than to describe.[9]

EXPERIENCE OF GOD IS LIKE A FLASH OF LIGHT

Ramakrishna Paramahansa underlines the power of experiencing an avatar, God incarnating as a human being. An avatar makes it easy to experience God.

> I have observed that a man acquires one kind of knowledge about God through reasoning and another through meditation. He acquires a third kind of knowledge about God when God reveals Himself to him, His devotee. If God Himself reveals to His devotee the nature of Divine Incarnation, how He plays in human form, then the devotee doesn't have to reason about the problem or need an explanation. Do you know what it is like? Suppose a man is in a dark room. He rubs a match against a matchbox, and suddenly, the light comes. Likewise,

> if God gives us this flash of divine light, all our doubts are destroyed.[10]

LOSING SELF-AWARENESS IN THE EXPERIENCE OF GOD

In his book, James presented numerous personal narratives to exemplify the nature of spiritual experiences. He identified the spiritual experience as a defining moment when the perception of God is aroused and reinforced by the overwhelming experience of love and happiness. Like a river that loses its identity in an infinite calm sea, the author of the passage, a Christian clergyman, felt that he was blending into a vastness. His mind was as quiet as Sunday morning, and he had the sense of being one with God. Based on a perspective that cannot be devalued by logic, he experienced an explosion of emotion and a renewed belief in God. His belief, founded in his experience, marked the beginning of living a spiritual life.

> I remember the night and the spot on the hilltop where my soul opened out into the Infinite, and there was a rushing together of the inner and the outer worlds. I stood alone with Him, who had made me and all the beauty of the world, love, sorrow and even temptation. I did not seek Him but felt the perfect unison of my spirit with His. The ordinary sense of things around me faded. For the moment, nothing but an ineffable joy and exaltation remained. It is impossible to describe the experience fully. It was like the effect of some great orchestra when all the separate notes have melted into one swelling harmony that leaves the listener conscious of nothing save that his soul is being wafted upwards and almost bursting with its own emotion. The perfect stillness of the night was thrilled by a more solemn silence. The darkness held a presence that was all the more felt because it was not seen. I could not doubt that He was there more than I was. Indeed, I felt myself to be, if possible, the less real of the two.
>
> My highest faith in God and his truest idea were born in me. Then, if ever, I believe, I stood face to face with God

and was born anew of his spirit. There was, as I recall it, no sudden change of thought or belief, except that my early crude conception had, as it were, burst into flower. There was no destruction of the old but a rapid, wonderful unfolding. Since then, no discussion that I have heard of the proof of God's existence has shaken my faith. Having once felt the presence of God's spirit, I have never lost it again for long. My most assuring evidence of his existence is deeply rooted in that hour of vision, the memory of that supreme experience and the conviction gained from reading and reflection that something of the same has come to all who have found God. I am aware that it may justly be called mystical. I am not acquainted enough with the philosophy to defend it from that or any other charge. In writing it, I have overlaid it with words rather than put it clearly in your thoughts. But, such as it is, I have described it as carefully as I now can do.[11]

ECSTATIC AWARENESS IN THE EXPERIENCE OF GOD

James characterizes his surreal experience of God as ecstatic in the following narrative. It is an intense emotional experience wherein he feels one with God and experiences His power, goodness and grace. He uses the word 'violent' to describe it. The author is unable to express his dialogue with God in black and white, but this challenge does not diminish the reality of the experience. Long after the initial feelings have ebbed, God still makes him emotional. The awareness of God prevails. He is invisible but present in him as awareness and consciousness.

When I experienced being raised above myself, I felt the presence of God—I was conscious of it—as if his goodness and power were penetrating me altogether. The throb of emotion was so violent that I could barely tell the boys to pass on and not wait for me. I then sat down on a stone, unable to stand any longer, and my eyes overflowed with tears. I thanked God for teaching me to know him, sustaining my life and taking pity on the insignificant creature and the sinner I was. I begged him that my life must be consecrated to the doing of his will. I felt his reply: I should do his will daily in humility and poverty, leaving him, the Almighty God, to judge. Then, slowly, the ecstasy left my heart; that is, I felt that God had withdrawn, and I could walk on, but very slowly, so firmly was I still possessed by the interior emotion. Besides, I had wept uninterruptedly for several minutes; my eyes were swollen, and I did not wish my companions to see me. The state of ecstasy may have lasted four or five minutes, although it seemed to last much longer. I think it well to add that God had neither form, colour, odour nor taste in this ecstasy of mine. It was instead as if the presence of a spiritual spirit had transformed my personality. But the more I seek words to express this intimate intercourse, the more I feel the impossibility of describing the thing by any of our usual images. At the bottom, the expression most apt to render what I felt is this: God was present, though invisible; he fell under no one of my senses, yet my consciousness perceived him.[12]

SPONTANEOUS JOY AND REVERENCE IN THE EXPERIENCE OF GOD

In this narrative, David Brainerd describes a spontaneous experience of God. He feels the realness of the experience in the awe and joy evoked by God's intuitive awareness. The author knows that he has seen God and experienced becoming one with God. His self-identity and sense of separateness disappear. The outcome of the experience is transformative.

Then, as I was walking in a thick grove, unspeakable glory seemed to open to the apprehension of my soul. I do not mean any external brightness or imagination of a body of light. Still, I had a new inward apprehension or view of God, such as I never had before, nor anything resembling it. I had no particular apprehension of any person in the Trinity—the Father, the Son, or the Holy Ghost—but it appeared to be Divine glory. My

> soul rejoiced with joy unspeakable. To see such a God, such a glorious Divine Being, I was inwardly pleased and satisfied that he should be God forever and ever. My soul was so captivated and delighted with God's excellence that I was lost in him. I continued in this state of inward joy, peace and astonishing till near dark without any sensible abatement and then began to think and examine what I had seen and felt sweetly composed in my mind all the evening following. I felt myself in a new world, and everything about me appeared different from what it was wont to do.[13]

ACCEPTANCE AND SUBMISSION IN THE EXPERIENCE OF GOD

James feels an upsurge of love, gratitude and freedom. His self-identity fades in the feeling of divine love that envelopes him.

> When I gave all up to him to do with me as he pleased and was willing that God should rule over me at his pleasure, redeeming love broke into my soul with such power that my whole soul seemed molten with love. The weight of guilt had lifted, dispelling the darkness within me. My heart became humble and brimmed with gratitude. My entire being, which had once cried out to an unknown God for assistance, was now infused with boundless love. It soared on the wings of faith, proclaiming, 'My Lord and my God, thou are my rock and my fortress, my shield and my refuge, my life, my source of joy, my present and my eternal inheritance.'[14]

EXPERIENCE OF GOD THROUGH SELF-ENQUIRY

Ramaṇa Maharshi describes his life-changing experience. He was motivated to understand what happens after death. In a few minutes of spontaneous self-inquiry without words, he experienced an awareness of God. From that moment onwards, he lived in unbroken knowledge of the truth. Other thoughts did arise; they came and went, but his awareness of reality remained. He exemplifies this using music as a metaphor. Many musical notes exist, but the *sruti* (smallest gradation of pitch) underlies them all.

Venkataraman had a life-changing experience. He spontaneously initiated a process of self-inquiry that culminated, within a few minutes, in his permanent awakening. In one of his written comments on this process, he wrote: 'Enquiring within "Who is the seer?" I saw the seer disappear, leaving That alone, which stands forever. No thought arose to say, "I saw." How then could the thought arise to say, "I did not see?"'

In those few moments, his identity disappeared and was replaced by a full awareness of the Self. That experience, that awareness, remained with him for the rest of his life. He did not need to do any more practice or meditation because this death experience left him in a state of complete and final liberation. This is very rare in the spiritual world: someone who had no interest in the spiritual life should, within a few minutes and without any effort or prior practice, reach a state that other seekers spend lifetimes trying to attain. I say 'without effort' because this re-enactment of death and the subsequent self-inquiry seemed to be something that happened to him rather than something he did. When he described this event to his Telugu biographer, the pronoun 'I' never appeared. He said, 'The body lay on the ground, the limbs stretched themselves out,' and so on. That particular description leaves the reader feeling that this event was utterly impersonal. Some power took over the boy Venkataraman, made him lie on the floor, and finally made him understand that death is for the body and the sense of individuality and that it cannot touch the underlying reality in which they both appear.

When the boy Venkataraman got up, he was a fully enlightened sage, but he had no cultural or spiritual context to evaluate what had happened to him. He had read some biographies of ancient Tamil saints and attended many temple rituals, but none of this seemed to relate to the new state he found himself in.

Sri Ramana reportedly described it later:

It was in 1896, about six weeks before I left Madurai for good, that this great change in my life occurred. I was sitting alone on the first floor of my uncle's house. I seldom had any sickness, and on that day, there was nothing wrong with my health, but a sudden violent fear of death overtook me. There was nothing in my state of health to account for it, nor was there any urge to find out whether there was any account for the fear. I just felt I would die and began thinking about what to do. It did not occur to me to consult a doctor or any elders or friends. I felt I had to solve the problem myself then and there. The shock of the fear of death drove my mind inwards, and I said to myself mentally, without actually framing the words: 'Now death has come; what does it mean? What is it that is dying? This body dies.' And at once, I dramatized the occurrence of death. I lay with my limbs stretched out as though rigor mortis had set in and imitated a corpse to give greater reality to the inquiry. I held my breath and kept my lips tightly closed so that no sound could escape, and neither the word 'I' nor any word could be uttered. 'Well then,' I said to myself, 'this body is dead. It will be carried stiff to the burning ground and there burn and be reduced to ashes. But with the death of the body, am I dead? Is the body I? It is silent and inert, but I feel the full force of my personality and even the voice of I within me, apart from it. So, I am the Spirit transcending the body. The body dies, but the spirit transcending it cannot be touched by death. That means I am the deathless Spirit.' All this was not a dull thought; it flashed through me vividly as living truths I perceived directly without a thought process. I was something real, the only real thing about my present state, and all the conscious activity connected with the body was centred on that I. From that moment onwards, the 'I' or self focused attention on itself with a powerful fascination.

> Fear of death vanished once and for all. The ego was lost in the flood of self-awareness. Absorption in the self continued unbroken from that time. Other thoughts might go like the various music notes, but I continued like the fundamental *sruti* note, which underlies and blends with all other notes.[15]

EXPLOSIVE ENCOUNTER WITH GOD

Different persons' first experience with God reveals many similarities. It isn't easy to describe how it happens, but what each person attains is similar.

The experience is profoundly personal and overwhelming. It is spontaneous, not reasoned and happens unannounced. The consequences of the incident are always dramatic. Intuitive knowledge of God is evoked. Understanding God as a continuing awareness endures long after a person's outlook changes.

James reveals facets of the spiritual experiences of God. The following quote touches on the inner nature of the spiritual transformation that transpires in an encounter with God.

> Neither an outside observer nor the subject who undergoes the process can explain fully how particular experiences can change one's centre of energy so decisively or why they often have to bide their hour to do so. All we know is that there are dead feelings, ideas and cold beliefs, and there are hot and live ones, and when one grows hot and alive within us, everything has to re-crystalize about it. Our explanations then get so vague and general that one realizes the intense individuality of the whole phenomenon.[16]

James writes that God initiates these emotions, which are His gifts to the person.

> How infinitely passionate a thing religion at its highest flights can be. It adds to life an enchantment that is not rationally or logically deducible from anything else. This enchantment, coming as a gift when it does come, is a gift of God's grace.

> Religious feeling gives a new sphere of power; it redeems and vivifies an interior world.[17]

Experiencing divine love is like a spiritual explosion that brings sublime joy, a feeling of confident optimism and security and a determination to be with God.

> Emotional occasions are incredibly potent in precipitating mental rearrangements. The sudden and explosive ways love can seize upon one are known to everybody. Hope, happiness, security, resolve and emotions characteristic of conversion can be equally explosive. And emotions that come in this explosive way seldom leave things as they found them.[18]

George Coe denotes that spiritual experiences do not correlate with anything in everyday life and are not evaluated based on the change in the person's disposition. Spiritual experiences are about attaining and becoming one with God.

> Those gracious influences, which are the effects of the Spirit of God, are altogether supernatural—quite different from anything men experience. They are what no improvement or composition of natural qualifications or principles will ever produce because they differ not only from what is natural and from everything that natural men experience in degree and circumstances but also in kind and are far more excellent.
>
> The ultimate test of religious values is nothing psychological, nothing definable in *how it happens*, but something ethical, definable only in terms of *what is attained*.[19]

POWER OF THE PRESENCE OF AND MEETING GOD

Swami describes the experiences of Krishna's contemporaries with Krishna in this excerpt.

> The mystery of the Krishna incarnation! That embodiment of sweetness is most captivating! Exquisite charm, unrivalled sweetness, incomparable love—the Krishna Form concretizes

> all these! That Form was the treasure-house of Bliss; it was the Ocean of Virtue; Oh, what Innocence! What Superhuman Excellence! The mere sight of Him is enough; listening to His words is enough; merely touching Him is enough; life will reach its goal! All rituals, all sacrifices and all scriptural ceremonies have as their goal only this: this sight, this listening, this touch. The gains accrued from the rites are nothing compared to those from sight, touch and listening to His voice. Ah! What immeasurable sweetness![20]

In Krishna's presence, people felt a spontaneous attraction for Him. Krishna's persona had a magnetic charm. A person's attention would naturally and effortlessly become focused on Him. They felt saturated with an emotion best described as love. With their mind blank, still and devoid of thought, they felt intense, never-experienced-before and inexplicable happiness. Being with Krishna—to see, talk and listen to Him—was enough for people.

UNEXPECTED MEETING

The first experience of God often occurs at an unexpected moment. Sheen writes:

> Divinity is always where one least expects to find it.[21]

The effect of the first meeting with God is heightened because of the suddenness of the experience. The metaphor of light instantly filling a dark room suggests the speed of the experience.

A STARTLING CONTRARIAN EXPERIENCE

The first experience of God is different from what people expect it to be. Sheen explains why.

> Divine power, which is infinite or limitless, is difficult for the human mind to comprehend. Every person carries an image of God in their mind that He is omnipresent, powerful, distant, inaccessible and so on. When they experience God,

> they 'see' that He is 'visibly' devoid of the presumed divine characteristics. They are surprised, and their ideas of what they envisioned God to be are shattered. The compelling nature of the meeting ensures they become amenable to change and spiritual renewal. He uses the metaphor of the bright sun and an eclipse to explain the idea. The sun's brightness is its natural state. When an eclipse occurs, it is contrary to the normal and gets noticed. When God assumes a human form and becomes accessible, 'hiding' behind normal human behaviour, it startles the person.[22]

Swami describes how He works and echoes the same idea. When God incarnates, He makes His attributes easy to recognize, experience and understand without being overwhelmed. Swami affirms His attributes of omniscience and omnipresence. He wants devotees to retain this awareness based on a belief that as God, Swami resides in everyone, watching and watching over.

> If I had come amongst you as Narayana with four arms, holding the Conch, the Wheel, the Mace and the Lotus, you would have kept Me in a museum and charged a fee for those seeking My darshan. If I had come as a mere man, you would not have respected My teachings and followed them for your good. So, I have to be in this human form with superhuman wisdom and power—and I show you, now and then, these miracles [...] I have come to guide and bless all *sadhakas*. I am neither man nor woman, old or young; I am all these. I am the inner spring in all that moves and exists. I am the energy, the power that propels and impels. I am the Knower, the Knowing and the Knowledge. Be whatever you like, do whatever you choose and remember that all you do is known to me. I am the inner ruler of all. I am seated in your hearts.[23]

In the following story, Swami dramatically evokes belief in a person by engineering an experience. He surprises and overcomes the lingering uncertainty of a devotee.

My father stayed at Prasanthi Nilayam instead of joining the annual *Rathothsavam*, the chariot procession of our family deity at our ancestral shrine. He only partly believed that Bhagavan was, in fact, Lord Venkateshwara. But he had felt it was not worthwhile to go to a distant place to worship a stone deity when he had the same deity in flesh and blood.

His mind was in turmoil as he sat on the sands opposite the mandir, waiting for the bhajan to begin. He was yet to identify Bhagavan as the Lord of Tirupati wholeheartedly. So, praying that on that day at least, there should be a bhajan with either Srinivasa, Venkatesha or Tirupateesha to convince him of His identity, he busied himself with the mental worship of his Lord at Tirupati. He was afraid that his family deity might be angry that he had abandoned him for some other. So, as compensation, he took up the long-distance mental worship of the deity. He mentally picked up Tulasi leaves, washed them, dipped them in sandal paste and offered them to the feet of His Lord. No, not of Swami, because he was still doubting His divinity, but of his family Lord at Tirupati. As he continued to do this, praying all the time that Lord Venkateshwara should forgive him for any lapse on his part by remaining at Puttaparthi, the bhajan began. The *Ganesha bhajan* ended, and the second bhajan started with the words '*Srinivasa, Venkatesha Tirupateesha, Satya Sayeesha.*' My father stopped his mental puja. Thrilled, he opened his eyes. Swami was standing before him, watching my father with a charming smile. He was delighted to see Bhagavan standing upright, just like Lord Venkateshwara. As my father looked at the lotus feet to offer his obeisance, he saw Tulasi leaves, wet with sandal paste and kumkum. The same leaves he had mentally pictured and offered as worship to Lord Venkateshwara only a few moments ago rolled from Bhagavan's feet.[24]

Aitken is unsettled and overwhelmed by the divine love he experiences with Swami. He describes his ecstatic feeling as spiritual intoxication. Meeting Swami is like experiencing God as a person who is reachable and accessible. Swami becomes the personal manifestation of God as love for each devotee.

> A visit to Puttaparthi can be unsettling. What he finds is something infinitely grander. (Experience) the grace of finding love embodied in this slight frame. And when you have love, who needs religion or anything else? This is the ultimate high for the seeker. Beyond this, ecstasy cannot go. For the soul in search of itself, here at Puttaparthi (or Shirdi), the wine of the spirit can be drunk neat.
>
> Sai teaching, in a nutshell, is the need to experience love. Shirdi Baba has enunciated its underlying mantra in the phrase *Sab ka Malik Ek* because love bestows this feeling of oneness. He is forced to acknowledge that what he sees in Sai is not just love personified but personalized.[25]

Schulman describes his first meeting with Swami. Swami startles him with His omniscience by revealing personal details and cajoles the author to find his true self before writing a book on Swami.

> 'You don't understand,' Baba said. 'I only told you "Write the book" because I wanted you. Understand? You. Not a book. The book is publicity. I don't need publicity. I don't want publicity. I want you. I want your faith. I want your love. Everybody here to see me thinks they have arranged it, but I arranged it. When the time is ready, I call all of those who need me to me when they are ready. No one can get here to see me otherwise. I want your soul because it is time now for you to stop vacillating. You have been trying Yoga. You went to Japan to study…' he fumbled for the word, 'Zen, Buddhism. You visited several Hindu saints in India to find the right master, but you have not found him yet. Am I right or wrong?'
>
> The writer instantly tried to recall whether he had ever mentioned these facts to Gokak. He did not remember having done so, but he might have. He decided, in which case Gokak could have mentioned it to Baba, placing in doubt, at least for the moment, whether Baba had demonstrated his much-advertised ability to tell one everything.

Baba looked at the writer, studying him, and then spoke in almost a whisper as if having read his mind.

'Your wife is better now,' Baba said in English.

The writer was startled.

'Before you came to India,' Baba continued in Telugu, 'you considered postponing the trip due to the discovery of a lump in her breast. However, two weeks later, when she revisited the doctor, the lump had disappeared. You briefly pondered whether I had something to do with it, but the doctor assured you that such occurrences were not uncommon, leading you to conclude that I had not played a role in it. Well, I did it. I took the lump away, so I am telling you this now. How else could I know of this if I didn't do it? You wondered if you had told Gokak about studying Buddhism in Japan, but you did not mention your wife and that problem to Gokak or anyone who knows me.'

The writer knew he was expected to speak but could only sit there in astonishment. Then he looked up at Baba, who was watching him.

Baba smiled.

'The relationship between a master and his disciple is very special,' Baba said. 'You think I am treating you badly because I said, "Go home. Don't write the book." I am doing this for a purpose.'

'What is the purpose?' the writer asked.

'That is for me to know,' Baba said. He laughed, and both Gokak and the writer laughed with him.

'Suppose a person has a thousand rupees in small coins,' Baba said. 'These are all of your anxieties, your problems. I want you to give them to me, your master, and he will give you a one-thousand rupee note. Do you understand?'

The writer nodded, but he wasn't at all sure he did.

'I am only concerned with you and your spiritual life,' Baba continued. 'Not your happiness because what you call happiness is only comfort, so I couldn't take you on the tour. I came to your hotel room. You saw me in a dream.' He laughed. 'Look how he looks at Gokak to see if he mentioned that to Gokak. You did not mention the dream to him; did he, Gokak?'

'No,' Gokak said, 'I don't remember him telling me a dream.'

'I came to your room,' Baba said to the writer, 'and saw you so unhappy and so ill, and you were very unhappy because you had come here to write this book. Am I right?'

The writer nodded.

'You didn't want to go on the tour,' Baba said in English, 'isn't it?'

'Not completely,' the writer admitted.

'So why should I take you with me?' Baba said, reverting to Telugu. 'I am so busy on these tours, and there is no time to be concerned with your comfort. So, I say I am only interested in your spiritual happiness, but my word for happiness, not your word. I am always in a state of happiness, so that is not my concern, but I only live to give satisfaction, joy and love to my devotees. That is the only reason I live.'

'If I...,' the writer started to say.

'Forget about the book,' Baba said in English, then added in Telugu, 'you were about to say if you write the book, you can help other people.'

'Isn't it?' Baba said in English after Gokak translated.

The writer nodded.

'First is self,' Baba said, 'then help. Find yourself first before trying to help others. Then you can help them later.'

'But I've come so far, all the way from...'

'Forget about far,' Baba said in English. 'Far is not important. No far, no near. Dear, only dear is important.'[26]

AFTER THE EXPERIENCE

Aitken writes that meeting and engaging with Swami is more about what He does with the person and less about the person comprehending Him. As Swami states in the previous excerpt, He aims to nudge a person Godward.

> Knowing and appreciating his ability to arouse the divine in anyone is more important than figuring out Sathya Sai.[27]

Aitken writes that experiences with Swami are designed to make a person fall in love with God. The intensity and strength of God's love are described as a raging fire, an irresistible fire that consumes everything in its way. Swami's love is an exploding wonder. Swami demands reciprocity from the devotee who experiences His divine love to experience, accept and submit to the power of His love.

> The most compelling definition of enlightenment lies (in) experiencing the grace of falling in love. It is an all-enveloping fire. Love is an exploding wonder that makes the most ordinary activity seem miraculous. Love is the ever-present grace. The demand of the Sai that we obey the dictates of love and surrender our assumptions, dogma and intellectual pride is realistic because the only thing most of us do readily surrender to is the power of love.[28]

The renewal of a person with an avatar is not without inner struggle. A person can become devout, attempting to change with a personified God, or be indifferent to Him, do nothing and lose a spiritual opportunity. Meeting and engaging with a personal God is a religious test. The sun can melt the wax and harden the clay, illustrating the potential for dual impact. Being with God can weaken or reinforce a person's ego. The person chooses what happens. God is accessible to everyone. However, each person decides to accept or deny God.

> He would act on one soul in one way and on another in another way. The sun shines on wax and softens it, whereas shining on mud hardens it. There is no difference in the sun, only in the objects on which it shines.[29]

Dr Gokak describes how Swami influences listeners, turning them inwards, evoking belief and confidence and motivating them on a spiritual quest. Swami's supreme authority, confidence and wisdom evoke a wellspring of divine strength and certainty.

> His impassioned eloquence keeps lakhs of people moved and spellbound. His discourses kindle in us the fire of hope and renewal. The confidence he inspires and the assurance he gives infuse us with new enthusiasm. They proceed from a centre of power that convinces us of its certainty and invincibility.[30]

The following excerpt describes Mahendranath Gupta's experience of meeting Ramakrishna Paramahansa for the first time. A diversity of emotions—wonder, fascination and attraction—are aroused in Gupta. He is captivated by Ramakrishna and, in His spiritual presence, feels rooted to the spot and speechless. He does not want to leave Ramakrishna's presence.

> It was spring Sunday when M. met him for the first time.
>
> They arrived at the main gate at dusk and went straight to Sri Ramakrishna's room. And there, they found him seated on a wooden couch facing the east. With a smile on his face, he was talking about God. The room was full of people, all seated on the floor, softly drinking in his words.
>
> M. stood there speechless and looked on. He felt he was standing where all holy places met.
>
> Sri Ramakrishna said, 'When hearing the name of *Hari* or *Rama* once, you shed tears and your hair stands on end; then you may know for certain that you no longer have to perform such devotions as the sandhya. Then only will you have a right to renounce rituals; rather, rituals will drop away themselves. Then it will be enough to repeat only the name of *Rama, Hari* or even *Om*.' He said, 'The sandhya merges in the Gayatri, and the Gayatri merges in *Om*.'
>
> M. looked around with wonder and said to himself, 'What a beautiful place! What a charming man! How beautiful his words are! I have no wish to move from this spot.'[31]

RIGHT TIMING OF THE ENGAGEMENT

Swami explains to Schulman the idea of right timing or spiritual readiness for a devotee. A person connects with God, or God connects with a person when the timing is right and the devotee is ready to accept, receive and develop.

> 'There is a special time and a special place for each man to find his master,' Baba said. 'It must be the right time and the right place.'
>
> 'Is this the right time and place for me?' the writer asked. 'You have to tell me,' Baba said. 'I cannot tell you.'[32]

FIRST DARSHAN OF SWAMI

The first darshan of Swami has a numinous quality. It is impactful and becomes a vivid, long-lasting memory, a defining moment in a person's spiritual life when they first engaged with God. The mind is alert and watchful in the encounter and captures subtle details of the incident. Father Mazzoleni narrates the experience of his first darshan. He is captivated by Swami and becomes emotional as tears well up in his eyes and begin to flow.

> A figure in orange was coming out with a calm and solemn step. His thick, curly hair, which made a large crown around his head like a regal diadem, was blown by a soft breeze and revealed his timeless face to those present.
>
> The group of men was a lake of white, and that of the women was a rainbow of colours. The temple was pink and blue, the trees an intense green. His robe stood out vividly in that festival of colours, which seemed like an enchanted garden full of lilies and meadow flowers. It was bright orange and fell straight, covering His feet, so He appeared as an eternal tree solidly planted in the ground. And the wind, to make Him even more fascinating, caressed His tunic, making it cling to a slender and powerful body.
>
> There was an ineffable silence in that atmosphere. Yes, there were many crows croaking and songbirds and parrots wheeling here and there, etched against a deep blue sky with swift passing clouds, and yet the overall impression made by the scene was that of great silence. The birds and clouds seemed nothing but

the image of our thoughts that come and go in a continuous whirlwind with a tireless pace. The silence was like pure consciousness, watching thoughts pass without being affected.

It seemed as if time had ceased to exist. No thoughts of family, problems, weariness or physical ills crossed my mind.

I was mesmerized by that Presence. Now, He was approaching the spot where I was sitting. Now and then, He would accept letters or gesture with His hand as if to say, 'Wait. Tomorrow. Patience! Stay seated.' He would stop, bend down over someone making a request and with a sweet and innocent voice ask, 'Eh?' like someone who hasn't understood or was pretending not to understand and wants to have the question repeated. Occasionally, He would stop, move off a bit and make circles with His hand, and a white powder, vibhuti, would flow from it. It all seemed normal to me; everything corresponded to the accounts I had read in the books.

While watching Him materialize the sacred ash, I noticed that I considered that action ordinary, and I was astonished that I wasn't amazed. 'How's this?' I said to myself. 'You're seeing something extraordinary, and you're not even surprised?' My indifference scandalized me.

He passed in front of me and gave me a broad smile, like the one a public figure might give to a friend he's known forever when he makes him out in the crowd as if to say, 'Oh, you're here too? Hi there!' I looked behind me because I was afraid that I had presumed to deserve attention that maybe was not for me, given that I had just arrived, but there was no one there. After He passed by, I had a shiver of indescribable joy that I could calm only by shedding a flood of tears.[33]

Paul Roberts describes his feelings on seeing Swami for the first time. He feels loved; emotions overcome him as tears flow. At that moment, he feels the pain of being unrecognized. During his six-month stay, he recognized that he believed in God. Swami has evoked belief.

We entered the ashram, which is known as 'Prasanthi Nilayam,' the abode of the highest peace (coincidentally, the meaning of

'Jerusalem'). I walked around the ashram. The large concrete buildings circled an inner enclosure marked by a small stone wall, dominated by a white-domed temple with an upper and lower veranda. The upper veranda had an extraordinary pair of huge silver doors emblazoned with the symbol of the world's major religions. The entire building was covered with moulded images ranging from elephants to what looked like flying armadillos. Seated on the sandy ground in front of this building, women to the right, men to the left, were about fifty people, mostly Indians, waiting for darshan. I was told that Baba would soon appear and that I should wait. Half a shifting, scratching, sweating hour passed, and suddenly, a strange hush fell over the silent crowd. Everyone began looking towards the low, pillared veranda of the temple. When he finally appeared, without warning, a tiny figure with a huge, frizzy bonnet of hair and a simple orange robe that covered his feet, I experienced an extraordinary sensation. It was love, certainly, but more being *loved* than being *in* love. So unexpected and so intense was this feeling that tears streamed down my cheeks as I watched Baba's slow, graceful movements. Later, I put this down to all the hype I had heard beforehand. Later still, I found it increasingly less easy to explain away.

Baba stood swaying slightly, gazing dreamily out over the semicircle of devotees, all eyes on him. He raised one hand as if testing for rain and appeared to stir the air with his middle finger. Then, with his other hand, he made a gesture that looked like he was writing on something invisible with his forefinger. His presence seemed suddenly vast and remote, disconnected from anything around it. There was an aura of stillness combined with a majesty that I have never since encountered in any other person, no matter how famous or powerful. He looked like someone in absolute control of all.

After some minutes, he moved slowly along the rows of adoring faces, pausing to take a note, bless a child or some religious object held up for his attention. Then, fifteen feet away from me, he stopped by an old man in a wheelchair

> and made a curious polishing motion with his right hand, palm down, from which suddenly poured a quantity of greyish powder into the waiting cupped hands of the man, who sobbed in gratitude. Baba pressed his thumb on the man's forehead, leaving a chalky mark, and moved on.
>
> As he drew still nearer, I trembled with almost painful emotions. My heart beat faster and faster. His dark, remote gaze swept over the people on all sides. He stood for a few moments when he reached me, gazing at me with a strange half-smiling, puzzled expression and kind bottomless eyes. I felt great mental peace and a rushing sense of release in my heart; for some reason, tears rolled down my cheeks.
>
> Then he passed and was gone without a glance my way. I felt oddly humiliated, spurned and jilted.[34]

Aitken describes the experience of seeing Swami. The encounters are intense and spiritually charged. He retains fascinating emotional and visual memories of the darshans. Swami describes meditation as identifying the mind with the divine form so that the mind recedes and ceases to exist. The darshan description is like meditation. The author is in a complete bond with Swami. His narrative is similar to Father Mazzoleni's experience described earlier.

> Sathya Sai has a slender but sturdy build. (He is) only five feet four in height, his presence is visibly enlarged by the grace of his bearing. Slim of hip, his shoulders are strong and suggestive of some numinous overhang of psychic wings. This charge of psychic energy is seen in his gaze and, again, in the fluidity of his lips. It is almost as if an inner grace propels his physical form. The eyes are soft with compassion and are boundless in their wonder. They often wear a soft, faraway look. Softly maternal, one moment, they can flash commandingly the next, as beautiful and as unpredictable as the weather in the high mountains of *Shivalaya*.
>
> So intriguing is Sathya Sai's psychic impact that the physical details tend to get blurred. To some, his complexion

> is golden like the sun, while a bluish tinge signifies the infinite to others. When he walks, Sathya Sai is the personification of grace.
>
> Though cut in the image of soft femininity, his mood is of masterfulness.[35]

Iyer writes that he never tires of seeing Swami and having darshan. Each darshan is spiritually energizing and kindles an upsurge of devotion.

> A hush ensues when he appears. The mind becomes silent. It is not an ordinary magnetism of a powerful personality. Time stops. It is as if the elements are paying homage to the Master.
>
> Deep within, reverence wells up.
>
> I can never get used to him, the first or the five hundredth time. The excitement, the anticipation and the yearning are all there. The response is spontaneous. It is not a result of thinking.[36]

The following narrative is a recollection of Mrs Ratanlal's first darshan of Swami 47 years after it occurred. The darshan evoked intense emotions. She felt she had seen God. During her second darshan, her behaviours have spontaneity. She jumps to her feet and sings bhajans to control crowds. The narrative has elements of the miraculous. She is discovering a way to build a connection with Swami.

> I had my first darshan when Swami visited Bombay in June 1965. We were waiting for Swami near the house where he was staying. We received information that it would take him nearly an hour to reach. I was an ulcer patient. I decided to walk to my house, just across the road, to have a glass of milk and return. I had just crossed the street when Swami's car entered the driveway. I returned a little while later, apprehensive about whether I would have his darshan. I had been informed that Swami retires after his meal and doesn't come out for darshan. I decided to sit opposite the house on the edge of Ridge Road. As I waited, I decided to start singing bhajans. I was sitting on the ground and singing. I started singing at 9:30 p.m. and

continued till 11:30 p.m. It was pitch-dark. Suddenly, I saw Swami come to the balcony. He saw me, gestured and said, 'It is very late. Come tomorrow morning at 7.'

As Swami spoke, I sensed a giant ball of light travel from him to me, hitting me in my heart. I spontaneously uttered, '*Narayan, Narayan, Narayan.*'

I returned home at midnight. Ratanlal was asleep. I woke him up and said, 'I have seen God. I could not "see" Swami's face, but I know he is God.' Ratanlal got annoyed and angry. I was dripping in sweat. I had been outside the house since morning. My hair was dishevelled. My sari was thoroughly crushed. He said, 'In your physical state, every person you see should be God. Why are you disturbing me at this hour?' I was irritated at his response. I picked up my sheet and pillow and slept in my mandir. I stretched out but could not sleep. How could I sleep after the experience? I got up at 2:30 a.m.

My niece Achala was born with very poor eyesight. She was clinically blind. Doctors said, 'God forgot to give her eyes when distributing them.' Her eyes had been operated upon, and the lens power in one eye was –13 and the other eye –14. I asked Achala to accompany me to Swami's darshan.

We reached the house and sat down for darshan. The intuitive feeling that Swami is God appeared to be strengthening. As soon as Swami came out towards the crowd, I started to cry. About 300–400 people were waiting for Swami's darshan. People began to stand up and extend their hands toward him. And Swami started signalling to the people, through gestures, to sit down. He got no response. I don't know what prompted me, but I jumped from the garden onto the verandah above, grabbed the mike and started singing bhajans. The crowd started following the bhajan and immediately became quiet.

Swami stared at me. He left the house immediately after the darshan finished.

Swami was to visit Atal's house after two days. They requested me to make arrangements and take care of the decorations and snacks for Swami.

> Three of us were in Atal's house: Ratanlal, Arun—he had a hole in his heart—and Achala. Ratanlal had very bad sinuses. Under the advisement of doctors, he was to travel to Switzerland for surgery. Arun's father had recently passed away. He had arranged for Arun to travel to America for heart surgery.
>
> I was singing bhajans. Swami came and saw me. He went to the living room and sat in the chair. After 15 minutes, he got up and asked me, 'Show me your hand.' He created vibhuti and asked me to distribute it to everyone. Achala was seated next to me. He asked Achala to remove her glasses and rubbed vibhuti on her eyes. Ratanlal and Arun were in different corners of the room. Swami went to Ratanlal and showered vibhuti on him. He then went to Arun, asked him to open the shirt, and rubbed vibhuti on his chest. After one month, the hole had vanished. Ratanlal went to the doctor, who found no signs of sinuses. He cancelled the tickets for Switzerland.
>
> This is how my relationship with Swami began in June 1965.[37]

Aitken relays the experience of his first darshan of Swami. He experiences intense spiritual energy and describes the spiritual jolt inherent in Swami's darshan experience.

> My first darshan of Sai Baba in Delhi (was), without question, the most electrifying presence of any holy man or, for that matter, any human being I had ever met (or have met since). He seemed to crackle with psychic static as though charged with energy so vital that you would receive a shock if you touched him.[38]

Brainerd describes his spiritual experience after a period of spiritual unrest. The contrast is from being sad to experiencing divine glory as light. He is captivated and filled with inexplicable joy.

> In a mournful melancholy state, I was attempting to pray but found no heart to engage in that or any other duty; my former concern, exercise and religious affections were gone. I thought

that the Spirit of God had entirely left me, but I still was not distressed, yet sad, as if nothing in heaven or earth could make me happy. Having been thus endeavouring to pray—though, as I thought, foolish and senseless—for nearly half an hour; then, as I was walking in a thick grove, unspeakable glory seemed to open to the apprehension of my soul. I do not mean any external brightness or imagination of a body of light. Still, I had a new inward apprehension or view of God, such as I never had before, nor anything which had the slightest resemblance to it. I had no particular apprehension of any person in the Trinity, the Father, the Son or the Holy Ghost, but it appeared to be Divine glory. My soul rejoiced with joy unspeakable to see such a God, such a glorious Divine Being, and I was inwardly pleased and satisfied that he should be God over all forever and ever. My soul was so captivated and delighted with the excellency of God that I was even swallowed up in him; at least to that degree that I had no thought about my salvation and scarce reflected that there was such a creature as myself. I continued in this state of inward joy, peace and astonishment till near dark without any sensible abatement and then began to think and examine what I had seen and felt sweetly composed in my mind all the evening following. I felt myself in a new world, and everything about me appeared with a different aspect from what it was wont to do. At this time, the way of salvation opened to me with such infinite wisdom, suitableness and excellence that I wondered if I should ever think of any other way of salvation; I was amazed that I had not dropped my contrivances and complied with this lovely, blessed and excellent way before.[39]

FEELINGS WITH SWAMI

Meeting Swami, even in silence, stirs profound emotions. Unexpectedly and spontaneously, spiritual awareness and comprehension are awakened within the individual to absorb the meeting. The person in Swami's presence recognizes they are with someone enveloped in spiritual love. This realization doesn't stem from conscious thought or logical reasoning and cannot be articulated through words. Instead, it is a state of unwavering assurance grounded in spontaneous thoughts and emotions, commonly referred to as intuition.

In *Ramakatha Rasavahini*, Swami shares the experience of King Janaka when he sees Rama and Lakshmana. He is stunned and rendered speechless. The mental disposition of devotees with Swami is similar to King Janaka's experience with Lord Rama.

> His (Janaka's) eyes fell on the two boys, Rama and Lakshmana. They struck him as embodiments of solar effulgence. He could not find words for a few seconds. He knew not where he was at the time. With great effort, he recovered enough awareness of the surroundings.[40]

Merton describes the post-experience state as one of perpetual contemplation. His experience is symptomatic of what happens to a person who has a spiritual experience and comes face to face with God.

> We are made to become one with God and proclaim the glory of God (and) live in perpetual contemplation. All day long, we turn our eyes to look at God.[41]

In the following citation, the student author feels a powerful kinship, bonding and desire to be with Swami.

> The first time I saw him, as he got out of his car and slowly walked through the large entrance of our school, I couldn't, for a second, take my eyes off him. Those incredibly expressive eyes and the charming countenance were something I had never before seen. I immediately felt a deep affinity towards him and an inexplicable longing to belong to Him.[42]

Schulman has a mysterious experience when he comes face-to-face with Swami for the first time. As Swami looked at him, he experienced what was akin to getting punched in his solar plexus and having his breath knocked out.

> After about ten minutes, Baba suddenly got up. Baba looked at the author for the first time. When their eyes met, the writer felt as if his breath had been knocked out of him. His ears started ringing. He felt completely disoriented. When Baba looked away, the ringing stopped.[43]

In the following three excerpts from her books, Reeves translates her feelings when she sees Swami during darshan. Her heart overflows joyfully, and she feels a deep spiritual conviction and confidence in Swami.

> (I found) a seat near the aisle. As He came by, my heart was hammering. Blood rushed to my head, and I felt momentarily paralyzed.
>
> He reached to take my letter. My heart was overflowing like a happy child's.
>
> He radiated love and kindness, soothing my troubled, anxious heart with His presence. He found me in the crowd, looking into my eyes without smiling, with a long, serious, contemplative gaze. I was filled with assurance and joyous delight.[44]

Reeves expresses her intense emotional reaction to Swami's presence.

> Baba was present. I was fortunate to sit in the front row facing Baba's chair. The closeness was so intense, too much to bear. When He glanced in my direction, I had to lower my eyes. I was breaking out in a sweat; my heart was pounding as if I had a fever. The feeling was uncomfortable, like being too close to God.[45]

In the third excerpt, she addresses how her mind stops working in Swami's proximity. She is an artist with acute powers of observation, yet cannot focus.

> Something happens whenever Baba is very close, and I lose my grasp of the physical reality. I try to observe details of His features to recall later, but I can't. In His immediate nearness, the divine aura surrounding Him blows the mind away. This happens every time Bhagavan comes near.[46]

Krystal's mind becomes blank in Swami's presence.

> Nothing else seems significant when one is in his presence. Every thought fades away, leaving one's mind blank.[47]

Aitken writes that meeting Swami is like coming face to face with Jesus after the resurrection, His divinity established without a doubt.

> Here is resurrection with a vengeance, the miracle of grace streaming forth before your eyes as the coordinates of love and longing meet and merge.[48]

John Hislop spotlights that his doubts vanished when he saw Swami.

> ...my intellectual doubts, which had gained considerable strength during the journey, could not survive even the first meeting with Baba. In his presence, doubt is like shallow water in the burning sun, disappearing in no time.[49]

Sandweiss cannot describe the excitement and emotions of being with Swami. The mind takes some time to grasp what the heart figures out quickly.

> This was my eighth trip. I was filled with excitement I could have at no other place but here. There is no way to describe the actual encounter. The mind cannot hold the vision that the heart grasps in this moment of intimate contact.[50]

MEANING INHERENT IN THE EXPERIENCE OF SWAMI

Many things happen when a person sees or converses with Swami for the first time. They are awestruck and experience profound love, their minds still infused with joy. They may have come to Swami with many questions, but they cease to be of consequence. This is when Swami connects with the person. It marks the beginning of a spiritual journey with Swami, the start of self-discovery. They find answers to profound religious questions through self-reflection catalysed by Swami.

Reeves describes her darshan experience and post-darshan reflections. Intense joy and spiritual longing are evoked in Swami's presence. Through an innocuous experience of His omniscience and overwhelming love, she feels Swami pierce into the core of her being. She realizes that she has nowhere to hide from God. He knows her inside out. She begins to believe that nothing can go awry because God loves her. He will not let anything untoward happen. The first stirrings of devotion fill her with this spiritual certitude. After meeting Swami, introspection and reflection restart on a religious basis. For her, God as Swami is a tangible reality, not a remote, inaccessible idea. This is a culmination of her 34-year search for God, a pursuit she first thought impossible.

> He looked directly at me, smiled and took my letter. Bending forward, He asked with a sweet, concerned, innocent expression on His face, 'Are you leaving?' I shook my head, saying no. Swami said, 'Stay, don't go!'
>
> I have never felt a joy comparable to this generated by Baba through His looks and words. I suddenly felt elevated, as if this was the crowning moment of my entire life, as my mind went over and over what Baba had said. Best of all, it was the love that reached straight to my heart. In my letter, I asked Swami for a sign to tell me if I was on the right path in my Sadhana and that it was not my imagination playing tricks with me. This was His reply.
>
> 'The Ocean of Love exists within Bhagavan. He can inspire a feeling of elevation and devotion through His presence. The joy and love evoked when a person thinks of Him is sufficient proof of Divinity. It is difficult to write about spiritual experiences and impossible to express the inner vision in words.
>
> When years of dreams (spiritual expectations) materialize in the form of Sathya Sai Baba, when His very Being (presence) is a manifestation of the dream, His words its dialogue (expression), His teaching its very essence, this is a realization.[51]

In this passage, Sandweiss recounts his initial encounter with Swami. During this experience, Swami offered him some candy, and in that simple gesture, a spiritual connection was forged. Swami's gaze seemed to convey a meaningful message, and this experience proved transformational for Sandweiss. He felt Swami's love and found it to be a catalyst for his belief and wholehearted acceptance.

> Then suddenly, he appeared. Quickly and gracefully, he walked up to us, smiling and joyful. He held out two pieces of candy, saying sweets, sweets. His blissful, loving gaze held my own transfixed. What a message in those eyes! They seemed to tell of an understanding beyond my comprehension. I felt a chill and a clear impression that this man knew and was responding to my despair.
>
> What was communicated in that brief moment? The world! Something broke inside of me. Some of Sai Baba's joy and love penetrated my soul [...] There was such love, gentleness, and caring in this man's presence.
>
> Who was he?
>
> Puffed-up self-worth and egotistical attachment to my particular values and beliefs seemed to shatter into dust, suddenly giving way to a sense of awe and mystery. I felt somehow transformed in one breathtaking, incredible moment.[52]

Sandweiss describes the same incident after many years. He attributes the timing of Swami's act of handing over the sweets to His awareness of the author's inner spiritual trauma. Sandweiss was reflecting on the purposelessness of his trip. The incident seemed outwardly innocuous, yet its timing and the evoked emotions made the experience vivid and memorable.

> He was coming to me. I could see in his eyes and smile that he understood my mind, with all its doubts and confusion. He chose this time to make personal, heart-to-heart contact with me. He extended his hand, which held two small pieces of candy, and said, 'Sweets, sweets, eat.'
>
> Instantly, my despair turned into exquisite happiness. How both omnipresent and personal his love truly is.[53]

Krystal articulates her reactions and emotions during her first darshan. She had reached the ashram with expectations, wanting to believe that Swami was the guru she had been searching for, but she wanted a confirmatory sign from Swami. Swami nonchalantly walks past her, and her expectations are belied. She becomes despondent because she is wary of restarting her search for a master. Swami unexpectedly turns around and talks to her, answering her question. Swami's smile dazzles her; her mind goes blank, and she loses her perception of time. This first dialogue is her sign, which answers a crucial spiritual question.

We entered the main gate and saw hundreds of people assembled and sitting, waiting. I remembered a visit to the healing shrine at Lourdes and once again felt the same overwhelming compassion that had welled inside me at the sight of all the hopeful people praying. The whole scene prompted me to ponder my reasons for coming here. The hope he held out to all waiting was the magnet that attracted me to him. I wondered if he would prove to be the right guide to lead me to that goal.

An almost audible hush came over the crowd after what seemed like hours but was less than one hour. By craning my neck, I could barely catch a fleeting flash of orange as Baba approached. Then he emerged into full view, my first sight of him in person. I had many different reactions in far too quick succession for me to be able to grasp them all at once. But of one thing, I was confident; he was more vibrantly alive than anyone I had ever seen in my whole life. He was shorter than I had expected. As I watched him from a distance, I noticed that his thick neck, shoulders and head, with its shock of black hair standing out all around it like a dark halo, all gave the impression that he was a large man. Yet I observed that his body was slight and extremely graceful.

He moved forward onto the driveway. Swami appeared to float rather than walk along it. He slowly drifted from one side of the driveway to the other between the rows of men and women. Sometimes, he stopped to speak to someone, confer a blessing, draw the symbol of Om on a child's slate and perform many other little loving gestures.

I watched, fascinated, determined to make no effort to attract his attention. Instead, I silently prayed for him to give me a sign to indicate if he was the Master I should now follow. He moved gracefully back and forth between the two sides of the driveway. I held my breath as he lightly drifted over to the women's side at a point just short of where I was sitting, but at no time looking in my direction. Then he moved past me and several feet beyond. As I watched, I thought, 'So that is my answer. He is not my guru.' Heavy-hearted, I realized that I must continue to seek further. No sooner had I accepted this decision than he wheeled around until he faced me directly and said, 'So you have come!' With this observation, his face broke into the most radiant smile I have ever seen, like the sun suddenly coming out from behind a cloud and lighting up everything it touched. I was so dazzled by it that I seemed to lose all sense of time or place, and my mind went blank, empty of its habitual, busy thoughts. I have no idea how long it was before he turned and continued. Time seemed to stand still.

As soon as Baba had made his rounds and returned, we drove back to the hotel. This time, I was oblivious to the wild drive. I was still glowing from the radiance of Baba's smile, which had pierced to the core of my being.[54]

In the forthcoming narrative, Swami begins building a connection with the author. He takes the initiative to engage in a dialogue, prompting Mr Ramana Rao to ask a question. Swami's response, while straightforward, carries profound wisdom that captivates the author's attention.

Baba turned towards me, patting me on my shoulder, and said, 'You neither hear nor talk. You are drowned in your thoughts. Come on. You have to ask some question.' This gave me courage. Clearing my throat, I asked, 'Is a man's future determined by his past deeds, Swami?'

'Yes,' he said.

Then why does not God grant man the knowledge of his earlier birth?' I ventured to ask.

'God knows the limits of the needs of man. He has given man an incredible body, five sense organs, functional and perceptive mind and intellect. When utilized correctly, one can comprehend any truth and attain divine power. In the current life, humans are forfeiting their inner peace by entangling themselves in desires, attachments, love and hatred directed at their possessions and relationships. He will be more stressed because of likes and dislikes beyond his capacity to manage if he also comes to know of his past! Therefore, oblivion of one's past is God's boon to man.

Let me give you an example. King Janaka, who accomplished spiritual scholarship, had the venerable sage Yagnyavalka as his guru. Janaka repeatedly appeals to his master to give him insight into his past, but Yagnyavalka refused to accept his wish by warning him that such knowledge would seriously disrupt his mental peace. Once King Janaka was so insistent on knowing the salient facts of his earlier life that Yagnyavalka could not resist any longer and, as one endowed with divine vision, disclosed, 'Oh king! The lady who is your wife now was your mother in your former life.' From that day, Janaka became an ascetic. When a spiritual giant like King Janaka could not stand the jolt of a peep into his past life, what do you think will impact an ordinary man?' Baba explained.

What a lesson![55]

Swami addresses Michael Goldstein's initial uncertainties during their first encounter. His very first words respond to a pressing question troubling Goldstein, demonstrating Swami's omniscience and his innate ability to attend to the concerns of a devoted individual.

On my first journey to India, I was worried that my past transgressions could prevent my spiritual progress. On the last day of my first visit to India, I sat in the Mandir for morning Bhajans just before leaving the Ashram.

While sitting in the Mandir listening to the Bhajans, I started to worry about my past errors. I felt useless and without hope because of my past. Although I knew I would always follow Swami, my past would not allow me to reach the end of the spiritual path. I thought past–past–past, an

> unsurpassable obstacle. Then suddenly, I felt a hand on my shoulder. It was Swami. He had entered the Mandir by the back door, approaching me from behind. He put his hand on my shoulder, looked me in the eyes, said, 'Forget the past, and carried on walking. I cried. I felt redeemed.
>
> The Lord said, 'Forget the past.' A load of past errors, sadness and guilt were removed.[56]

In the next excerpt, the protagonist reflects on her experience of the ashram, the emotions of the people visiting and Swami. Swami's dialogue reveals His awareness of her thoughts, leaving her to reflect and discover.

> For the first few days, I did not think much of Baba. What impressed me was the following. I was thinking, 'There is one thing very spectacular about this ashram.' In those days, only about 25 or 30 people would be there. They experienced significant difficulties getting there, having to use bullock carts. Yet when they left, they would have tears in their eyes. Baba used to see them off in the olden days and lift the children into the bullock carts, help them to get into the carts and all that. Everybody would be in tears. And Baba, too. He was quite visibly moved.
>
> Then I was sitting on the veranda in Puttaparthi one day and thinking to myself, 'Many people come to my house as guests, but when they leave, I don't think they are so sorrowful or that I am so sorrowful. What is it that makes people sad to leave Baba? What is it that they get?' Pondering along these lines, I just thought, 'It is the love which he gives, probably, that is the great thing about Baba.' While thinking this, Baba came from behind and told me, 'You are thinking along the correct lines.'[57]

Swami often dramatically surprises or jolts people by doing something unexpected. The nature of such an experience becomes a trigger for reflection, intensifying their search for meaning. Baskin reflects on her inner thoughts while interacting with Swami. Initially, her resistance is evident in her peculiar responses to His questions. However, Swami's replies are even more enigmatic. When she silently expresses her aversion to His appearance, He presents her with a medallion bearing His distorted image, conveying a message without words. Baskin gradually comprehends that Swami is entirely unlike what she had anticipated. She becomes aware of the profound and all-encompassing nature of His love, ultimately grasping the unique and exceptional qualities that set Swami apart.

> The following morning, still with high temperatures and dressed very inappropriately, we went to the interview. Sai Baba sat on the floor with us in a small room. He turned to me and asked, 'What do you want?' I could not think, but, by my answer, the welfare of animals was uppermost in my mind. It would be a great relief if He protected me from that pain. I answered, 'Something to protect animals.'
>
> He asked, 'Do you like my image?' I hesitated a moment before answering because at that time, I did not particularly like His physical appearance. He certainly did not fit my concept of what a Holy Man should look like, but how could I say this tactfully? So, to be polite, I answered, 'Yes.' He again waved His palm in a circular motion and materialized a porcelain medallion that He handed me. When I looked at the medallion, I was stunned to see a most unbecoming, out-of-proportion likeness of His face, complete with a missing front tooth!
>
> What to make of it all? So far, everything had shocked my expectations so severely that I might have felt unsound had it not been for the fever numbing my mind.
>
> That evening, I thought about my first encounter with Sai Baba. I certainly did not recognize His divinity instantly, as many claim to do. As I observed His every movement, gesture and expression throughout the interview, I knew I was not looking at a human being. I did not understand what He was, but I knew what He was not. I realized after much deliberation that what I had not discerned in Sai Baba was the assertion of the ego: the human element. To see this is beyond description; it can only be experienced. The materializations

> were undoubtedly amazing but secondary. They were done in such an open, spontaneous and natural way that they left no question about their authenticity. They undoubtedly were part of His nature, as creation is an inseparable part of the creator. His superhuman love, in itself, was the greatest miracle I had ever witnessed. It was so all-encompassing that the universe melted away when He focused it on me, and only He and I existed.[58]

Baskin appreciates the futility of trying to understand Swami by rationalizing Him. The narrative reveals a deepening belief and acceptance.

> The more I discovered about Him, the more was left to discover. Deep introspection, trial and error and a desire to know the truth are the tools needed to begin understanding Sai Baba's mysterious ways, the total of which we can only hope to learn a minuscule part.
>
> The only question I asked Him was if the baby I was carrying would be all right, as I was worried that my illness might affect the child. He assured me that the baby would be a healthy one. Those few words said by anyone else would have meant nothing, but the moment Baba said them, they carried the power to completely lift the burden of worry from me. Though they did not answer my problems verbally, the solution was to be found in my state of mind. He had transformed the inner self instead of the outer.
>
> We stood up as Sai Baba left the room. As we started to walk out, my mother let out a cry of delight upon discovering she could move her crippled toe, 'Look, I can move my toe. It's fixed!' she exclaimed. I, too, was astounded at witnessing such a miracle. Even though I had seen Baba touch her toe, I never thought He could fix it or even knew it was broken as we hadn't told Him. I had naively categorized miracles as more difficult to perform than others. Omnipotence was a concept too complex for me to grasp at that point. Also, how He gently touched her toe—without words or display

> of power—was surprising. I would have expected a certain amount of showy demonstration to emphasize such a miracle. How many false concepts do I have to eliminate? How many opinions and ideas have been formed erroneously throughout my life? The spiritual path has been and continues to be a purifier of the mind.[59]

Schulman details an interview with Swami. The meeting occurs at the end of the trip, forming the basis of his book. He is honest about his expectations and emotions. Swami responds to him during the meeting, answering his unarticulated thoughts and giving him what he wants. Swami describes the purpose of the gift.

> He placed a hand on each of the writer's shoulders, transferring an inner warmth and affection and forming a bond between them. Baba then pushed his right sleeve up over his elbow and, with his fingers spread apart, his palm down, made a slow, rotating motion as he closed his fingers. When he opened them, his palm was covered with vibhuti.
>
> The writer was disappointed. He had been looking forward to receiving a gift from Baba, but he didn't want vibhuti. What he had hoped to get was a picture of Baba.
>
> Baba laughed. 'Why didn't you tell me you don't want vibhuti?' he said in English. 'Alright, I will give you what you want.'
>
> He made the same motion with his hand, and when he opened his fingers, a small colour photograph on aluminium, about three inches square, had materialized in his palm.
>
> 'Keep it in your pocket,' Baba said, 'until you have me in your heart. Then you won't need a photograph.'[60]

SWAMI STAGE-MANAGES THE EXPERIENCE

Ramana Rao reflects on his first meetings with Swami and all that transpired—the darshan, the induced emotions, the dialogue and the inner struggle to accept. He realizes that Swami was controlling or stage-managing their encounters. The insight becomes evident as he recognizes Swami's perfect timing in their interactions. Swami engages with him only when he is mentally ready to listen, understand and accept change. Swami moves when His intervention will have the desired spiritual impact on the person.

> Wc would have gone by the eleven o'clock bus. Narayana Rao stopped us. If Baba had delayed by a few seconds in sending for us, we would have left the Ashram. How did he time his message perfectly to the second? That means his eyes were watching our movements and even thoughts closely. If he knows I don't wear a sacred thread or am averse to wearing Vibhoothi on my forehead, what does he not know about me? Fantastic.[61]

DIALOGUE WITH SWAMI

Gupta, the author of *The Gospel of Sri Ramakrishna*, gradually developed a reverent attitude towards Ramakrishna Paramahansa. The humbling occurs through the slow destruction of his pride. The process is similar to the experiences of people with Swami. Ramakrishna helps Gupta understand spiritual ideas using metaphors and emphasizes the role of God in assisting devotees to know Him. A devotee is never alone.

> Ramakrishna: 'Are you married?'
>
> M: 'Yes, sir.'
>
> Master (with a shudder): 'Oh, Ramlal! Alas, he is married!'
>
> Like one guilty of a terrible offense, M. sat motionlessly, his eyes fixed on the ground. He thought, 'Is it such a wicked thing to get married?'
>
> The Master continued, 'Have you any children?'
>
> M., this time, could hear the beating of his own heart. He whispered tremblingly, 'Yes, sir, I have children.'
>
> Very sadly, Sri Ramakrishna said, 'Ah me! He even has children!'
>
> Thus rebuked, M. sat speechlessly. His pride had received a blow. After a few minutes, Sri Ramakrishna looked at him kindly and said affectionately, 'You see, you have certain good

signs. I know them by looking at a person's forehead, eyes, etc. Tell me, now, what kind of person is your wife? Has she spiritual attributes, or is she under the power of avidya?'

M.: 'She is all right. But I am afraid she is ignorant.'

Master (with evident displeasure): 'And you are a man of knowledge!'

M.'s ego was again severely shocked.

Master: 'Well, do you believe in God with form or without form?'

M., somewhat surprised, said to himself: 'How can one believe in God without form when one believes in God with a form? And if one believes in God without form, how can one believe that God has a form? Can these two contradictory ideas be true at the same time? Can a white liquid-like milk be black?'

M: 'Sir, I like to think of God as formless.'

Master: 'Very good. It is enough to have faith in either aspect. You believe in God without form; that is quite all right. But never for a moment think this alone is true and all else false. Remember that God with form is just as true as God without form. But hold fast to your conviction.'

The assertion that both are equally true amazed M.; he had never learned this from his books. Thus, his ego received a third blow, but since it was not yet completely crushed, he came forward to argue with the Master a little more.

M: 'Sir, suppose one believes in God with form. Certainly, He is not the clay image!'

Master (interrupting): 'But why clay? It is an image of Spirit.'

M. could not quite understand the significance of this image of Spirit. 'But, sir,' he said to the Master, 'one should explain to those who worship the clay image that it is not God and that while worshipping it, they should have God in view and not the clay image. One should not worship clay.'

Master (sharply): 'That's the one hobby of you Calcutta (now Kolkata) people—giving lectures and bringing others to the light! Nobody ever stops to consider how to get the light himself. Who are you to teach others?'

'He who is the Lord of the Universe will teach everyone. He alone teaches us who has created this universe and made the sun and moon, men and beasts and all other beings. Who has provided means for their sustenance; who has given the children parents and endowed them with love to bring them up. The Lord has done so many things; will He not show people how to worship Him? If they need teaching, then He will be the Teacher. He is our Inner Guide.'

'Suppose there is an error in worshipping the clay image, doesn't God know that He alone is invoked through it? He will be pleased with that same worship. Why should you get a headache over it? You had better try for knowledge and devotion yourself.'

This time, M. felt that his ego was completely crushed. He said to himself: 'Yes, he has spoken the truth. What need is there for me to teach others? Have I known God? Do I love Him? I haven't room for myself in my bed, and I am inviting my friend to share it with me! I know nothing about God, yet I am trying to teach others. What a shame! How foolish I am! This is not mathematics, history or literature that one can teach others. No, this is the deep mystery of God; what he says appeals to me.'

This was M.'s first argument with the Master and, happily, his last.[62]

The engagement of a person with Swami is both simple and complex. A person engages with Him in an interpersonal way. They can see Swami, be with Him and talk to Him through the concepts of *darshan* (seeing), *sparshan* (touching or contact) and *sambhashan* (dialogue). This association has another important characteristic: mystical and spiritual engagement. A person often gets direct answers to their religious questions, or Swami creates situations for meaning to arise within them through reflection. Swami is available; He can be engaged but remains elusive and an enigma. An engagement with Him is always a process of inner discovery. Swami indirectly answers Raja Reddy by asking a rhetorical question.

> I went there; I saw Bhagavan and was most attracted by His gentle, loving voice and speech. And then He moved His hand in the air in His usual inimitable style. I then asked Him why He was waving His hand in that manner. After all, since I was educated, I was a little inquisitive. But Swami didn't reply directly. He said: 'Then why are you wearing a tucked-in shirt?' I said: 'This is how we should be in our college.' (He) answered it indirectly![63]

Reddy narrates how he became Swami's devotee. His experience suggests that Swami helps evoke knowledge in a person, triggered through incidents that motivate self-reflection. A listener has to be sensitive and aware to recognize, absorb and comprehend that knowledge.

> I had finished my studies and was absorbed in my sadhana (spiritual practice). Because spiritually, I am an incorrigible introvert—that's what I would say of myself! I used to have my meditation, bhajans, yoga sessions, etc.
>
> So, with that background, I went to Baba. And the very first question I asked Him was: 'Are You a realized soul?'
>
> He is not given to give direct answers! He just pointed to a light in the room with His hand. He said: 'This is the hand; this is the hand's shadow on the wall. There is no such realization.'
>
> What He meant to say is: 'I am the Original! You're the shadow; there is nothing to realize for Me! You have to realize!' That's how it was. I had to read between the lines.
>
> And then, of course, I was absorbed by Him—it was irresistible! His power was something else! And I became His regular follower.[64]

Roberts writes about his inside-out transformation with Swami. He describes being with Swami as a test, a passing through fire. With Swami, he understands or realizes his belief in God.

> The *Shivarathri* Festival, the Night of Siva, is held on a full moon in late February or March. This was the most important holy day of the year for Baba's devotees. A huge crowd gathered in

the Poornachandra (literally Full Moon) Hall as darkness fell. People had been arriving from all over India and beyond during the previous days. The atmosphere crackled with expectation. Brahmin pundits chanted the Vedas as drums thudded and discordant reed horns wailed. The drums and pipes reached a deafening pitch when Baba himself finally entered the packed hall, accompanied by a procession of priests. He looked different, somehow swollen and pained, the way an expectant mother can. Taking his seat behind a little desk on the stage, he seemed uncharacteristically withdrawn and preoccupied as various students from his colleges and sundry devotees delivered very dull speeches. Finally, he rose and spoke in Telugu, pausing.

At the same time, Dr Bhagvantham, a dry and pretentious older man who had been an eminent nuclear physicist before retiring to the ashram, translated what he was saying into what was just about English. The translation was so tedious that Baba frequently interjected straightforward phrases to hurry along Bhagvantham's rambling and ponderous paraphrases. As usual, the speech summed up the significance of the holy day, pointing out that the act of creation was the merging of the material with the divine and that we should all try to do the same, blending our lower natures into our higher ones. *Be good, do good, see good*—the message was so straightforward I wondered how Baba found the patience to keep repeating it. Just as his speeches always seemed to begin at no particular point, so did this one stop in the middle of a sentence as Baba suddenly began singing a bhajan.

The hall echoed his lead, repeating each phrase, the tempo growing toward a restrained frenzy until the bhajan abruptly stopped. The chants had quite a rigid form when sung by devotees, but Baba, who had composed them all, prolonged or curtailed them at will. There was a plaintive and honeyed sweetness to his voice. That night, the mood was more subdued than usual, as if we were less preoccupied with our egos and trying to out-sing one another. After a mere three or four bhajans, Baba began one that consisted entirely of the phrase

Om Sivaiah, Om Sivaiah, Shambo Shankara Om Sivaiah—a tremendous booming hymn to Siva, Destroyer of Worlds, Cosmic Dancer. Unlike the previous bhajans, this one appeared to have no end, and Baba sank into his chair and fell silent, letting the chorus continue without his lead.

A sense that something significant was happening descended. The crowd continued to repeat the one phrase in low, restrained voices. Baba conducted with his finger, his body occasionally contracting as if in pain. *Om Sivaiah, Om Sivaiah*—the throbbing chant continued with solemn power, every eye in the room fixed on the tiny figure. After fifteen minutes, he suddenly clasped his throat and convulsed, rocking back and forth in his chair. Only fifteen feet away, I thought I saw a kind of dreamy agony in his eyes. There was something genuinely awesome, rather than frightening, about this spectacle. The bhajan was gradually increasing tempo now, the entire hall thumping with it like the great heart of some vast machine. Then Baba lurched forward, opening his mouth. Inside it, I glimpsed an odd green glow. He heaved violently, his eyes closing as if he were in pain.

Then, with one hand, he began to pull what looked like a large, crystalline egg from his mouth. Indeed, so large was it that blood appeared at the corners of his lips as the object came through. Like a new baby, it was suddenly out. He caught it in a handkerchief, wiped it clean, then transferred it to his other hand as he dabbed at the blood around his mouth and smiled, every bit the proud new mother. The crowd roared. It was such an extraordinary sight that no one seemed sure how to respond. Baba stood, holding up this egg of greenish crystal, inside which a light pulsed like a heartbeat, like something alive. Then something burst inside my heart, and I started sobbing uncontrollably. At that moment, it was exceedingly hard to doubt that Baba was indeed who he said he was. Here was the symbolic re-enactment of Creation itself: the Siva–Shakti force, the yin and yang, the mighty opposites, the bisecting circles giving birth between them to the *lingam* that represents life itself, life plucked from nothingness. Because of what I felt and saw, I have never for a moment thought that he had swallowed the object earlier and then regurgitated it. Long after Baba left, leaving the glowing, pulsing *lingam* in a little stand on his table, everyone sat as if held like spokes on a wheel to the hub of creation symbolized before us, chanting bhajans until dawn broke. It seemed the only conceivable response to what had happened.

One day, several months after arriving in Puttaparthi, I suddenly felt it was time to leave. On the day I made up my mind to leave, Baba told me he would talk to me. I was shocked. Finally, I walked over the compound to the door of Baba's living quarters. I had wondered for months what was behind it. I stood looking into a tiny and virtually bare concrete room. It smelled nice, at least, of the incense that burned in the temple. I've never encountered that fragrance anywhere else. Several people sat beside me; no one spoke. Baba appeared from the compound outside at the end of the darshan. He stood looking at us. He said something about seeing God in everyone and then, rolling up a sleeve, waved his hand and slowly produced a giant rosary of pink stones. It seemed to emerge from a hole in space just below his palm, swinging in a circle until it was all present in its new dimension. I was no more than a yard from his hand. He presented this sparkling *japamala* to an old Chinese woman, beckoning her and her husband to follow him through a door covered by a cloth flap. Soon—or maybe not—the couple emerged in a daze, followed by Baba, who beckoned someone else inside that other room, always referred to as his living quarters.

Muffled grunts could be heard, and then this person would emerge as if stunned. What was he going to say to me? I didn't want to leave anymore. Finally, I was inside that room. I recall being amazed by how small and bare it was. My room at Nagamma's (rented room) was more extensive and comfortable, and I regarded it as penance. This was also the first time I had ever really stood beside Baba. Like the room, he was unbelievably small. As I looked down into his eyes, trying to think of something to say, I began to shake, gasping with emotion. Quite involuntarily, I said, 'I love you, Baba,' over and over and over again. He hugged me, his hair soft as lamb's wool in my face. This surprised me. I'd imagined it would be wiry. *Baba*, I thought absurdly, *the Lamb of God*. Looking down at him, though, I had the odd impression that I was looking up at him. 'Baba loves you, too,' he said. He meant it; I could *feel* it. To *be loved*: that was not the same as to *love*. I had never let myself *be loved* before, I realized. And I was so grateful that I merely wept more. It was all I could do.

Baba then delivered a summary of my life and a breakdown of my personality in machine-gun bursts that had me reeling, nodding humbly, speechless. With all my faults, there I was, 'the thing itself'. It seemed to be his way of reassuring me that there was nothing he did not know about me and that none of it bothered him. As he usefully confided, the total was 'much confusion'. I had to agree. He reassured me that he would sort things out. It was a workman-like statement. 'Thanks,' I managed. He'd moved back by now and circled his hand in the space between us. Expecting some trinket, I was surprised to see a white, oily substance appear in his palm. Somehow, I knew what he wanted to do, so I lifted my shirt and let him rub this substance into my chest. I kept thanking him profusely. Then he said, 'Don't worry. I am always with you. Baba loves you.' I hardly said a word throughout the interview, yet I emerged knowing I had been given what I most needed: love and reassurance. I felt, and still feel, inexplicably closer to him than to anyone in the world. The next thing I knew, I was back in the antechamber.

The subsequent few days are a blur. I recall walking around in a daze, so happy I couldn't speak. It once crossed my mind to start walking across the great subcontinent and never stop questioning what was undeniably true again. Perhaps I should have done that, but I didn't. When I eventually tried to tell people what had happened, I was not even sure what *had* happened. Words failed; they did not adapt to the feelings I wished to express. A week later, I could no longer return my consciousness to wherever it had been. It was like waking from a beautiful dream and realizing that you could never explain *why* the dream was beautiful. I was only sure of one thing again: I should leave Puttaparthi as soon as possible.

As my bus finally turned onto Bangalore road, I felt enormous relief, as if I had survived some dreadful test and passed through the fire. I hardly knew that person who had arrived there the previous September. Something of him had been burned away, some part I didn't miss. Even the searing air now seemed kinder and cooler. As many have attested, before and since, Puttaparthi is a crucible.

In Baba's teachings and within the strict routine of ashram life, I understood something fundamental about myself: I believed in God and had to believe for anything to make sense.[65]

VIVID MEMORY OF THE FIRST CONVERSATION

Salian narrates the story of his first conversation with Swami. The event is a consequential milestone in his subsequent relationship with Swami. He believes this was when Swami selected him for spiritual development and engagement.

I got picked up from the wayside by the divine master who has patiently, lovingly chipped off the unwanted facets of this rock. The first sculpture process is for the sculptor to pick out the rock and mark it for future sculpting. He did this when I was just a four-day-old student. We were having breakfast in the hostel. We were served *idlis*, and I commented to a friend, 'What is this? They are giving just four idlis. I used to eat ten at home.' This was an innocuous comment I gently made into my friend's ear. I am sure even the person serving us could not hear the conversation.

We ate breakfast and sat for darshan in Trayee under the Ashoka trees. I was sitting in the fourth or the fifth row in front of the Trayee door. Bhagwan came out, glided down the stairs, took a few steps, looked straight at me and went out for darshan. I was sitting amongst the new boys and started getting nudges from behind, 'Swami looked at you, Swami looked at you.' I also felt that Swami looked at me without knowing what was coming.

He went out, gave darshan, came back and from a distance of about 15 feet, he asked me something. That was the first time that I heard his voice without the microphone. I could not decipher what he was asking. Suddenly, everybody around me burst out, '*Idli* Swami, *Idli* Swami.' Swami walked a few more steps and asked me, 'How many idlis?'

I told Swami, 'Four.' I said this plainly, in a matter-of-fact way. He looked into my eyes and asked, 'Do you eat ten idlis?'

My head was buzzing. I could not hear the following question from Swami. My secret was known to all.

I fumbled and said, 'No, Swami. Yes, Swami.' I did not know what to answer. Swami enquired, 'Big idli or small idli?'

I made a gesture showing the size and said, 'This idli, Swami.'

Swami replied, 'That is not the truth.' He continued, 'It is big but not a thick idli.' He described the exact shape of the idli.

He did not have to do that. He had put the stamp on it (me), the rock, a mark for sculpting at a future date.[66]

THE SCAFFOLDING OF BELIEF

The initial encounters with Swami are emotionally overwhelming and pregnant with intuitive insights, yet belief develops gradually. Reeves realizes in hindsight how Swami gently and slowly guided her self-reflection until she accepted Him.

The first time I saw Sai Baba, I strongly felt He had been with me all my life. Nothing about Him—His appearance or mannerisms—was unfamiliar. Like my father, he was close to me, yet I could not believe in His Divinity. Baba masterfully

> guided my self-inquiry and spiritual development until I became aware of a growing surrender to His will.[67]

Iyer describes his first interview with Swami. Upon entering Swami's presence, he is acutely aware of his unsteady faith, which evokes a complex blend of emotions, including love and fear. He narrates an incident that accents the fragility of his budding faith. Throughout his interactions with Swami, he consistently experiences the kindness and love that have become a hallmark of their relationship.

> In my first interview, I was scared and excited at the same time. In every meeting with Swami, one can feel the energy. I remember the encounter. There was nothing to distract me. I could feel the benevolence, the warmth, the love. It was very intense and powerful.
>
> You don't see him as a short person. He is large, huge and magnanimous. You feel tiny and puny in his presence. This feeling never diminished. It was the first time, regardless of familiarity or frequent recurrence.
>
> He cornered me and asked me, 'What do you want?'
>
> My mother had asked me to check with Swami about my sister. She had been married for eleven years but was not blessed with a baby.
>
> Swami said, 'I will give Prasad. In eight months, a baby boy will be born.'
>
> Swami gave Prasad from the basket and asked me to send it by registered post. I came out with my fragile faith. I have to wait eight months, and the baby has to be a boy. For my faith, I had to wait eight months.
>
> It was a boy.[68]

In a person's relationship with God, belief crystallizes and consolidates in personal experiences. The incidents seem ordinary but are realized as God's handiwork in hindsight.

During Ramana Rao's first visit to Prasanthi Nilayam, he had persistent headaches through the night. The pain became unbearable. He implored Swami to relieve his suffering, promising to believe in

Him if the headache subsided, a commitment he temporarily forgot until Swami brought it up in a conversation the following day. Swami displayed an uncanny awareness of the incident's details, instilling faith in Ramana Rao. The author subtly altered how he addressed Swami, reflecting his evolving belief.

> I slept in the open in front of the Mandir. I woke up suddenly at eleven in the night with a headache. I opened my suitcase; I had forgotten to bring the small plastic case containing household remedies. Within fifteen minutes, it developed into a splitting headache. Whom could I wake up in the dead of night to find out if they had any tablets? I walked in the cool breeze for some time. It was to no avail. I kept a wet handkerchief on my forehead, with no effect. The headache was on the increase.
>
> Just then, a tourist bus arrived. About sixty to seventy people got down and silently started preparations to sleep. I went to a group of men talking among themselves in a low tone and enquired if they had some medicine for my headache. None of them seemed to understand English.
>
> I tried to explain through gestures what I needed. One of them appeared to comprehend. He took out a bottle and asked me to hold out my hand. I noticed that it contained some pungent oil. I withdrew my hand and asked for a tablet. He assured me through gestures that a massage with that oil would cure my headache. I shuddered at the thought of massage on top of this insufferable headache.
>
> In a state of helplessness, I went and sat on my bed. There used to be an idol of a lotus in front of the Mandir. In front of the lotus, there used to be an idol of Ganesh. About ten members who had alighted from the tourist bus walked around the Mandir silently with folded hands, prostrated in front of that idol and smeared on their foreheads ashes of the burnt incense sticks lying on the ground as if it was vibhuti.
>
> My headache became unbearable.
>
> Suddenly a thought occurred to me. I waited till all those ten people disappeared and went and stood in front of the

Ganesh idol and looked at Baba's room. I fervently appealed in the silence of my heart, 'Baba, my friend, one of your devotees brought me here. I would not have suffered from this terrible headache if I were in Hyderabad. I have heard enough about your miraculous powers. This is a crucial test. I will bow before you and wear this ash on my forehead. If my headache is cured, you are God or a fraud.' I knelt on the ground, applied a little ash, paid obeisance to him, stood up, walked away and lay in my bed.

Around four in the morning, a student from Pataskala woke me up with some irritation. I got up reluctantly, got ready and sat in the row next to my friend. Baba selected two batches, one after another, without any deviation in his procedure to avoid us. I was least surprised since I was more than convinced that it was a punishment inflicted on my friend for bringing along with him an unworthy fellow like me.

I packed my luggage and was ready by half-past ten. We loaded our luggage into (the) car and started. Our car had hardly moved forward a few feet when a student from *Patashala* came running and stopped the vehicle. The student informed, 'Swami is calling Mr Desikachari and his friend wearing dark glasses (me).'

Led by the student, we went up the stairs right into Baba's room. There was a couch shaped like a coiled serpent with a five-headed hood. Baba was sitting on that. He greeted us with a smile and asked us to sit. My friend pulled me down to Baba's feet and paid his obeisance. I folded my hands in reverence and sat by my friend's side at Baba's feet. Baba asked me, 'Hey, Rowdy! How is your headache?' I blinked at him, not knowing what he was talking about.

'What headache, Swami?' asked my friend after looking at my blank face.

'Ask your friend,' Baba said, looking at me smiling. I stared at him silently, not knowing what to say.

'Hey, Rowdy! Speak up. Has your last night's headache gone?' Baba asked, patting my cheek affectionately. I only

> recollected last night's excruciating headache and my challenging Baba's divine powers. I must have instantaneously gone to sleep after I lay down and forgotten in the morning in my hurried preparations for our return journey.
>
> 'My headache is gone, sir, gone, Swami,' I said, bewildered, while correcting my way of addressing Baba.
>
> 'He did not tell me anything, Swami,' my friend said. It was true.
>
> 'He has forgotten. He fought with it for over an hour like Gajendra, didn't you?' He looked at me with the same sweet smile. For the first time, I touched his feet with reverence as in utter astonishment at his graphic description of my fateful headache.[69]

Ramana Rao reflects on his experiences with Swami's omniscience and power. Swami had done two things. One, He had identified him from among many people on Hyderabad's streets. Two, He had mysteriously and miraculously taken care of a persistent headache. He reflects on his relative insignificance, and his ego shrivels up. The desire to examine Swami diminishes.

> Perhaps Swami noticed me dumbstruck with awe, so he asked my friend, 'Come on, Desikachari! Ask something. You are fond of spiritual subjects.'
>
> 'Swami! A man is supposed to pay for his deeds. Can't he escape his retribution with God's grace?' asked my friend.
>
> 'Nothing is impossible for a man who has acquired God's grace,' Baba explained. Not familiar with philosophical phraseology, I could neither comprehend nor attempt to understand what Baba was saying. I was fascinated by the sweetness of his voice. I was enchanted by the recapitulation of his earlier statements directed at me. If he could tell that he had seen me in Dr Boorgula Ramakrishna Rao's house, he could identify every one of the thousands present here. He knew how much and how long I had suffered from headaches and the challenge I had thrown at him. My God![70]

The experience of the Samaritan Woman in the Bible has similarities with Mr Ramana Rao's meetings with Swami in the preceding two citations. The Samaritan Woman engages in a dialogue with Jesus. She uses different titles to address Jesus, changing as the conversation progresses. The varying titles reveal her developing faith. She first addresses Jesus as a Jew, then calls Him a Man, then Sir, then a Prophet, followed by the Messiah and finally the Saviour of the world and Redeemer.

This meeting symbolizes God's direct accessibility, without choice, favour or barriers, when He comes as a person, an incarnation. The metaphor used to characterize the nature of the meeting is an ambush, alluding to the impending effect of meeting Jesus as an incarnation and the transformation of the Samaritan Woman.

The story is split into three segments to appreciate its spiritual significance. The first excerpt highlights a few attributes of Jesus as an incarnation. One is His omniscience, the ability to know a person's heart. Two is His ability to attract, engage and captivate a person drawn to Him. Three is always being available for a person to connect with Him.

> The time was noon, and Our Blessed Lord sat down at Jacob's well. It was rather unusual for a woman to come in the heat of the day to draw water. As she filled her pitcher, she sought to avoid Our Blessed Lord. But to her surprise, the Stranger beside the well addressed her with a request: give me a drink.[71]

Jesus asks her for water as she fills her water jug. She does not recognize Jesus and asks him how a Jew asks her for a drink. Sheen explains the spiritual meaning of asking for water. According to him, it signifies how Jesus asks people who come to Him to empty themself of all unnecessary thoughts, ideas and beliefs so that He can fill them with God. Jesus is the divine giver and not the receiver of anything.

> There must always be an emptying of the human before there can be a filling with the Divine.[72]

The dialogue between Jesus and the Samaritan Woman continues, and He slowly reveals His omniscience, an awareness of her life. This becomes her spiritual turning point as she realizes she is talking to the Messiah.

The woman saw in Him only a weary man. Her eye could not penetrate beneath the outward form of the Divine. She saw the Jew but not the Son of God. But she grows in respect for Him as she adds:

You have no bucket, and this well is deep. How can you give me living water? Are you a greater man than Jacob, our ancestor, who gave us the well and drank from it himself, he and his sons and his cattle too? *John 4:11,12*

He answered that He was greater than Jacob:

Everyone who drinks this water will be thirsty again, but whoever drinks the water I give him will never suffer thirst any more. The water I shall give him will be an inner spring always welling up for eternal life. *John 4.13,14*

She could not understand grace or heavenly power under the analogy of water for the body. She continues:

Sir, give me that water, and then I shall not be thirsty nor have to come all this way to draw. *John 4.15*

She was confused. She imagined that His promise would exempt her from the toil of coming to the well every day.

Jesus saw that she had failed to comprehend the spiritual lesson. He changed the conversation to reveal Himself:

Go home, call your husband and come back. *John 4.16*

The woman answered:

I have no husband. *John 4.17*

This was an honest and truthful confession. Our Lord answered:

You are right in saying you have no husband. *John 4.18*

Then He continued:

You have had five husbands. The man you now live with is not your husband; you told me the truth. *John 4:18*

Jesus revealed his omniscience. The penny dropped, and she realized who she was with. She answered:

I know that Messiah (that is, Christ) is coming. When he

comes, he will tell us everything. *John 4:25*

In answer to her nascent belief, Jesus answered:

I am he, I, who am speaking to you now. *John 4:26*

Sensing the magnitude of the revelation, she hastened into the city to call the others:

Come and see a man who has told me everything I ever did. Could this be the Messiah? *John 4:29*

Her earnest manner convinced the men who followed her back to the well. After seeing Jesus, they said to the woman:

It is no longer because of what you said that we believe, for we have heard him ourselves, and we know that this is the Savior of the world. *John 4:42*

Her belief was stronger. At first, Christ was to her a 'Jew', then a 'man', then 'Sir', then a 'Prophet', then 'the Messiah' and at last the 'Savior of the world' and 'Redeemer from sin'.[73]

In the experiences with Swami and Jesus, Ramana Rao and the Samaritan Woman modify how they address Swami and Christ, respectively. How the experiences unfold is characterized by the unexpectedness of what comes next. The meetings appear to be planned by Jesus and Swami for maximum impact to achieve the evocation of belief. God has to amaze a person to create a willingness to accept and believe. There is a slow scaffolding of faith after the experience. Feelings for God begin to arise; the defences come down, and the person starts to engage with God. With Swami, the process of discovery occurs over time. Despite the initial impact, the mind takes time to accept. Spiritual answers are never straightforward. Logic does not always work. Conviction in God is different from acceptance of God.

> Miracles are no cure for scepticism. Some will not believe whatever happens. No divine sign or experience can evoke complete conviction if the person is unwilling to recognize their experiences. Sometimes, the intellect fails to win the heart in the struggle of the head and the heart.[74]

Iyer tests Swami to build his fledgling faith in the following excerpt. He conducts different experiments to test Swami's responsiveness to him until Swami gives a dramatic, unexpected and immediate response to his request for instant feedback on his thoughts.

> I put Baba to the test. Swami did small things to increase my belief.
>
> And I tried experiments. I would say, 'If you are God, step on my fingers as you walk by. Swami, please do this for my faith.' And he would come close, stand on my fingers and talk to someone.
>
> Baba would usually stop the Bhajan of a slow singer after the first beat. And I would pray to Baba to take the bhajan to three speeds. I would implore, 'Just do it for me.' And Baba took it to three speeds. He was looking at me and smiling. The happening was not a coincidence.
>
> A question often crossed my mind, 'Does he know what I am thinking?' The mind wavers at the beginning of the association. Even when Swami responded to my prayers, I would question, 'Was it a coincidence? Maybe he didn't know what I was praying for?'
>
> Swami, in a physical form, is 'like' a human. A question would cross my mind, 'When he is talking to someone else at that moment, does he know what I am thinking?'
>
> Once, when Baba was giving darshan, I got this 'weird' desire, 'Do you know what I am thinking? It can't be a coincidence if you respond to me now. If you know what I am thinking, look at me now.' And he just didn't look at me but beckoned me. I went running, and he handed me the letters.
>
> I was genuinely seeking faith. I was telling Baba I needed belief. I needed to accept a teacher who I know knows everything that goes on within me. By this time, I had read the two books: *Man of Miracles* and *The Holy Man and the Psychiatrist*. I had to find my own experience and my faith.
>
> They were these simple steps, like building blocks; I started accepting and getting to know Swami.[75]

Developing belief is not a smooth process. It is like a person gingerly treading on a frozen lake, uncertain whether the ice will hold them.

Schulman is alone with Swami. No conversation ensues. He is struggling with his feelings for Swami. Suddenly, he feels an upsurge of a love of the kind he has never felt before. He feels alone, isolated and scared. He fears the loss of his self-identity and self-control in front of Swami's overpowering love. He is struggling with giving up logical thinking to discover the reasons for his coming to Swami. It all began with a book writing project. His emotions suggest that his trip has taken a different turn. This is when Swami starts to talk, trying to soften his uneasiness. Swami confirms that the author's coming to Him was masterminded by Swami; He draws people who are spiritually ready. The concept of readiness is unexplained.

> They were silent for a time.
>
> The writer stood beside the couch and waited. There was nothing he could say. A kind of warmth and closeness he had never known before was spreading through his consciousness, frightening him. He felt in danger of being smothered by it, but it wasn't the intensity that disturbed him. It was the sudden realization that this feeling was love—he thought it was love—different from any other love he had felt, heard about or read about. It may have been this inability to define what he felt that caused him to panic suddenly. In less than a minute, he had become a displaced person, feeling emotionally isolated in an unfamiliar darkness. To cope with this perplexing anxiety, the only defence he could find was to shut it off.
>
> Baba watched him for a time with intensity.
>
> 'You cannot run away from me,' Baba said. 'As I told you, no one can come to Puttaparthi, however accidental it might seem, without my calling him. I bring only those people here who are ready to see me, and nobody else can find his way here. You understand when I say ready, there are different readiness levels.'
>
> Baba laughed. 'You wonder why I called you here instead of the millions of others because you don't like how you feel for me. Isn't it? And it makes you worry why I called you.'[76]

James explains why surrendering to God is emotionally challenging. A person who has grown up exercising agency will have to give up control over their life and accept God's all-encompassing involvement and role. For this to happen, a man's ego must weaken and dissolve. This struggle creates spiritual anxiety. James' writing describes Schulman's experience in the previous excerpt.

> The 'surrender': Give up the feeling of responsibility, let go of your hold, resign the care of your destiny to higher powers and be genuinely indifferent as to what becomes of it all. A critical point must be passed to get to it, and a corner must be turned within one. Something must give way; a native hardness must break down and liquefy, and this event is frequently sudden and automatic and leaves on the subject an impression that external power has wreaked on him.
>
> Whatever its ultimate significance may prove to be, this is undoubtedly one basic form of human experience. With those who undergo it in its fullness, no criticism casts doubt on its reality. They know they have felt the higher powers giving up the tension of their will.[77]

Prof. Christian Moevs' understanding of the spiritual journey on his initial understanding is explained by the following excerpt.

> It is the surrender of the finite itself; you must be willing to let go of what you think you are to awaken to the unlimited possibility of what you really are. The encounter with Sai Baba awoke me to the reality of Christ and spiritual life and truth.[78]

5

LOVE BEYOND MEASURE

Spiritual seekers are both amazed and unsettled when they experience God. The emotions experienced defy description and yet are spiritually significant. Through this experience, the devotees become aware that they are with the Divine. They do not conclude this by reasoning, using their mind and intellect. The awareness is embedded in the experience of divine love.

FEELINGS AND REASONING IN SPIRITUAL LIFE

It is necessary to recognize the role of emotions and intuition in belief formation. A growing body of research suggests that reason and emotion complement, not conflict with, one another in decision-making. There was a time when decisions and conclusions about any matter were expected to be grounded in logical reasoning rather than influenced by subjective reactions and feelings towards the subject. It is now widely accepted that rational thinking and evoked emotions about an issue inform each other. Reasoning-based perceptions help refine a person's feelings and, in turn, help evaluate and validate logical conclusions. Decisions and judgements based on either reasoning or sentiments alone are fallible.

People discover meaning based on their feelings and reasoning on the spiritual path. When people attach importance to something, it is based on their feelings about it. Emotions motivate people to seek information, knowledge and understanding to justify their feelings. Without feeling deeply about an issue, there may not be any reason to do anything. Emotions play a role in identifying what is pursued and what becomes a passion and goal.

INTUITIVE PERCEPTION

To a layperson, God is an enigma. The experience of spontaneous love for God makes it easier to comprehend an inexplicable God. Aitken describes the role of emotion in recognizing God. Through his experience with Swami, he realizes that love is a means of experiencing the mysteries of the divine. A person who meets Swami becomes intuitively aware of spiritual insights in their experience of unexpected and spontaneous love.

> Imponderables such as the nature of the divine are beyond the comprehension of the average enquirer. To anyone blessed with the maddening experience of love, at least a ray of light is available for viewing such imponderables. When love smiles, our understanding is strangely enhanced. Love gives wings to the seeker. The Sathya Sai phenomenon makes sense only to a lover. Through love, we can experience the mystery of the divine, a realization entirely different from the fruits of any intellectual analysis.[1]

Ramakrishna Paramahansa emphasizes the role and power of an avatar. God is infinite and limitless. He confines Himself and becomes an avatar to become accessible to people, giving them an experience of divine love and teaching them how to love God. Each person has to engage with God to experience and realize Him. He uses the metaphor of a cow and milk to underline the strength and value of learning through personal experience. Knowing a cow's features is useless for a person seeking nourishment. They have to drink milk to realize the cow's value. Similarly, God can only be understood and recognized through personal effort and direct experience.

> However great and infinite God may be, His essence can and does manifest itself through man by His mere will. God's incarnation as a man cannot be explained by analogy. One must feel it for oneself and realize it by direct perception. An analogy can give us only a little glimpse. By touching a cow's horns, legs or tail, we feel the cow herself, but for us, the essential thing about a cow is her milk, which comes through

> the udder. The Divine Incarnation is like the udder. From time to time, God incarnates Himself as a man to teach people devotion and divine love.[2]

Engaging with an avatar is the easy way of experiencing God. Ramakrishna Paramahansa explains the good fortune of associating with an incarnation. God as infinite and endless is a challenging idea to visualize and comprehend; where does He begin and end? However, when God becomes an incarnation, He limits himself and becomes tangible and understandable to everyone. He allows each person to experience, recognize and realize Him. An avatar makes spiritual experiences easily accessible to everyone. It is a blessing and good fortune to associate with and experience an avatar.

> Who can comprehend everything about God? It is not given to man to know any aspect of God, great or small. And what need is there to know everything about God? It is enough if we only realize Him. And we see God Himself we but see His Incarnation. Suppose a person goes to the Ganges and touches its water. He will then say, 'Yes, I have seen and touched the Ganges.' To say this, he doesn't need to touch the whole length of the river from Haridwar to Gangasagar.[3]

Manning highlights that even a brief experience of God is transformative. The duration of the experience is unimportant. Even a moment's glimpse of God's power and magnificence is adequate to awaken belief in God.

> A fleeting glimpse of God (is a) powerful transforming experience of his incomparable glory that awakens a dormant belief in God. It is an intuitive understanding and realization that God, filled with transcendent brightness, wisdom, ingenuity, power and goodness, is within.[4]

Rani portrays Swami's powerful capacity to change people's mindsets and thinking. She experiences His power on her first visit and is willing to listen and accept everything from Swami.

> His aura was very powerful! He could really transform our whole thinking in a very short time! I could accept anything

> on the first visit within a few days! He gave us an experience of His Power. On my first visit, I could understand; we had Baba's blessing to understand that He had infinite power.[5]

Manning encapsulates the overwhelming nature of the encounter with God. He emphasizes that those who experience God find it impossible to fully comprehend and articulate their experience when confronted directly by God. He employs phrases like shattering collision and helplessness to vividly convey the aftermath of meeting God.

> How do we deal with a glimpse of God? What happens in the silent, empty mind, in the shattering collision with the glory of God that God's vision entails? Can a person look, focus and stare at the majesty and holiness of a living God? Do we have any inner resources when God accosts us?
>
> The awareness of God is essential to all authentic spiritual experiences, and it evokes self-forgetfulness, adoration and a keen look at the wonder of God.[6]

St John of the Cross writes that in the presence of God, a person feels calm and aware of being with God but cannot describe it.

> Such a person can only say that he is satisfied, tranquil and contented, conscious of God's presence, and that, as it seems, all is going well with him, but he cannot describe the state.[7]

Underhill underlines the challenge of sharing spiritual experiences for easy understanding by others. She suggests that conveying an indescribable and overpowering experience may need an artist's creative talents, imagination and linguistic prowess to make it more accessible and fathomable to others.

> In the descriptions of the joy of illumination—in the outpourings of love—it is only by oblique methods of the artist that the wonder of that vision can be expressed. When essential goodness, truth and beauty are apprehended by the heart, whether the heart is that of a poet, painter, lover or saint, the experience is best creatively communicated.[8]

James identifies the touchstone by which spiritual seekers know they have experienced and are with God. Extreme and inexplicable joy or happiness engulfs the person in the proximity of God. The strength and authority of the evoked intuition signify that they have been and are with God. The awareness and understanding of the experience are not an outcome of discursive thought. This description mimics the experiences of devotees with Swami.

> The presence of God is experienced in its reality—indeed only experienced. The mark by which the spirit's existence and nearness are made irrefutably clear to those who have ever had the experience is the incomparable feeling of happiness connected with the nearness, which is, therefore, possible and a good feeling for us to have (and is) the best and most indispensable proof of God's reality. No other proof is equally convincing.[9]

INITIATION INTO SPIRITUAL LIFE

This excerpt narrates a personal experience of God, marked by overwhelming sensations of love and joy. The protagonist deeply yearns for God and earnestly desires His presence. Through prayer, he witnesses the personification of Jesus, a tangible and palpable experience. Overwhelmed by this encounter, tears stream down his face, and he prostrates himself at the feet of Jesus. Amid this, he is enveloped in divine love, gradually regaining his composure. This experience serves as a defining moment in his spiritual journey, akin to an initiation into religious life. Many individuals who come into contact with Swami express similar sentiments and profound emotions.

> All my feelings seemed to rise and flow out, and the utterance of my heart was, 'I want to pour my whole soul out to God.' The rising of my soul was so great that I rushed into the back room of the front office to pray. The room had no fire or light; nevertheless, it appeared to me as if it was perfectly lit. As I went in and shut the door after me, it seemed like I had met the Lord Jesus Christ face to face.
>
> [...] I saw him like any other man. He said nothing but

> looked at me to break me right down at his feet [...] for it seemed a reality that he stood before me, and I fell at his feet and poured out my soul to him. I wept aloud like a child and made such confessions as I could with my choked utterance. It seemed to me that I bathed his feet with my tears, yet I had no distinct impression that I touched him that I recollect. I must have continued in this state for a good while. As soon as my mind became calm, I returned to the front office [...] the Holy Spirit descended upon me in a manner that seemed to go through me, body and soul. I could feel the impression, like a wave of electricity, going through and through me. Indeed, it seemed to come in waves and waves of liquid love, for I could not express it in any other way. It seemed like the very breath of God.
>
> No words can express the incredible love shed abroad in my heart. I wept aloud with joy and love, and I do not know, but I should say I bellowed out the unutterable gushing of my heart. These waves came over me, one after the other, until I cried out, 'I shall die if these waves continue to pass over me.' I said, 'Lord, I cannot bear anymore,' yet I had no fear of death.
>
> How long I continued in this state, I do not know. But it was late evening when a choir member came into the office to see me. He found me in this state of loud weeping and said to me, 'Mr. Finney, what ails you?' I could make him no answer for some time. He then said, 'Are you in pain?' I gathered myself up as best I could and replied, 'No, but so happy that I cannot live.'[10]

Hislop has a similar experience with Swami. The emotions evoked in the meeting are beyond his imagination, unlike anything experienced before.

> There is nothing in Western tradition to prepare a person for his first meeting with Bhagavan. We were seated in a small room with several people. All attention was on the slender, elegant, graceful form of Baba. His deep, luminous eyes, the sweet and warm smile and the fascinating quality of His voice blended into an irresistible charm. One's critical questioning mind stops its restless activity. Remembrance of the world and

its problems fell away from consciousness. There remained just a feeling of quiet happiness. Although Baba was speaking, one was surrounded by quietness.

In that peaceful state of being, one's awareness deepened without effort, and there was a perception that some aliveness, something unknown, was in one's heart. In a moment, the realization came that a current of love was moving in one's dry heart, and then it was clear that the source of the current of love was Bhagavan—nay, more, that the sweetness of *Bhagavan* Himself was there, with life, in the heart.

How could Sri Sathya Sai Baba, a stranger never seen before, come into the heart of a mature man and bring about a change from within, a change from which there is no turning back? Indeed, God is the only stranger who can do this.

All care dropped away, and only the happy, blissful state of the present was real. The experience was so real that tears came to my eyes. The ecstasy that had come with Baba's presence became more intense when He answered questions and spoke of spiritual matters. The depth and wisdom of His words carried such a thrill of truth that it almost seemed that my consciousness could not bear the intense joy that filled my heart and mind.[11]

BREAKDOWN OF INTELLIGENCE

Manning emphasizes that beyond the intense emotional aspect of encountering God, there lies an experience of love in that meeting that is beyond measurement and all-encompassing. All other emotions pale in comparison to the awareness of this divine love. In the direct presence of God's glory and brilliance, a person's intellect becomes incomprehensible.

> When the trembling subsides, we realize that 'omniscient' and 'compassion' are only hints of the ineffable God. The substance of belief and confidence lies in the conviction that immense, infinite and immeasurable love is beyond these preliminary clues or signs. We are drawn into a deepening and direct awareness of the divine incomprehensibility.

> The effects of 'beholding God'—contemplating the Lord's glory—are profound and far-reaching. The aptitude to appreciate the grandeur of the divine, born of the brush with God, begets (a) spirit of speechless humility and breathless amazement at the overpowering splendour of God.
>
> Abraham Heschel, an American Rabbi, said to his friend, '...never once did I ask God for success or wisdom or power or fame. I asked for wonder, and he gave it to me.' Confronted with the vision of divine majesty, however fleeting and obscure, one becomes reluctant to speak and share the experience because language cannot convey what is grasped only intuitively. Intellect surrenders to the mystery of God. Spiritual reading, meditation and reflection inevitably yield to silent reverence. To love and worship God is to recognize God's unfathomable greatness and the devotee's nothingness.[12]

Sandweiss finds it futile to describe his experience with Swami in two settings: one when he is with Swami and the other when he reflects and contemplates his experiences with Swami. In both contexts, he experiences his mind quietening, thoughts ebbing and disappearing and a vast empty space, limitless and endless.

> When one contemplates or experiences Baba, something strange happens to the mental processes. They get fuzzy and fade out, and one perceives an intense inner vastness where words and concepts have no place. I have struggled to express this glorious inner experience of expansion and boundlessness in some concept or description, but that is a futile task![13]

Aitken articulates his emotions during Swami's darshan. He mentions that one never becomes accustomed to darshan; each encounter is fresh, distinct and brimming with love. It is never a routine experience and should be approached with utmost seriousness. A person must maintain focus and attentiveness to fully appreciate darshan's momentousness.

> Never does the thrill of a Sathya Sai darshan pall nor its tangible glow fail to hearten. It is a moment of rare love.

> I have never failed to be uplifted by the sight of this stand-in for the divine. This baffling stream of energy between him and his disciples works its magic on the audience. Here is the climax to my search to witness divine grace in action.[14]

Father Mazzoleni describes the reality of Swami intuited by him in his experiences with Swami. He connects the emotions experienced with Swami, of being engulfed in His intense and inclusive love, and the evoked sentiments of joy, serenity and patience as a convincing confirmation of His reality.

> Anyone who has seen or met Sai Baba or heard Him speak has come away with an experience of love, security, truthfulness and fullness. After an initial shock that overcomes anyone not accustomed to omnipresent energy, everyone who has made contact with Sai Baba feels he has contacted a higher Reality full of peace, mercy, sweetness and forbearance. Ultimately, the direct experience of Sai's physical presence proves its reliability.[15]

MAGNETISM OF GOD

The basis of a God–devotee relationship is reciprocity. God responds to a person as soon as they reach out, and the person begins to feel an attachment, adoration or love for God.

Ramakrishna Paramahansa explains this idea using the example of the tidal influence of the sea in a riverine estuary. As the river reaches the ocean, the delta of a river experiences tides; ocean water flows upstream during high tides. Similarly, a devotee begins to feel God as soon as they turn towards God. The closer they believe they are to God, the more palpable their experience of God will be.

> The nearer you approach God, the more you feel His love. As the river approaches the ocean, it increasingly feels the flow of the tides.[16]

People react emotionally to Swami even before they see and experience Him. The following narrative exemplifies this. As Father Mazzoleni becomes aware of Swami, he is motivated to learn about Him by reading, talking to others and listening to stories about Him. These activities, with Swami as the subject, are emotionally charged experiences.

> Nothing in my life has given me as much joy and filled me with so much bliss as studying this person. This in itself is extraordinary. When I devote myself to studying Sai Baba, His work and His teaching, I never tire of it, even when learning and analysing things that I already know (or think I know). I always benefit from it: it is always uplifting and refreshing.[17]

Father Mazzoleni uses an experience to highlight how thinking about Swami and talking about Him is spiritually inspiring and uplifting.

> Ever since I learned about Baba, I have noticed that people never tire when they talk about Him. You can go on for hours describing His divine games and miracles, His encounters with His devotees and His ways of drawing them to Him, and you forget even to eat.
>
> Another thing I have observed ever since I have been involved with Sai Baba is that talking about Him warms you and recharges you with new energy. At times, remembering a story about Him or recalling one of His characteristic gestures moves the heart so profoundly that unless you are talking to someone who does not know Baba, you are liable to dissolve into tears of joy. When I often speak of Him, I see tears in the eyes of people I met for the first time, who, until that moment, had always felt distant from faith and religion.[18]

In the *Bhagavatha Vahini*, Suka elucidates the profound experience of listening to and reading about the adventures of Lord Krishna. These narratives evoke intense feelings of love and affection within him, saturating him with pronounced bliss. Suka helps Prakshith believe in the spiritual strength and efficacy of listening to the stories of Lord Krishna. The power of the stories of God personified as an avatar is the essence of *Bhagavatham*.

> There is an inexpressible sweetness in God when He incarnates that attracts and captivates a person by absorbing them in

> His playful and light-hearted activities, manifesting His divine attributes. I have listened to the description of the beauty and sweetness of God. Even I get delighted and thrilled when I hear the glory of God revealing His divine attributes. I could not remain at peace; I rejoiced like a madman, thrilled by the bliss I derived from listening and reading. His sweet pranks intoxicated me with infinite joy.[19]

In *Ramakatha Rasavahini,* Surpanakha, Ravana's sister, recounts memories of her powerful emotional experience of seeing Lord Rama and Lakshmana, even though Lakshmana disfigures her. A pull towards Rama is induced in Ravana from her vivid portrayal of Rama.

> Surpanakha said, 'Brother! The very sight of those Princes rendered me so entranced that I lost all awareness of myself and the surroundings. What shall I speak of the ecstasy I derived by conversing with them? They bubble over always with joyful smiles; they know no other attitude or reaction. They are captivating representations of the God of Love. I have never so far set eyes on such beauty.'
>
> The courtiers and ministers listened to this description with awe and delight. Her words confounded even Ravana. The picture of Rama she drew gave him great joy and peace when he contemplated it. Deep within him, he wanted to see that inspiring embodiment of divine charm.[20]

In *Ramakatha Rasavahini*, Swami describes Janaka's ecstatic experience with Rama and Lakshmana. Janaka compares his feelings when in the company of Lord Rama to the experience of *samadhi* (profound contemplation of God undisturbed by thought or emotion).

> Hearing these words and filling his eyes with his majesty and the charming loveliness of the boys (Rama and Lakshmana), Janaka experienced supreme delight, the delight he often derived in Samadhi! He felt that the boys were actual embodiments of divine splendour. Though he repeatedly tried to look elsewhere, his eyes thirsted only to see those charming lotus-like faces that showered Brahmic illumination! Janaka significantly suppressed

> the outward expression of his inner ecstasy and sat looking intently at them in humility and reverence.[21]

EXPERIENCING GOD'S LOVE IN SILENCE

Father Mazzoleni describes Swami's love as natural, numinous and unconditional. It has the power to evoke a response from every receptive heart.

> No one can condition the experience of the bliss and love that radiate from the person of Sai Baba. No one whose heart produces profound feelings can resist being fascinated by Him.[22]

A student author, Ravindra Shroff, describes Swami's love as a multi-sensory experience. All his five senses focus, engage and are absorbed in Swami.

> He embodies all charm, grace, glory and love. His face fascinates the smile that soothes, the voice that thrills and the advice that illuminates.[23]

Another student author, Prakash, elaborates on the diverse emotions and ideas on seeing Swami during darshan. He struggles to express his feelings.

> A Saffron-robed, petite figure with that halo of beautiful hair has just emerged from the gate and is slowly gliding down the pathway. The ups and downs of worldly turmoil fade, filling me with happiness and love for God. There is immediate rapport and contact with Bhagavan. I am eagerly feasting my eyes upon the Red-robed figure. My heart skips a beat. His words fill me with *ananda*, and touching His feet brings bliss. It is an inexplicable experience. How can I even describe the impact His words have on my heart? It is experienced as love and joy in God's presence.[24]

Aitken experiences intense sentiments with Swami.

> Sathya Sai Baba arouses in me a feeling so maddeningly beautiful.[25]

In the following excerpt, Aitken is writing about the experience of Rajmata of Jind with Swami. In Swami's presence, she experienced a deep, profound love. She was neither able to describe her experience nor use reasoning to explain how an intuitive awareness of Swami as God arose within her.

> In his presence, what you register is the ineffable realization that you are face-to-face with the miracle of love. (She) who understands the limitations of words and does not need logic, seems to have got it right when she keeps reminding me: 'I don't believe Sai Baba is God. He's something much more.'
>
> That just about sums up my experience of being in love.[26]

Aitken's own experience is emotional. Swami's presence evokes a feeling of peace. All questions vanish in the experience of divine love. He is aware that he is with God, an understanding that needs no justification.

> In Sai Baba, I encountered the light of the unwavering love that sustains and gives meaning to existence. For this particular student, the Sai aura is the greatest wonder discovered.
>
> Sathya Sai easily possesses the most charismatic of presences I have experienced. My heart spontaneously responds to his divine aura. Sathya Sai has the ability to arouse in me the most profound love and move my soul so deeply that all mental questioning is stilled. I know what I feel, and that buoyant reality is beyond verbal definition. I feel indescribably graced.[27]

Abhijit, a student author, experiences Swami's all-encompassing love.

> Thoughts pass through my mind till the time the red-robed form comes close to him. He has an innocent look on His face. He pretends not to know anything. And the Lord enquires about my name and from where have I come. Unable to answer, I stand rooted to the ground, drinking in the beauty of His effulgent form. The curl of hair, the lotus face radiant with the pan-reddened lips, the heart-melting smile and the soft lotus eyes are so full of love that they seem to envelop me with a tenderness you do not find anywhere in the world.[28]

A devotee who came to Swami when the ashram infrastructure was underdeveloped describes their numerous hardships. Nothing mattered. They were drawn to Swami, and they experienced divine love in His proximity.

> We thought we would be disturbed, but we were not worried. It didn't bother us that we did not have a toilet. We happily managed. We didn't have tap water. We had to draw water from the well and walk all the way from the Patha (old) Mandir to Chitravathi to wash our clothes. And return like a washer-man. We were not used to all this! And yet, we used to cry on leaving Puttaparthi! Can you believe it? We didn't want to go back home! What did He do? It was an overnight change! I consider us very blessed.[29]

EXPERIENCING GOD'S LOVE IN HIS PRESENCE

Ramana Rao describes how he was drawn and fascinated by Swami. Every action of Swami is seen as an affectionate gesture, and he experiences being transformed into a child.

> Folding the right sleeve of his *kurta* (a loose collarless shirt that is knee-length. Swami's kurta is longer, till his feet), he waved his hand in circles four or five times briskly in front of my eyes and said, 'Here, take this prasadam (consecrated sacred offering).' We held out our hands. I had seen Baba creating vibhuti for his devotees in the same fashion twice before. When we entered his room, my friend Desikachari did padanamaskar (knelt and placed his head at Baba's feet). Swami's hand touched his head as a blessing and patted my cheek. When he was materializing prasadam with the same hand, I watched intently. 'Go on, eat it,' Baba urged when out of his fingertips fell a spoonful of wheat-coloured granular powder in our hands. When I put it in my mouth, it was deliciously sweet and melted on my tongue instantaneously.
>
> Glancing at me, Baba said to my friend, 'Good! Your companion does not like vibhuti. I have created something to

> eat. This fake Brahmin doesn't even wear the sacred thread. How can I expect him to apply vibhuti on his forehead?' He again patted my cheek lovingly and said, 'I just said it for fun, Bangaru (translated as gold, an affectionate term for precious)!' His affection transformed me into a child petted by a loving mother.[30]

Sandweiss captures the spiritually powerful experience of making focused eye contact with Swami. Swami's eyes captivate and grip him. He is drawn to Swami, experiences His love and transforms into an innocent and trusting child.

> I looked deeply into his eyes. They were like an ocean of love. You could merge into those eyes; you could melt into those eyes. His eyes spoke of omniscience and love. I was immediately transformed into an innocent child.[31]

Baskin experiences Swami as a love that flows, omniscient and aware, and His words are always spiritually reassuring.

> So uniquely different was He from any being she had ever seen. Pure love, capable of uplifting and transforming, radiated from Him. His words were soft, consoling and awakening, revealing His total awareness of every aspect of our lives. Every thought, action and feeling we experienced was bare before Him.[32]

In another piece, Baskin describes her experience with Swami as an incomparable and intense spiritual joy.

> Sai Baba sat on a chair, and we gathered around Him on the floor. The atmosphere was joyous and electric as Baba talked and joked with us. During that hour, time stood still. Each moment was eternal. No experience, even the most thrilling I recall, could compare to the joy of being in His presence. I was beginning to experience a blissful state, which grew in intensity as time passed.[33]

Father Mazzoleni is speechless and feels intoxicated with the experience of Swami's abundant divine love after meeting Him.

> We all stepped out of the interview room with our hearts full of silence. We were like people invited to a banquet and coming out satiated, intoxicated with the nectar of an infinite love we had never experienced before that moment.[34]

Gupta ruminates on his first meeting with Ramakrishna Paramahansa. He feels the pull of the Master as he desires to return to him.

> M. wondered, 'Who is this serene-looking man drawing me back to him? How wonderful it is! I would like to see him again.
>
> He said, "Come again." I shall go tomorrow or the day after.'[35]

Gupta recounts how he was continuously absorbed in thinking about Ramakrishna Paramahansa after the first visit, keen to return as soon as possible.

> No sooner had M. entered the room than the Master laughed aloud and said to the boys, 'There! He has come again.' They all joined in the laughter. M. bowed low before him and took a seat. Before this, he had saluted the Master with folded hands that day. He had learned to fall at his feet.
>
> The Master explained the cause of his laughter to the devotees. He said, 'A man once fed a peacock with a pill of opium at four o'clock in the afternoon. The next day, exactly at that time, the peacock came back. It had felt the intoxication of the drug and returned just in time to have another dose.' M. thought this a very apt illustration. Even at home, he could not banish the thought of Sri Ramakrishna for a moment. His mind was constantly at Dakshineswar, and he had counted the minutes until he should go again.[36]

BELONGING TO GOD

Tillich, the philosopher–theologian, writes about the important meaning inherent in the experience of God; it is a sign to a person that they belong to God. The person must believe they are God's property and accepted by God without any precondition.

> God accepts you. Believe that you belong to God. You are his possession. Surrender. Submit. Accept. Desire nothing. Do nothing. Give up the intent.[37]

Sandweiss shares an experience that creates a feeling of spiritual reassurance in him. As he witnesses Swami performing Narayan Seva, he is overcome with emotion. He envisions the scene as a manifestation of God's love, with Swami assuming the role of the divine father.

> Today has been trying but extraordinary. Baba walked amongst a crowd of the gathered poor, giving food and clothing. It was beautiful. He was so impressive. Tears came to my eyes as I felt for the first time the possibility that a father, all-knowing and comforting, could exist in human form.
>
> I remember sitting in meditation and seeing a small light in the distance. I wondered whether I could be looking through a distant window, and I felt that if only I could get close enough, I would see Him. I was struck with this experience as I watched Baba lovingly give and care for the poor. It was as if I was looking directly through the window at the loving father, and tears rose.[38]

PERPETUAL AWARENESS

Swami simplifies the meaning of constantly living in a state of awareness and oneness with God.

> Suddenly, Swami asked me, 'Who is God?'
>
> I ventured hesitatingly, 'Swami, God is love.'
>
> Swami said, 'What else?'
>
> I replied, 'Swami, God is omniscient, omnipotent, omnipresent.'
>
> He paused and added, 'When you think of God, in what language do you think about God?'
>
> I replied, 'English.'
>
> He then queried, 'When you think of God, are you thinking of words that describe God or are you thinking of God?'

It was a profound question. I remained silent.

Swami said, 'Close your eyes. Listen to your heart. You will know the answer.'

I sat there, attempting to still my mind. He got up, went to the interview room, returned and looked out through the window at the devotees.

Swami said, 'God is. It is simple. All the rest is imagination.' He explained, 'Every time you try to describe God, you limit him. But God simply is: *Tat sat tat sat*.'[39]

Swami describes the meaning of *Om Tat Sat* and how to live in awareness of oneness with God.

> When you perform an activity (*kriya*) as an offering to the Lord, your good, what is good for others and the highest good (*swartha, parartha and paramaartha*) all merge! First, you and I become we. Next, He and we become one. The individual soul, the 'I' (*jiva*), should accomplish identity first with the creation (*Prakriti*) and then with the Supreme Divine (*Paramatma*). This is the significance of the mantra *Om Tat Sat* (which connects the individual's identity with the universal *Brahman*). 'He' and 'I' are always there; the spiritual practice (*sadhana*) is also there. Just as the sun is inseparable and is never apart from its rays, any aspirant should part with their sadhana under no circumstances. It is only then they can be said to be one with Om.[40]

Living with Swami or in His proximity is an extraordinary opportunity. You see him as a human, experience his grace and realize he is not the diminutive figure. He is the fullness of God, an incarnation, God in human form.

> To be with Baba at close quarters is an unforgettable experience. His wonderfully human touch, showing tender concern for all, is expressed most naturally. The grace of a rare being seems to shine through him, and when he stayed for three days in Mussoorie, I got a distinct impression of an abiding awareness.

> Typically, we view grace as a portion of the divine, but here, the fullness of Providence seemed to brim over.[41]

Aitken intuits Swami as living in perpetual awareness and oneness. Swami explains the meaning of constantly living in a state of awareness and oneness.

In the first paragraph, Swami explains the meaning of a changeless God or truth–awareness–bliss.

> God remains changeless in all three periods of time. So, we call God the very form of being–awareness–bliss (*sat, chit* and *ananda*). *Sat* means being. *Chit* means awareness. The combination of *sat* and *chit* is *ananda* (bliss). *Sat* is the changeless form of God. God is attribute-less; He has no attributes whatsoever. His nature is changeless.[42]

He uses a metaphor of the sun reflecting in moving water to explain the meaning of a changeless God.

> The Self (Atma) appears pure to the one with a steady mind. How? When the water is still and there is no wind, the sun's reflection can be clearly seen in the water. When there is movement in the water due to the wind, the sun's reflection also appears to be moving. Similarly, God appears to be moving or changing to those whose minds are wavering. Know that God does not move or change. It is only the reflection that has movement, not the sun.[43]

Swami highlights that living in a state of awareness is to possess complete knowledge and wisdom. The knowledge He alludes to is experiential knowledge or wisdom, not bookish knowledge.

> Chit means total awareness. You say, 'I have read many sacred texts and am a great scholar. I am a man of wisdom.' What is this knowledge? What is it that you call wisdom? You consider that wisdom lies in knowing the essence of all sacred texts. But sacred texts give only minimal knowledge. So, one cannot say one has acquired total wisdom by reading the Vedas, the Upanishads and the Brahma Sutras. Out of the infinite wisdom,

you get just a little bit. This is not full wisdom. This is not full awareness. When you know what awareness is, you will understand that it is total knowledge, total wisdom.

Only God has total wisdom.[44]

God is inexplicable, incomprehensible and endowed with awareness and understanding. These two qualities lead a person to live in continuous bliss. Swami describes this as the underpinning of *sat–chit–ananda*.

> God is eternal and endowed with total wisdom. When we combine the two divine qualities of eternity and wisdom, we get permanent bliss. Eternal bliss is that which never declines. To have such everlasting joy, we should install God, who is the very form of truth (*sat*), in our hearts. Awareness of the divine form of God is *chit*. When we combine these two, bliss will emerge quite naturally.[45]

Swami elaborates on the idea.

> The love present in everyone is sweet, like sugar. Wherefrom do you get love? It comes from God. It is the reaction, reflection and resound of God in everyone. The nature of love is sweetness. This is *sat*. Whatever you may do, it will never change. Its sweetness remains as it is. That is *sat*. Next is *chit*. Associate *chit* with *sat*. Only then will you experience bliss (*ananda*). When being (*sat*) and awareness (*chit*) are combined, it becomes bliss (*ananda*). That is the divine quality of *sat–chit–ananda*. How do you get this bliss? You get it by the combination of *sat* and *chit*. It is not worldly happiness. It is divine bliss. Then, everything in your life will have divine bliss. So, God has these three permanent qualities: being–awareness–bliss (*sat–chit–ananda*).[46]

Swami underscores the practical implications of the idea and awareness of oneness with God. He coined the term constant integrated awareness when a person lives in perpetual awareness and understanding of God.

> This awareness is Constant Integrated Awareness, which is changeless. It is *chit*. This awareness is there in our words, in our actions, in our feelings and in every part of our body.

Without awareness, you cannot live even for a moment. This awareness is the very form of God. If you understand and investigate these spiritual principles and put them into practice, you will have divine bliss.

There is only one changeless principle: constant, integrated awareness (*Prajnanam*). The Upanishads declare *Prajnanam Brahma* (*Brahman* is supreme consciousness). You must develop Ekatmabhava (feeling of oneness) to attain that state. Though the bodies differ, only one Atma dwells in all living beings. The human bodies are like pots, and the mind therein is water. The one moon reflects in all the pots. It is only reaction, reflection and resound everywhere.[47]

LOSE YOUR HEART TO GOD

Living in a state of awareness and oneness with God is the same as losing one's heart to God.

Swami always encouraged us to learn new bhajans, and He would sing them to us repeatedly until we sang them with ease. One evening, He tried to teach us *Prema Mudita Manase Kaho*, but it was too difficult for us. So, Swami, on the spur of the moment, began to sing Telugu folk songs from His boyhood days. He sang for a full hour, and I then understood the real meaning of the word sweetness as I listened to His voice. That night, He took my heart (and), He never gave it back.[48]

6

ACCEPTANCE AND ACTION

DETERMINATION TO BE WITH GOD

Tolstoy writes about his transformation after encountering God. He attributes a divine will and purpose to God and uses his life to highlight a characteristic of religious transformation. Living an ordinary, mundane life is not an option after experiencing God. He uses the metaphor of being in a boat in a hilly stream swirling downhill to describe his life's uncontrollable nature before the spiritual experience. He changes from a lack of purpose and life control to living with a determined spiritual purpose.

> I returned to the belief in that Will which produced me and desired something of me. I returned to the belief that my life's chief and only aim is to be better, i.e., to live according to that Will. And I returned to the belief that I can find the expression of that Will in humanity. I returned to a belief in God, in moral perfection and a tradition transmitting the meaning of life. Only this difference was accepted unconsciously, while now I knew I could not live without it.
>
> What happened to me was something like this: I was put into a boat and pushed off from an unknown shore, shown the direction of the opposite shore, had oars put into my unpractised hands and was left alone. I rowed as best I could and moved forward, but the further I advanced towards the middle of the stream, the more rapidly the current bore

> me away from my goal. And the further I went, I forgot the direction given to me. In the centre of the stream, being borne downstream, I lost my direction and abandoned my oars. I floated and was carried far. I heard the roar of the rapids in which I would be shattered. I recollected myself. I was long unable to understand what had happened to me. I perceived innumerable boats that unceasingly and strenuously pushed across the stream, and I remembered about the shore, the oars and the direction and began to pull back upwards against the stream and towards the shore. That shore was God; that direction was tradition; the oars were the freedom given me to pull for the shore and unite with God. And so, with a renewed determination, the force of life was restored, and I again began to live.[1]

Underhill vividly depicts the impact of the initial experience of God, which closely resonates with the experiences of individuals with Swami. This encounter fills a person with profound awe and reverence for the magnificence of God. What is imagined as a divine being beyond the scope of human experience is now understood as permeating all creation and being accessible and reachable. Underhill emphasizes that the first encounter should lead to a conscious effort to cultivate a personal relationship with God. She refers to this process as participation, noting that it is neither easy nor straightforward; it demands a change or self-transformation.

> (There are) two fundamental ways of apprehending reality [...] eternal and temporal, transcendent and immanent [...] They comprise the twofold knowledge of a God who is both Being and Becoming near and far [...] There is first the apprehension of splendour [...] Godhead is perceived as transcendent yet immanent in the created universe [...] the reaction of the self takes the form of awe and rapture rather than of intimate affection [...] This experience [...] must pass beyond the metaphysical rapture or splendour stage and crystallize into a willing response to the reality perceived; a definite and personal relationship must be set up [...] The awakening of the self,

> the self and the absolute life. To be a spectator of reality is not enough. The awakened subject is not merely to perceive transcendent life but to participate therein; a drastic and costly life-changing experience is required.[2]

Belief in God is kindled in a person through experience; they feel extraordinary and awe-inspiring emotions, intuit knowledge and understand and comprehend God as a relatable person. This belief is based on recognizing and accepting God and understanding that God is real and palpable, not an idea or concept. God becomes an embodied other, personified, made flesh or incarnated. Realizing they have had an authentic encounter with God transforms into a desire and intention to live a spiritual life.

Underhill characterizes the spiritual turning point, centred on their experience of God, as the moment when a person sees and becomes new.

> When the intuitions are born and the eyes open to new light, life's stress, desires and uncertainties are forgotten. In this recognition of reality, all things are made new. Conversion of this sort has three marked characteristics: a sense of liberation and victory, a conviction of God's nearness and a sentiment of love towards God. It is a sudden, intense and joyous perception of God immanent in the universe, of the divine beauty, power and splendour of that more meaningful life in which the individual is immersed and of a new life to be lived by the self in correspondence with this dominant fact of existence.[3]

Sheen emphasizes the power of Jesus to transform every person who came to Him.

> No one who meets Christ will return the same way he came.[4]

He then writes about the all-encompassing change in a person when they turn towards God. Jesus identifies it as a second birth. It symbolizes the complete renewal of a person to be with God.

> Unless a man has been born over again, he cannot see the Kingdom of God. Spiritual life (is) different from physical or intellectual life. Spiritual life is a gift from (God). Every person

> has a first birth. Jesus said (that) a second birth is necessary for spiritual life. It (is a) regeneration, not an improvement.[5]

Accepting God and embarking on a spiritual journey becomes more accessible based on the promise of God. Conviction in God's commitment to their spiritual progress transforms the nature of a person's spiritual journey.

Swami highlights how God accompanies and assists aspirants on their spiritual journey. God is constantly present, readily accessible and responsive to aspirants.

> Life is a pilgrimage where man drags his feet along the rough, thorny road. With the name of God on his lips, he will have no thirst; with the form of God in his heart, he will feel no exhaustion. The company of the holy will inspire him to travel in hope and faith. The assurance that God is within call, that He is ever near, will lend strength to his limbs and courage to his eyes. Remember that with every step, you are nearing God, and God, too, takes ten steps toward you when you take one step toward Him. There is no stopping place in this pilgrimage; it is one continuous journey, through day and night, through valley and desert, through tears and smiles, through death and birth, through tomb and womb. When the road ends and the goal is gained, the pilgrim finds that he has travelled only from himself to himself, that the way was long and lonesome but the God that led him unto it was all the while in him, around him, with him and beside him! He was always divine. His yearning to merge in God was but the sea calling to the ocean! Man loves because He is love! He craves melody and harmony because He is melody and harmony. He seeks joy for He is joy. He thirsts for God for he is composed of God and cannot exist without Him.[6]

A JOURNEY THAT BEGINS AND ENDS WITH GOD

The divine encounter is the beginning and end of a journey. In the following excerpt, a student author highlights the importance of finding

Swami. He becomes a devotee's guide and protector on a journey that begins and ends with Him.

> To have found the avatar is to have ended the search for God in one sense. But, in another sense, it is to have begun it. Bhagawan offers the unique opportunity to have the goal as the guide.[7]

The first divine experience is typically God expressing His love for a person. The experience is a powerful motivation, igniting restlessness within people for a lasting and profound relationship with God. Henri Nouwen writes that the journey to become one with God marks the commencement and culmination of spiritual life. As devotees progress, they seek what they have already discovered, recognizing that their pursuit of God is an ongoing and transformative process.

> Being the beloved is the origin and the fulfilment of the life of the spirit. I say this because as soon as we catch a glimpse of this truth, we are put on a journey in search of the fullness of that truth, and we will not rest until we can rest in that truth. When we claim the truth of being the beloved, we face the call to become who we are. Becoming the beloved is an incredible spiritual journey we have to make.
>
> Augustine's words, My soul is restless until it rests in you, O God,' capture this journey well.
>
> I know that I am always searching for God, always struggling to discover the fullness of love and constantly yearning for the complete truth tells me that I have already been given a taste of God, of love and truth. I can only look for something I have already found to some degree. How can I search for beauty and truth unless that beauty and truth are already known to me?[8]

THE DIVINE EXPERIENCE: AN END AND A BEGINNING

A divine encounter brings about two enduring transformations within an individual. Firstly, it fundamentally shifts how they contemplate life and matters of spirituality. Secondly, this shift in perspective leads to changes in behaviour that align with their religious experience. The individual becomes acutely aware of the reality of God's presence—real, close and accessible. As a result, their thoughts and actions undergo a substantial transformation. In the subsequent piece, Gardner identifies behaviour modification as the crucial indicator of authentic change.

> Changing minds must involve changes in behaviour. Changes that occur 'within the mind', if they do not result in the present or future change of behaviour, are of no interest.[9]

In Marie-Alphonse Ratisbonne's spiritual experience, belief is turning towards God, changing life's direction, focusing and striving towards a new goal. The development is depicted as emerging from darkness into light, seeing something new and developing an intuitive awareness of a new reality. The similarities of this experience with those with Swami are unmistakable.

> I did not know where I was: I did not know whether I was Alphonse or another. I only felt changed and believed in myself as another me; I looked for myself in myself and did not find myself. From the bottom of my soul, I felt an explosion of the most ardent joy; I could not speak; I had no wish to reveal what had happened. But I felt something solemn and sacred within me. I can say that in an instant, the bandage had fallen from my eyes [...] One after another, they rapidly disappeared as the mud and ice disappeared under the burning sun's rays.
>
> I came out from an abyss of darkness and was living perfectly. But I wept. Infinite mercy had saved me. I (was) overwhelmed with wonder and gratitude upon entering that church. I was in darkness altogether, and on coming out of it, I saw the light's fullness; without any knowledge of religious doctrine, I now intuitively perceived its sense and spirit. I felt those hidden things by the inexplicable effects they produced in me. It all happened in my mind, and those impressions, more rapid than thought, shook my soul, revolved and turned it, as it were, in another direction, towards other aims, by other paths.[10]

In the next incident, Swami explains and vividly reinforces the need for a drastic change in his thinking, spiritual alertness and behaviour. Swami asserts His expectations for the desired changes in behaviour. It is akin to starting a new life. Spiritual life is a new beginning.

> How did he put me on the track? There is a lot of activity in the hostel. However, no one did guide me. And all of a sudden, Swami started to give the direction.
>
> I had been a resident of the hostel for five years. I used to go inside the interview room around 2:30 p.m. He would then take me inside the dining room for food. One day I reached the mandir and was told by the person on duty, 'Swami has already come.'
>
> I felt, 'Okay, Swami has come. I am a bit late.' I went inside. Swami was standing. He was angry. He asked me, 'What do you do?'
>
> I replied, 'Swami, I didn't do anything.' He asked me, 'Why are you late?'
>
> I did not reply. I could not have said to Swami, 'Swami, you came early.'
>
> Swami had a letter in his hand. He said, 'See what people are writing about you?'
>
> I replied, 'Swami, what has happened?'
>
> He continued, 'People are writing that you are a very talkative boy. You don't have discipline. Your warden has written about you. See this. Everybody is writing negative things about you. They are saying that Swami is wasting His time on you. They are saying Swami is getting a bad name because of you.'
>
> I felt helpless and thought that my effort to become better and worthy of Swami was futile. Swami is getting a bad name because of me, even though I am trying my best. I said, 'Swami, I follow what you say.' I said this and couldn't hold or control myself. I started crying. I was a twenty-two-year-old boy uncontrollably sobbing.
>
> Swami put his hand on my head and touched my forehead

> to his chest. I experienced an unearthly peace and stopped sobbing. He made me sit down. He sat on the chair of the interview room and endearingly said, '*Bangaaru*, when you were a small child, did you run around in the home naked without clothes?'
>
> I smiled and replied, 'Yes, Swami.' The tears were gone. Swami then asked me, 'Will you do it now?'
>
> I replied, 'No, Swami.'
>
> He continued, 'But today, are you ashamed that you used to run around naked as a child?'
>
> I said, 'No, Swami.'
>
> He then said, 'What was considered normal for that age is acceptable for that age. What is natural for this age is accepted for this age. Likewise, the actions and behaviours one engaged in before Swami's interaction were typical for that particular age and period. However, once Swami initiates communication and guidance, it becomes necessary to relinquish the old, "natural" way of life and strive to lead an ideal and spiritually-aligned life.'
>
> I realized that it was the master who could give you a fresh start. Once he has touched me, ordinary life is no longer satisfying (acceptable). I have to lead and live a life of being touched by the brilliance of the divine master.[11]

Dr Bhagvantham writes that the meeting with Swami is a turning point in the beliefs, attitudes and lives of innumerable people who meet Him.

> An interview has been the turning point in the lives of many devotees. In that private room, many sceptics have changed into ardent believers. Many sorrowing people found unexpected solace (and many) have had their first experience of divine love and divine touch. It has often been said that 'Man cannot comprehend divinity unless God lays His unseen hand on him and helps him do so.' Baba has done this to many people.[12]

Dr Gokak conveys the same idea. He writes how Swami nonchalantly sows belief in people's hearts.

Baba's lasting appeal lies in the human touch, his ability to enter into the hearts of men and plant a seed of faith.[13]

Changkakoti describes his moment of change. He uses the metaphor of catching fish and reeling in the line as being pulled by God. It exemplifies how Swami innocuously and gently brings a person closer to God.

In the old hostel, we were just about 60–70 students. On his darshan rounds in the Sai Ram shed, Swami often walked into the dining hall. It was just before the Dussehra celebrations. Prof. Amrendra requested Swami's permission to put up a play on Shankaracharya for Dussehra. Swami said, 'Yes, yes, very good.'

Prof. Amrendra then asked Swami to identify a student to play the role of Shankaracharya. Swami looked around, saw me and said, 'Why not Rupak?'

This was a step in my moving closer to Swami. He was directing the play even though Amrendra wrote it. It was a play within a play. He was bringing me closer and closer. Giving me direct guidance on how to enact the role.[14]

Sandweiss recounts his feelings when he met Swami. He describes the experience of change as magnificent, a transformation based on a fresh and distinctive perspective of the world created by Swami.

It is possible to have a profound inner reaction in which an amazing new vision of the world opens up, and one feels that he is coming home again. This magnificent transition took place within me.[15]

Hislop affirms that Swami motivates people to live spiritually.

Baba inspires people who turn to him. He encourages interested men and women to change from an ordinary, conventional life to a life based on spiritual values.[16]

Hislop describes Swami's dramatic impact on him and his spiritual mindset, beliefs and thinking. At the outset, he confesses the difficulty in revealing the profundity and intensity of Swami's influence on him. On seeing Swami, the author immediately and intuitively recognized and realized Swami as the trusted font of spiritual knowledge. He experienced his mind disengaging from the world and his consciousness becoming inward-focused and centred on Swami.

> Upon meeting Baba, I immediately knew that here was the true source of wisdom. It is difficult and probably impossible to express in words the effect of that first meeting with Baba. My entire being was profoundly affected and changed. Immediately, Baba became the centre of my life and has remained so. In his presence, at that first meeting, the world fell away from me, my consciousness was drawn inward and, at a most subtle level of awareness, Baba appeared in my heart.[17]

Sandweiss points to Swami's greatest miracle: His capacity to instil spirituality in individuals. In Swami's physical presence, he felt enveloped by His love. That experience of divine love turned him Godward.

> Sai Baba's greatest miracle is his ability to turn people Godward. 'I felt enveloped in His presence in a highly charged aura of love. Many are transformed on the spot in such a profoundly spiritual and holy atmosphere. And almost everyone coming into his presence can feel this deeply moving climate.'[18]

Living a spiritual life requires considerable effort. The self-transformation that follows meeting God is more than intellectual acceptance. The touchstone of real change is behavioural change. The following excerpt recounts the reflections of the author after meeting Swami. She recognizes the scale of impending spiritual change, an awareness of the need for determination and the significant effort required to manifest change.

> I tried to sort out the many varied reactions and impressions of my first experience with Baba. I was sure his influence would strongly impact all areas of my life. My reactions to him were very positive. But to enable the experience to work in my daily life instead of remaining merely a meaningful memory would, I was sure, entail great effort and dedication.[19]

HESITANT BEGINNINGS

The spiritual experience has two participants: God and an aspirant. God is eternal, constant and consistent. An aspirant's relationship with God evolves. They bond in a spiritual experience. God reveals Himself to the aspirant. Devotion is awakened within the seeker who desires to forge a deeper connection with God.

The following narrative details Schulman's struggles to understand Swami. Doubts assail him as he attempts to clinically examine Swami. Swami is gently assisting him in turning inward and spiritual. He wants the author to reflect on who he is, his truth and his motives before labouring to understand Swami.

> 'Why do you waste your time and energy trying to explain me?' Baba said, 'Can a fish measure the sky? If I had come as Narayana with four arms, they would have put me in a circus, charging money for people to see me. If I had come only as a man like every other man, who would listen to me? So, I had to come in this human form, with more than human powers and...' he groped for the word, 'wisdom.'
>
> 'Then you are God...'
>
> 'First, you have to understand yourself. I told you that. And then you will understand me. I'm not a man, and I'm not a woman. I'm not old, and I'm not young. I'm all of these.'
>
> Here was a human being, or what looked like one, curled on a studio couch, his legs tucked beneath him like a teenage girl, and there was nothing the writer could think of that would allow him to accept the idea that this person with the afro hairdo and orange dress could actually, literally, be God.[20]

When individuals initially turn towards God, their beliefs and feelings about God may be in their early stages of development. People may embark on their spiritual journey with healthy scepticism, gradually refining their understanding as they experience God. Swami's interactions symbolize the spiritual dimension of His engagement with everyone, even in seemingly mundane conversations. For Him, all discussions serve a purpose, contributing to the individual's spiritual growth.

> 'What do you know about me?' Baba asked. 'Do you believe in me like I said you have to believe in me?'
>
> 'Not yet.'
>
> 'Then how can you write about me? You are like a child. When I fulfil your desires or bring laughter to your life, you express love for me. However, in the next moment, if I become occupied and cannot attend to your needs immediately, you may exhibit frustration or anger toward me.'[21]

Belief in God is different from the acceptance of God. Belief is not acquired by conducting a scientific experiment to research and understand God. An aspirant's purity of conviction and intensity of search are precursors to God revealing Himself and helping them affirm their belief. Ramakrishna Paramahansa emphasizes the importance of yearning and perseverance in spiritual effort.

> He who seeks God with a longing heart can see Him, talk to Him as I am talking to you. Believe my words when I say that God can be seen. God does not reveal Himself to a man unless he dives deep. Only after such a plunge, after the revelation of God through His grace, are one's doubts destroyed. Unless you plunge into God with a yearning of heart, you will not comprehend Him. Nothing can be realized without His grace. Strive with a longing heart for His grace. You will see Him through His grace, and He will talk to you.[22]

Swami uses an allegory to explain how God should be understood. Just as a moon is seen in the sky through its luminosity, God, who is love, can only be understood with love.

> When the moon comes up in the sky, you can see it directly. You do not require the aid of a torchlight, a petromax lamp or any other artificial light. You do not need another light because we can look at the moon by the light reflecting off the moon. Similarly, if we want to go near God, an embodiment of love, or to understand God, it becomes possible only by using love and His characteristics.[23]

Aitken reflects on his first meeting with Swami wherein he experienced Swami's spiritual power and intensity. Thereafter, he felt excluded and remote. He learned to accept and surrender his ego to bond and engage with Swami.

> Despite the charged aura I had experienced during my first meeting with Baba, I felt excluded. The price of having Sai Baba as a guru was to surrender entirely to him in love.[24]

INITIAL STIRRINGS OF KNOWLEDGE

Individuals begin their spiritual journey believing that God is real and reachable. The basis of this conviction is their religious experience. Ramakrishna Paramahansa points out.

> A man is ignorant so long as he feels that God is far away. He has knowledge when he knows that God is here and everywhere.[25]

The consciousness of the absolute, a sense of God's presence, is a vivid experience. A person feels the reality of God deep within themself. Aitken brings to the fore the emotions and intuitions evoked in a person when engaged with Swami. They induce a confident conviction that they have experienced divinity. A person becomes aware, and questions or doubts cease to matter.

> People experience the abundance of divinity when they confront Baba and, through love, intuitively know that it took theologians centuries to work out. The critical factor is the presence of Sathya Sai Baba. Then, all questions become immaterial. All mental chattering is stilled in the fullness of the heart's certainty.[26]

James zeros in on the personal nature of religious experiences and how they produce meaning for the person undergoing them. The intensity of evoked perceptions in the person having the experience endows them with unambiguous recognition and acceptance.

> They (these experiences) are as convincing to those who have them as any direct sensible experiences can be, and they are, as a rule, much more compelling than results established by mere logic. One may indeed be entirely without them. But suppose you do have them and have them at all strongly. In that case, the probability is that you cannot help regarding them as genuine perceptions of truth, as revelations of a kind of reality which no adverse argument, however unanswerable by you in words, can expel from your belief.[27]

Sandweiss says that Swami aroused an awareness, belief in God and conviction about Swami's reality. He describes this as Swami's invaluable spiritual gift.

> He has awakened me to the existence of a higher reality and has convinced me of his greatness. His significance and meaning for me are profound. He has given me a precious gift.[28]

Father Mazzoleni writes that seeing Swami is a unique spiritual benediction and grace.

> Someone who sees Him has already received an enormous gift.[29]

Ramakrishna Paramahansa explains how the enkindling of belief is God's gift because only God reveals Himself. God's grace is easy to acquire and is essential for Him to enter a person's heart and evoke devotion. An aspirant has to surrender and accept God in humility. He uses a story to communicate the idea vividly. A police sergeant is doing night rounds with a lantern covered on three sides. His face is in darkness. We must request that he turn the light on his face to see him. Similarly, we must pray to God to turn the light on His face and reveal Himself.

> You may try thousands of times, but nothing can be achieved without God's grace. One cannot see God without His grace. Is it an easy thing to receive the grace of God? One must altogether renounce egotism; one cannot see God as long as one feels 'I am the doer.'

> God doesn't readily appear in the heart of a man who feels to be his own master. But God can be seen the moment His grace descends. He is the Sun of Knowledge. One single ray of His has illuminated the world with the light of knowledge. One can see God only if He turns His light toward His face.
>
> The police sergeant does his rounds in the dark of night with a lantern (a reference to the lantern carried by the night watchman, which has dark glass on three sides) in his hand. No one sees his face, but with the help of that light, the sergeant sees everybody's face, and others, too, can see one another. However, if you want to see the sergeant, you must pray to him, 'Sir, please turn the light on your face. Let me see you.' In the same way, one must pray to God, 'O Lord, be gracious and turn the light of knowledge on Thyself, that I may see Thy face.'[30]

In this parable, Ramakrishna Paramahansa illustrates what happens to a person when they face God's power and glory. They know without a doubt that they are with God. They do not need any confirmatory evidence.

> The king dwells in the innermost room of the palace, which has seven gates. The visitor comes to the first gate. He sees a lordly person with a large entourage, surrounded by pomp and grandeur. The visitor asks his companion, 'Is he the king?' 'No,' says his friend with a smile.
>
> He repeats the same question to his friend at the second and the other gates. He finds that the nearer he comes to the innermost part of the palace, the greater the glory, pomp and grandeur. When he passes the seventh gate, he does not ask his companion whether it is the king; he stands speechless at the king's immeasurable glory. He realizes that he is face-to-face with the king. He hasn't the slightest doubt about it.[31]

A student author, Satish Chandra, writes that he responds to the experience of Swami's love by loving Him because of the inherent joy.

To love Him for the sheer joy of loving Him.[32]

St Augustine describes the meaning of his love for God. The basis of his love is a certainty, a belief about an unbreakable bond with God.

> My love for you, Lord, is not an uncertain feeling but a matter of conscious certainty. With your word, you pierced my heart, and I loved you. But when I love you, what do I love? It is not physical beauty, nor temporal glory, nor the brightness of light dear to earthly eyes, nor the sweet melodies of all kinds of songs, nor the mild odour of flowers and ointments and perfumes, nor manna or honey; it is not these I love when I love my God.
>
> Yet there is a light I love, a food and a kind of embrace when I love my God, where my soul is floodlit by light which space cannot contain, there is a sound that time cannot seize, a perfume which no breeze disperses and where there is a bond of union that nothing can part. That is what I love when I love my God.[33]

THE FEELING OF ASSURANCE AND BELONGING

The experience of God's love is an intense and powerful awareness of His continuous presence. The feelings that form the basis of a connection with God are belongingness, security and being chosen and accepted by Him. After the experience of God's love, the understanding and feeling felt during the encounter persist in life. James points this out.

> 'God surrounds me like the physical atmosphere. He is closer to me than my breath. In him, literally, I live and move and have my being.
>
> Sometimes, I seem to stand in his presence to talk with him. Answers to prayer have come, sometimes direct and overwhelming, revealing his presence and powers. Sometimes, God seems far off.
>
> I have the sense of a presence, strong and at the same

> time soothing, which hovers over me. Sometimes, it seems to enwrap me with sustaining arms.'
>
> Such is the human imagination and the convincingness of what it brings to birth. Unpicturable beings are realized and realized with an intensity almost like that of a hallucination. They determine our attitude as decisively as the attitude of lovers haunted by the feelings of the other. A lover notoriously has this sense of the continuous presence of his idol, even when his attention focuses on other matters. He cannot forget her; she uninterruptedly affects him through and through.[34]

Hislop writes about a similar experience with Swami.

> Love was unmistakable, and that Baba was this love was equally unmistakable. It seemed to me that only God Himself could enter my heart as love, and since then, this feeling of divine presence has never changed. There is no way I can deny my own direct experience.[35]

Nouwen recaps his thoughts when he experiences God's love. He is overwhelmed by the experience and believes God is faithful, dedicated and responsive. God is not a distant being. He is close by, like a continuous presence, and accessible. The author experiences God's tenderness and care. The underlying feeling is of being related to God, being God's property and being one with God. The perceptions of security and assurance arise from this sense of belongingness.

> I listen to the inner voice attentively; I hear words that say, 'I have called you by name. You are mine, and I am yours. I created you with my own hands. I love you and care for you as a mother. Wherever you go, I will be with you; wherever you rest, I keep watch. I will not hide from you. You will realize me as your own as I know as mine. You belong to me and will be with me wherever I am. Nothing can ever separate us.'[36]

Sandweiss narrates a story wherein Swami describes His personal and personalized engagement with each person.

> He was overcome with reverence and cried, 'Oh, Swami, I love you so much. I want you only to be my private Swami.'
>
> Swami replied, 'But I am your private Swami, just for you. I am everybody's private Swami. I come to everyone personally according to their need and in a most pleasing form.'[37]

Nouwen feels that God has chosen him as a recipient of His grace.

> To live a spiritual life, I must believe that (God) has chosen me. When I understand that He has picked me, I know He wants to bring me closer to him and love me. When love chooses, it chooses without making anyone else feel excluded. Love is all-encompassing. It possesses everyone.[38]

Swami explains God's idea of a person's selection in the following excerpt from a letter. The selection of the person is an expression of His love.

> I will never ask anybody anything for my own sake. There is nothing in this world that I can desire. Everything I possess is being used for the sake of devotees. I can as well do things myself. But because of 'human effort', I sometimes assign responsibilities and get things done through devotees. Rama gave the task of building the bridge on the sea to Hanuman, not because He could not reach Lanka on His own. It is to show the world devotees' capabilities and provide them with ideal examples.[39]

SELF-CONFIDENCE

The initial stirrings of belief in God are tentative. A person may doubt the authenticity and understanding of their religious experience. Developing a solid and unwavering belief in God is like curing concrete: it needs time to solidify. Spiritual self-confidence is the conviction that the person has met or experienced God and an increasing belief that God is near and reciprocates their love. Confidence is a precursor to the emergence of stable and steady faith. The excerpts in this section include narratives of diverse people engaging with Swami in different ways, each on a journey of belief.

> The religious experience is a personal encounter with God. It endows a person with spiritual conviction or faith based on their personal experience with God.[40]

Mrs Ratanlal describes how her devotional relationship with Swami evolved. She visited Swami often but continued concentrating on her ritualistic prayers. She believed her prayers would reach Swami. Swami rarely spoke to her. However, He used to sing Meera bhajans in her presence. She became increasingly apprehensive about her devotional relationship with Swami, even though He often gave her assurances to make her a devotee. Swami slowly and gently enabled her to develop a devotion-based relationship with Him. He made her recollect a personal moment when she had uniquely expressed her affection for Krishna. She remembers and cherishes the moment her relationship with Swami transformed.

> Each time we came to Swami, a new relationship cycle would start in the early days. We never took anything for granted. Past experiences with Swami do not predict his engagement on a recent trip.
>
> Swami used to call Ratanlal to his room on the first floor of the mandir. But he never used to talk to me. He would call us for an interview in the old interview room on the last day of our stay. Private discussions with Swami took place behind the curtain. Swami used to stand on the steps, his face at our eye level or a slight angle, looking at us, and we used to stand on the floor, half covered by the curtain. In the interviews also, Swami spoke to Ratanlal. During the interview, he would start singing Meera bhajans. Listening to him, I used to start crying.
>
> Swami would ask us to come back for Navrathras.[41] I was particular about doing my nine days of Navratri puja. Ratanlal would tell Swami, 'Swami, she is unwilling to come because she has to start her puja in Bombay.' He further commented,

> 'Swami, she has no devotion for you. Her only interest is in doing puja in her mandir.'
>
> Swami used to tell him, 'Don't worry, I will make her my devotee.' He emphasized this by adding, 'Understand.'
>
> I began to have a complex. Swami was not talking to me. Yet, at the same time, whenever he called us, he would sing Meera bhajans and I used to cry.
>
> In one interview, he said, 'You are my son, Giridhar Gopala.[42] You are my son, Giridhar Gopala.' I didn't understand him at that moment. The connection dawned on me later. The mandir in our house in Bombay had statues of Krishna and other deities. An incident happened when the mandir was under construction. The small pratimas[43] or idols arrived before they were scheduled for installation in the mandir. I used to hug them and treat them like my children. But when Swami said, 'You are my son, Giridhar Gopala,' I thought Swami was joking. I didn't take it seriously. Then it hit me![44]

Sandweiss narrates his thoughts after he met Swami. He experiences and acknowledges Swami as a divine manifestation. The experience is unsettling because all his past beliefs need to change. Even though he is shocked and unsettled, he decides to become a devotee.

> Amazing! Unbelievable! Unthinkable! The most extraordinary experience!
>
> All of this delivers a crushing blow to my previous beliefs and value systems, and it is painful to give them up. But when I see what appears to be concrete evidence of our existence beyond time and space in a human being who not only demonstrates this reality but also teaches us how to attain realization of this higher self, then I must listen. I am seeing concrete evidence of such a reality.
>
> When one finds a teacher of this calibre, all one can do is follow him, which means complete surrender, as exemplified in the Bible.
>
> I am humbled now by the feeling that I am not in charge of my destiny, that I am not the doer; God is the doer. Nevertheless,

> I must muster whatever strength I have to do my duty as best as possible, live a righteous life and do what a great master such as Baba says. There is no other choice.
>
> I feel a great sense of helplessness and vulnerability in the face of Baba's incredible power; my fundamental beliefs are shaken.
>
> I am like a newborn baby, awed at what I see and beginning to recognize this new reality without knowing how to become a part of it. I don't have confident faith, and I don't feel protected by it.[45]

Sandweiss identifies his uncertainties at the moment of spiritual commitment. He juggles his hesitation to commit on one side and desire for understanding on the other. The narration exemplifies that confident belief requires work.

> Faith does not come easily. Questions continued to haunt me, and confusion and doubts kept me from joining Sai activities.
>
> I still had no idea who Baba was. I was attracted to Sai Baba's personality, emphasis on human values and how he lived these values. Sai Baba offered a profound teaching level that intrigued and challenged me.
>
> While the questions kept coming, I held on tightly to Sai Baba, fearing that I might miss out on his supreme promise: that he could transform my life. I wanted to be free from fear. I wanted to have faith.[46]

Erlendur Haraldsson writes that his belief in Swami slowly matured. He became a devotee as he experienced Swami.

> I would say that from the beginning, I felt a personal attachment to Baba rather than spiritual faith. As the attachment grew and we understood him better, seeing him daily, our faith increased. That is how we became devotees.[47]

Ramana Rao writes how he is impressed by Swami and His persona. He intuitively understands that Swami's humaneness hides something. A desire to inquire and learn more is evoked.

> This was my first experience when I sat at Baba's feet. When I came there, I didn't know whether Baba was God. I could have asserted one way or another if I had seen God before. Baba didn't have four faces like Brahma, four hands like Vishnu or three eyes like Shiva. He did not have a *Nandi*, *Garuda* or *Hamsa* as his *Vahana*[48] as our mythological Gods. When he went out, he used his two legs to walk in the ashram and a motor car. He did have some extraordinary powers, which he used for the welfare of those who came to him for succour but not for personal aggrandizement. He is good, great and generous. Whether he is God or not, he is rendering more extraordinary service to humanity, moving amongst us, than God, an invisible, silent witness. I decided to go to Puttaparthi more often to study this miracle man closely.[49]

Schulman summarizes a group interview with Swami. His writing suggests that he is evaluating the interview proceedings with a scientific mindset, looking for miraculous happenings as a test of Swami. Initially, he does not give credence to another person's cure but later becomes reflective. The narrative is characteristic of a period of formative faith when people analyse God and their feelings for Him.

> Baba, in his early forties, was slightly over five feet tall. He wore a bright orange silk dress that hung loosely down to his chunky bare feet, but the first thing one noticed was his Afro-electric hair standing straight out from all parts of his head like a black, kinky halo five or six inches wide. He spoke gently and sweetly to each of the seven people in the room but did not reveal anything about anyone's past or future. He confined his remarks to platitudes about God, love and devotion. Then, just before Baba ended the audience, he materialized a ruby ring, which he gave to the novelist, and a handful of ashes, which he gave to the woman in the group. Baba was talking to someone else on the other side of the room when he suddenly stopped in the middle of the sentence and turned to the woman.
>
> 'I will cure your appendicitis,' he said as he materialized the ashes. 'Take this in water for three days.'

> She had suffered an attack of appendicitis the night before and was in great pain. No one had mentioned her attack.
>
> She followed the instructions, and three days later, when the pain had disappeared, she had two reputable doctors in another town examine her thoroughly. Neither of them could find a trace of appendicitis.
>
> The writer was not particularly impressed. Only later, when he tried to reconstruct what he had seen, did he begin to wonder if he had been witness to something extraordinary.[50]

The following narrative is a continuation of the previous one. Swami sits amongst the group, and the author is adjacent to Him. Schulman's examination manifests in bending to see Swami's downward-facing palm. Swami is helping the author test Him to develop belief. The author felt amazed at other people's passive reactions to extraordinary incidents during the interview. For devotees who believe, miracles with Swami are everyday occurrences and expressions of God's attributes.

> First, Baba had pushed the sleeve on his right arm up the elbow, and then he held his palm up, showing his empty right hand. Slowly, he turned his palm down and held it motionless for a few seconds. His fingers were apart. Nothing could have been concealed between them. Baba was seated in the middle of the floor. Others were also seated on the floor in a semicircle around him. The writer was sitting a few inches from Baba's right hand. Knowing it might be rude, he nevertheless bent forward to examine Baba's hand as he turned his palm downward. There was nothing hidden between his thumb and the fold of his hand. Then, Baba slowly closed his fingers and turned his hand over simultaneously. In one continuous motion, he opened his fingers, revealing the ring the first time and the ashes the second time.
>
> What puzzled the writer each time he recalled the incident was that neither he nor anyone else in the room had reacted with surprise, delight or amazement at what they had seen. Baba had materialized the objects so effortlessly, with so little importance attached, that they accepted what he had done as

> casually as if he had scratched his head or coughed. Neither had they questioned how Baba could have known about the attack of appendicitis.[51]

Father Mazzoleni narrates an interview with Swami. The location and his mental condition vis-a-vis Swami contextualize his experience in the interview room with Biblical stories. Initially, he wonders whether he is like an unwanted wedding guest turned away because he is not wearing wedding clothes. The clothes symbolize belief and giving up the old for the new in the parable of The Great Banquet narrated by Jesus. His mind is hyperactive from then on. At first, he doubts himself, but when Swami engages him in dialogue, his inner ruminations become spiritual conversations. Finally, Swami guides him and the discussion, which mirrors his mental and physical condition. He later realizes that conversations with Swami have a profound import. They are often not what they seem—simple encounters with an incarnation wherein God comes as a man. Upon reflection, the underlying meaning of the conversations with Swami is understood.

> I was not sure about what I was doing. I was afraid that when I went in, Sai Baba would say to me, 'Who called you?' thus relegating me to the fate of the wedding guest in the famous parable of Jesus, who the master ejected because he was not wearing the proper wedding garment. With a certain step, Baba returned and entered the interview room, followed by all of us. I sighed in relief.
>
> Sai Baba went to sit on a chair in the corner of the room. He was very small, and in the room, he no longer had that imposing appearance that He takes on at darshan. He was very human, and my brain was already beginning to devise theories.
>
> 'So, this person is supposed to be God in flesh and blood? He doesn't look like a God. He looks more like a little wizard.' My mind was busy searching for plausible explanations.
>
> The skin of His face was extraordinarily luminous, and only later, thinking about it, did I realize that I didn't see it olive-toned as it usually is but bluish like the clouds of a mid-summer thunderstorm. The luminosity of His face gave

the impression that under the translucent skin, a light shone through. It certainly was not the face of a 56-year-old man but instead of a pure and angelic adolescent.

The minute He was seated on the chair, His eyes fixed on mine, and He asked me, 'How are you?' My English was halting, but I had encountered that phrase in all my English courses, and I knew how to answer it, 'Fine, thank you!'

It was like a farce in which one of the actors, I, in this case, had got stuck on the only line he knew. Sai Baba, who had leaned forward a little to ask me that question, drew back a bit with an expression that meant, 'Are you sure?' while I was biting my tongue for having answered in such a foolish way.

After this, He turned His attention to me again to ask me, 'How are you?' I was deeply grateful to Him for giving me that second chance so I could correct my previous answer.

I had no intention of asking Him for a physical cure. I had left Italy with a very clear purpose. I knew He had the power to manipulate matter and heal and touch the hearts of men to show them the main road that leads to the final destination. But to speak to Him in front of everyone about my moral state and desire to receive directions so I could get on that road seemed immodest to me. So, having no alternative, I answered Him by saying I had kidney problems.

'Yes,' He said, 'I know.' And He began with a detailed description of the disease. Francesco translated. The gist of His whole discourse was that I should not worry about the illness, that He would take care of me and that the origin of all ills is in my mind. 'Dispel depression,' He said to me, 'and don't think about the future.' These two warnings made a deep impression on me because they accurately described my mental state at the time: emotional highs and lows and deep torment about the future.

I asked myself why on earth He had devoted so much of His precious time to give attention to a problem that, for me, was not important. Perhaps because I should have prioritized it. When you meet Sai Baba, everything happens in an extrasensory dimension; you are stunned and no longer understand anything about what is happening around you. You understand the message He leaves you with only later, often much later.

Thus, while I didn't understand why He emphasized my illness when what I wanted to ask Him was spiritual, I later understood that you could only attain spiritual discipline and final realization when you have refined and cared for the primary instrument, the body.[52]

Swami extends a helping hand to Rani Maa to develop confident belief when she is troubled with doubt and uncertainty. He explicitly states that He is open and willing to be tested by devotees to help build their beliefs. He asks her to be demanding and confront doubt by asking Him for evidence of His omnipresence.

My sister and I were in the room, and Swami came into the room. He looked at us and said, 'You are not convinced yet that I am God. You have got doubts about My divinity, is it not?' He asked us a straightforward question.

We kept quiet and just looked at Him, which meant 'Yes!' We couldn't tell Him directly; He knows everything, so why should we?

Then He said, 'It is but natural! It's nothing unnatural. How can you believe if somebody just comes and tells you, "I am God!"? There's nothing wrong; it is very natural!' Then He said, 'But there's one thing you must do to remove your doubts. You can't always live with doubt, so try it! If I am God, I must show Omnipresence; nobody else can be Omnipresent—only God can do that!' He said, 'You must test My Omnipresence!' He insisted, 'You have to do it! There is no other way! Only then will your doubts go.'

How could we test His Omnipresence in Puttaparthi? He is already here!

He said, 'When you return to your respective places, test Me whether I am available as Omnipresent! You have to do it for your own sake!'[53]

Schulman is ambivalent about Swami when the time comes for him to leave India after being with Swami for a while. He does not know whether he believes in Swami. In His inimitable way, Swami emphasizes that He will be with him even if he doesn't believe in Him or tries to forget Him. For Swami, the relationship expresses His nature: the promise of proximity and responsiveness to a devotee's stated and unstated needs. Swami's comments vividly demonstrate that God's promise is His nature, His spontaneous love of a person and is not a transaction preconditioned by or a response to the evocation of belief in the person.

> Baba rubbed his hands as hard as he could on the writer's chest, massaging it vigorously to stimulate the writer's spiritual circulation.
>
> 'I am always with you,' Baba said. 'Even when you don't believe in me and try to forget me, even when you laugh at me or hate me. Even when I seem to be on the opposite side of the earth, you need material things to remind you, isn't it?'
>
> He pushed up his sleeve and rotated his open palm as he closed his fingers. When he opened them, he held a gold ring with his picture painted on porcelain in the centre, surrounded by sixteen stones that seemed to be diamonds. He put the ring on the writer's finger. It fits perfectly. 'I am in you,' Baba said, 'You are in me. Don't forget that. We cannot be separated.'[54]

A REFLECTIVE STRUGGLE

The initial stirring of belief is embryonic and needs to be nurtured and strengthened. St Augustine highlights that God's grace enabled him to hold on to his belief despite hesitating.

> There was a firm place in my heart for the faith. In many respects, this faith was still unformed and hesitant. Yet my mind did not abandon it but drank more daily. You did not allow fluctuations in my thinking to carry me away from the faith I held.[55]

The engagement with Swami creates an urge to know and be with Him. The initial inspiration to believe manifests as behaviours motivated by a desire for a deeper personal and spiritual relationship with Him.

> We returned delighted. Bhagavan had utterly charmed us. It created a natural urge to read more about him, to know more of him, to see more of him and to be in his presence as much as possible. Our trip to Puttaparthi further strengthened the silent bond between Bhagavan and ourselves.[56]

Hislop writes about the power and influence of God's love, spiritual wisdom and universal experience with Swami. This induces every person who comes into contact with Swami to become religious and try to learn Swami's teachings.

> His wisdom, the love so strongly felt when one is in his presence, and his extraordinary power over the natural elements and human circumstances contribute to the remarkable reverence in which he is held and to the almost irresistible attraction felt by people of all ages and races when they see him or begin to pay close attention to his teachings and life.[57]

Aitken describes the dichotomy of belief and what it takes to establish a steady relationship with Swami. Being with Swami, getting to know Him and believing in Him as a divine incarnation are spiritual struggles. When people see Swami or are in His presence, they focus on His persona. Their mind ceases to wander. When they are away from Him, the mind plays games. To overcome the vacillations, uncertainties and hesitancy of belief and to commit and bond with Swami, the effort becomes to find the inner Swami. Aitken uses a metaphor of tides to suggest that this fluctuating engagement with Swami ends when He is experienced within.

> For a seeker, the Puttaparthi experience veers from an outward single-minded focus on one person to the inner struggle to establish the truth of that eternal presence within. The battle against the mind's doubting is fought a hundred times daily and lost only to be won back briefly at darshan. But slowly,

> the ocean of love reclaims the sandy shore of the devotee's doubts. The tidal conflict will continue, but the devotee will find firm ground beneath his feet one day. The waves continue to wash over him, but he is not swept away. The realization dawns that Sathya Sai can be (and is) recognized as divine because of the devotee's capacity to achieve this state.[58]

The following four excerpts are Reeves' reflections.

She is narrating her own life story with Swami. Her writings reflect the nature of her inner struggle that shaped her relationship with Swami. Her wavering thinking mirrors the ruminations of Tolstoy or St Augustine with God. The narratives depict how Swami moulds people's spiritual mindset through inner trials, which are their ways of thinking.

Swami rarely gives direct answers because self-discovered knowledge and understanding are stable, robust and have deep foundations.

The inner conflict on the spiritual journey to establish a stable engagement with Swami is an emotional roller coaster ride. In the following excerpt, Reeves recognizes that her unmanageable ideas, concentration and self-interest influence her. There are moments when Swami acknowledges her, and then she feels spiritually close to Swami. At other times, Swami does not recognize her, and then she assumes that she is far away from Swami. These scenarios do not reflect the reality of her spiritual relationship with Swami. They are her imaginations and projections onto Swami. Moreover, there is a need to always be careful in the relationship with God. A devotee should refrain from attributing reasons and interpretations to Swami and His behaviour, characterizing the engagement based on personal expectations and conjectures.

> The day before yesterday was a day of disappointment and rejection. I felt hurt. Baba did not notice me; instead, He ignored me.
>
> Yesterday, I concentrated on the higher self and did not allow my ego to assert, become dominant and take over. I named November 11th my new birthday, when my ego-less self was born.

The mood changed again today. I waited for Baba to call me for an interview. He seemed to call everyone except me. Should I accept the endless waiting? Is this my fate? The uncertainty overwhelmed me. I became angry again. Feeling sadder, I had to get away. With my sandals broken, I decided to walk barefoot to the Gokulum.[59] The cows were not visible. I could see Sai Gita[60] over the wall of her shelter. The atmosphere was peaceful. I calmed down.

I became self-centred about my pain and blamed Swami for my miserable state. He was the cause of my grief. I even doubted His significance. And finally, I broke down, shedding tears.

I returned to the ashram just in time for Baba's darshan. The pain was still raw. I wanted to be near enough to see Him yet distant and stood outside the low wall surrounding the darshan area.

I saw Baba walking out of the mandir. My eyes were fascinated and absorbed in His graceful form and elegant, charming walk. I was affected and emotionally stirred by the darshan. I seemed to be engulfed by intense energy emanating from Him. I looked down, feeling uncomfortable about the thoughts that crossed my mind earlier. In my mind, I begged for forgiveness from Swami, the embodiment of pure love.[61]

The next piece depicts Reeves' continued self-inflicted emotional turmoil. Her experience symbolizes the spiritual journey of a person who has to cross the minefield of uncertainty with God and develop firm belief after experiencing God's attributes and reciprocity. The emotional oscillations continue until a person recognizes that their engagement with God is not of two equals. The logic of God's decision-making is very different from human reasoning. The scale at which God decides is very different from a person's perspective. A person may want an immediate reaction and response from God to their concerns. In contrast, working according to a spiritual timescale and paradigm, God will respond at the appropriate time, which may lead to a delayed response.

I prepared a birthday card for Swami. I placed it in an envelope and took it for darshan. Yesterday, I offered Him the envelope. He stopped with a lovely smile, pointed to the mandir verandah and said, 'Tomorrow morning. You too, California.'

I did not expect this. The outpouring of love and emotion in His presence makes the expectation of an interview/meeting with Swami recede from the mind. I was speechless with mounting excitement. Did this mean that I would have an interview? Indeed, if Swami said so.

I was a bit scared. On the one hand, there was the fear of not knowing what may happen. On the other hand, I doubted my readiness to face Him. It was a long, sleepless night. I kept my mind focused on Him, mentally repeating Om Sai Ram.

Hobi and I sat in the front row facing the mandir with anticipation and excitement. Swami appeared and started walking towards us. He was smiling and looking at us. As He came closer, He abruptly turned towards the men's side.

He took letters and selected people for interviews. He did not call us.

Throughout the morning, He walked on the verandah. It seemed He was glancing at us. Inevitably, I wondered if He remembered the promise given yesterday. The morning passed. I felt we were like puppets on strings held in Baba's hands.

During evening darshan, He stopped before me and motioned for Hobi to go for an interview. I felt that He didn't seem to notice me because He called people sitting around me. I wanted to ask Swami if I could also go, but it was impossible to utter even a word. I was too shocked to think or speak.

I went up the hill behind the temple, sat on the rock and sobbed like a child. Baba had ignored me. I sincerely wished to give Him my loving greeting card for His birthday.

Different uncontrollable thoughts jumbled in my head as I reacted to my pain. I didn't know what I was thinking. I was using logic to alleviate my suffering. I believe that God doesn't hurt people. Why was He being cruel to me? Was

> Baba behaving like a human? Unable to endure the stress, I wanted to escape. I decided to leave Puttaparthi first thing in the morning.
>
> After the morning congregation dispersed, I sat under the palm trees. Suddenly, Swami appeared from the interview room and walked towards me. The birthday card was with me. I had decided not to give it to Baba. I involuntarily brought the envelope to my lap. Baba was looking at me from a distance. I was unsure of what would happen. As He stopped before me, His eyes were on the envelope. He looked at me and said infinitely sweetly, 'Oh, a very good artist,' and remained standing there, smiling, and stretched His hand for the card.
>
> My face must have displayed all the emotional drama of the recent past. His behaviour revealed His awareness of my feelings. He continued walking along the darshan line, occasionally looking back at me.
>
> A feeling of love for Baba filled my heart. The residual anger and resentment had vanished. I guess His thoughts, logic and vocabulary are different from my own, and at the same time, I felt immersed in a calming and comforting love radiating from Him, an illuminating and healing love.[62]

She finally accepts the undulating nature of her relationship with Swami. A person's spiritual struggle to establish an enduring relationship with God is within the person and not with God.

> When we arrived in Brindavan, every darshan was bliss. Seeing Baba in the morning and evening was enough. Then, envy started to arise. I wondered why certain devotees repeatedly get called for an interview while we have been waiting for months, desperate for Baba's encouragement and love. In my desire to catch Baba's eye, I was jealous and resentful of others. During darshan, I felt Baba was avoiding us; He was not coming near where I was sitting. The feeling of rejection intensified until it became a feeling of resentment.
>
> I wrote a letter enumerating all my complaints and held it up in darshan. Baba was accepting letters from everyone. He

turned away before reaching me. I felt that He had purposely turned away. He was aware of the contents of the letter.

I was so unhappy with Baba that I doubted Him and demanded a clear sign that cannot be misconstrued as an overworked imagination. I felt I needed the sign at this stage of my spiritual development.

Nothing happened.

I have settled into a peaceful acceptance of the present, enjoying the will of Bhagavan, His beauty, and the intense tranquillity that a person feels radiates from His presence. Is this the meaning of flowing with the divine current, not struggling or fighting it?

I can still picture the beautiful darshan this afternoon in my mind. On His return to the mandir with His back towards us, I could see the sun's golden glow encircling him and the light of His robe surrounding the dark crown of hair. The feeling of supreme peace and tranquillity was of another realm. Baba is beyond the mind's limitations, beyond verbal descriptions. On occasions like these, the longing to merge with God is intense. I yearn to be absorbed in God like a drop of water into the ocean.[63]

The following narrative is a reflective self-appraisal by Reeves as she alternates between thinking of Swami as a human and an avatar. On the one hand, she wants and expects immediate personal answers to her prayers from Swami; on the other hand, she aspires to accept Him as an incarnation of God.

I arrived in Prasanthi Nilayam six months back. One loses all sense of time here. Six months seem forever or like six days and no doubt like six seconds for Bhagavan.

I have changed very much but not enough yet.

I am very attached to Him as a person. Or, as some say, His physical form. I am stumbling through the consequences of this attachment and the associated pain. On the one side, I try very hard to give up the constant need for acknowledgment of Swami's love. I continuously want to be assured and reassured through recognition. On the other side, I am happy, silently immersed in the joy of His proximity, His darshan and receiving His grace in many subtle ways.

I am constantly assessing how far I have travelled in a spiritual sense in the last six months. It is challenging to self-judge. I know that my heart and vision have expanded, the anguish and uncertainty of the search have ended, and yet the journey continues to be complicated. It isn't a little bit easier. I must constantly keep pace with Baba, the bright light leading the way. At times, He moves too far ahead. Even when the flame is hidden by the nine vices like ego, pride, jealousy and anger and when there is an impulse to pull out from this journey, it takes all my intellectual and mental prowess to keep my mind on God. This is when the spiritual path holds such sweetness and great joy as no other.[64]

Sharon Sandweiss describes her spiritual quest and struggle of 13 years to understand and accept Swami as an incarnation. Her narrative mirrors inner anguish, restlessness and an ultimatum to Swami to respond to her inner ordeal. Her story mirrors that of Reeves'.

We went to India for Sai Baba's 50th birthday. I was miserable. My ego screamed for attention, and Sai Baba didn't glance at me.

I was eager to return home, and I felt that Sai Baba had ignored me because he was unhappy with me, and I was certainly disappointed with him.

The feeling of being unloved by Sai Baba is difficult to eradicate because deep within, I knew I couldn't explain something I didn't fully understand.

I went to India in 1980 for Sai Baba's 55th birthday, and Sai Baba was very gracious. Amidst the bustling festivities, he granted us a private interview in a small room. Despite Sai Baba's affectionate demeanour, my mind was filled with questions as I silently departed from India, earnestly asking Sai Baba to dispel my doubts. In 1985, we (went) to India for Sai Baba's 60th birthday.

I was the unhappy one. I suffered, complained and loudly

proclaimed, 'I'm not going to return to this place again. I'll hold Sai Baba in my heart in the comfort of my own home!'

Within five months, (we) made another quick trip to India. Despite my previous proclamations that I would never again visit Sai Baba, I was on a plane heading back to India for the sixth time. It was 13 years after my first trip to India in 1972. This time, I made a silent vow to stop complaining and be receptive. Then, perhaps, I would feel Sai Baba's love.

At the very first darshan, Sai Baba motioned for me to go in for an interview. He had signalled to me first before Sam! I was incredulous because I had been convinced that Sam was the one Sai Baba loved and that I was sliding in on Sam's coattails. Sai Baba was attentive and told me very little of a personal nature. I left the room feeling dissatisfied and yearned for deeper contact with him.

Sai Baba emerged from the temple. As he walked toward me, dazzling rays of sunlight sparkled and danced in his dark hair. I was stunned; he was so beautiful. I gasped at his beauty; my heart opened to Sai Baba's love at that moment.

In the next moment, Sam was motioning me up to the temple. We had been called in for another interview! I floated in, and Sai Baba asked me, 'How are you?' 'I'm so happy,' I answered. There was much more given than a material object in this beautiful gift. Sai Baba's love was all-consuming and transforming when directed toward me. My heart burst with love for him. Finally, I knew that he loved me.

Suddenly, I was unfettered and free! I had been given the gift of faith.

I began to experience Sai Baba as divinity. His glory and authority awed me. Energized and inspired, my love for Sai Baba began to spill over into every aspect of my life.[65]

TIP OF THE ICEBERG

St Augustine describes how the first experience of God occurs: how an inward-focused mind metaphorically goes deeper and rises higher to experience God as awareness and knowledge. God is eternal and changeless wisdom; an aspirant experiences Him and then returns to the world.

> An ardent affection toward the eternal being lifted our minds. Step by step, we climbed beyond all material objects and heaven, where the sun, moon and stars shed light on the earth. We ascended further by internal reflection and dialogue, marvelled at your works and entered our minds. We moved beyond them to attain the region of inexhaustible abundance [...] where life is the wisdom by which all creatures come into being, both things which were and will be. But wisdom is not brought into being but is as it was and always will be.
>
> Furthermore, this wisdom has no past and future, only being, since it is eternal. To exist in the past or future is not the property of the eternal. And while we talked and panted after it, we touched it in some small degree by a moment of total concentration of the heart. And we sighed and left behind the first fruits of the Spirit bound to that higher world as we returned to the noise of our human speech where a sentence has both a beginning and an ending.[66]

In the following conversation, Ramana Maharshi identifies a man's true nature and what needs to be done to make the fleeting peace experienced in his presence last. His description mimics St Augustine's.

> Devotee: (I) felt peace in His presence, which lasted sometime after. He added, 'Why is it not enduring?'
>
> Maharshi: That peace is your real nature. Contrary ideas are only superimpositions. You may say that you acquire this peace by practice. The wrong notions are given up by practice. This is all. Your true nature always persists. These flashes are only signs of the resulting revelation of the self.[67]

Father Mazzoleni depicts his meeting with Swami as extraordinarily transformative. He believes his initial awareness and experience are the tip of the iceberg. There is knowledge to be discovered: the iceberg below the waves.

> The things you understand upon meeting Him may be enough to revolutionize your life. However, they are only a tiny part of what you did not know then and will gradually discover in subsequent events.[68]

ACCEPT AND CHANGE

Tillich pictures belief as a state of being grasped by God.[69] The birth of belief is not an event but a moment when belief evokes or a person says I believe. It is the moment when God becomes the basis of a person's life; the relationship with God becomes the disposition that permeates and influences their life. Tolstoy distinguishes between knowing about God and living for and with God. He wants to live a life seeking God.

> 'But my perception of God, of Him whom I seek,' I asked myself, 'where has that perception come from?' And again, at this thought, the glad waves of life rose within me. All that was around me came to life and received meaning. But my joy did not last long. My mind continued its work.
>
> 'The conception of God is not God,' I said. 'The conception is what takes place within me. I can evoke or refrain from evoking the conception of God in myself. That is not what I seek. I seek that without which there can be no life.'
>
> But then I turned my gaze upon myself, on what went on within me, and I remembered that I only lived when I believed in God.
>
> I live, really live, only when I feel Him and seek Him. 'What more do you seek?' exclaimed a voice within me. 'This is He. He is that without which one cannot live. To know God and to live are the same thing.'
>
> 'Live seeking God, and then you will not live without God.' And more than ever before, all within me and around me lit up. And the light did not again abandon me.[70]

In the following citation, Justice V.R. Krishna Iyer, a judge of the Indian Supreme Court, writes how Swami changed him from a sceptic to a believer, an experience he likens to the opening of the eyes.

> And in the presence of Light, eyes open, cries stop silent, hopes of sight rise brightly. This is the experience when divinity's presence kindles the divinity in each of us. Baba is such a presence.
>
> I turned to him in the most profound sorrow that virtually broke my being. I changed my earlier role of sceptic and critic into an objective searcher of truth to the extent my low level of intelligence allowed. After that, I had a rewarding series of experiences that were elevating, comforting, verifiable and veracious.[71]

Sandweiss acquires a new perspective on life after meeting Swami. His experience mimics Tolstoy's journey of belief. He begins to see and think about everything in his life using 'Sai spectacles' and how Swami would look at it. His life and purpose take on a new meaning as he describes this process as aligning with Swami, consciously shaping himself according to Swami's teachings. There was a time when Sandweiss wanted to test Swami and His teachings using his professional knowledge and experience. Initially, he approached this cautiously, even considering Swami's speeches mere platitudes. However, because he now believes in being enveloped by Swami's divine love and safeguarded by His watchful presence, he overcomes all hesitation, wholeheartedly embracing Swami and transforming his perspective. The change manifests as his willingness to unquestioningly accept everything, even things he was uncomfortable with earlier.

> One of my most amazing insights has been experiencing how dramatically one can change upon seeing this higher reality. Everything seems different.
>
> I can't describe what happens during this sudden change, only that I can see my life powerfully affected by this experience and vision of a new reality colouring everything I see.
>
> To experience such a phenomenon, I am feeling more of Baba's love and protection; my feelings of apprehension and worry a few days ago are quieting. His smile is electrifying;

he can change from a child to a lion in the wink of an eye.

I see my task in the near future as having to come to terms with some aspects of my life to align myself more fully with Baba.

I struggled terribly against what I thought to be Puritan moralism, yet after witnessing Baba's greatness, I can do nothing but fully accept what he says. He is genuinely so magnificent.[72]

In the upcoming incident, Swami orients Salian's mindset, who seeks an opportunity to serve and be with Him. He helps Salian clarify the significance of living in His proximity. The key is for an individual to learn to perceive God in everything as God truly permeates everything. These ideas manifest in the narrator's reflections. During the *Vishwaroop Darshan*, he ponders whether Arjuna perceived everything as being transformed into Krishna or if he saw Krishna infused within everything. Salian grasps the lesson that he must fully accept that he is in God's presence and seize the spiritual opportunity of being with an incarnation.

(Swami taught me the) nature and expression of belief I should have with him. (I was travelling with Swami in the car) Swami was sitting on my right. Suddenly, Swami said, 'What can you see?'

I replied, 'Swami, I can see Swami.'

Swami then said, 'That is different, sir. What can you see—do you want to see Rama, or do you want to see Krishna?'

My brain started to click. I realized that Swami was asking me about the form I wanted to see him as or what vision I wanted to have. This was a dilemma. I was with Swami. I was getting all the good things that we have read in books.

In contrast, Mr. Hislop said that he saw the blue form of Krishna. I momentarily thought that this was my chance. And then I held back. Do I want to see anything? I am seeing Swami. Why do I want to see anything else? So, I replied, 'Swami, I don't want to see anything else. I only want to see you Swami.'

Swami responded, 'Being smart! Enough of Vedanta. Tell me what you want to see. Do you want to see Narasimha avatar?'

I said, 'No, Swami.'

He then queried, 'Do you want to see the old man? Shirdi baba? You can see the old man.'

I said, 'No, Swami. I want to see Swami.'

He was insistent, 'Tell me. I am asking you repeatedly, and you are not answering.'

With Swami insistent, I thought, let me take a chance and say something non-controversial. I told Swami, 'Swami, I want to see the Vishwaroopa.'

When I said I wanted to see Vishwaroopa, Swami leaned back in his seat, pointed his hand outside and said, 'You see it every day, and you don't understand it. You see it every day. You don't comprehend it.'

Swami was quiet. I looked through the window for fifteen minutes, trying to understand what Swami had just told me. I was wondering. What is it that he has shown Arjuna on the battlefield? Was it some tangible form that Krishna showed Arjuna? Or was it a change in Arjuna's perception, an insight that suddenly, he could see God in everything? Everything was present there. Nothing had to be done. There is no such thing as the future and no such thing as the past. There is birth, there is death, there is fire, there is forest and there is everything, planets and everything in the divine form. What did Lord Krishna do? These became the thoughts in the mind of a young twenty-two-year-old. Swami was able to mould a mind that knew nothing other than chemistry. This was the master stroke of the master sculptor for a person who has not read anything.

We came back from the drive. We entered Trayee Brindavan. We went walking towards the dining hall. There is a small bridge there. Mrs Ratanlal was standing at the edge of the bridge. Swami was climbing down the five steps. I was behind Swami. I could see his hand gestures. I imagined his expression as he was talking to Mrs Ratanlal. He appeared to be telling her, 'See this buffalo' (Buffalo is a metaphor for feeble thinking).

Mrs Ratanlal confirmed my intuition about Swami's dialogue by saying, 'What has the boy done now?'

> Swami replied, 'The boy has got a chance to serve Swami and is asking me for Moksha.'
>
> The profundity of this comment brought about a change in my attitude and the goal of my life. Swami changed perceptions of what life is and is not, what is essential and what is unimportant in life.[73]

GOAL

After an experience of God, a person desires to always be with God. They want to perpetually enjoy the bliss of being with God. A momentary experience of God is not the same as living with God, a life of continuing awareness of God. This dichotomy, the ups and downs of being with and without God, motivates them to embark on their spiritual journey.

Ramakrishna Paramahansa uses the metaphor of milk to distinguish between two spiritual dispositions: one, being aware of God's existence, and two, doing something with the awareness, striving to experience and realize Him. Knowing about God is like being knowledgeable about milk and its properties. Endeavouring to experience God after learning about Him is deriving nourishment by drinking milk. Conviction-based belief inspires a person to consciously seek God. Belief in God becomes unshakable when a person experiences Him and can see and talk to Him. Belief formation begins after the first experience of God ends. Having found God, a person must seek Him to develop a stable and enduring connection with Him.

> That God exists may be known by looking at the universe. But it is one thing to hear of God, another to see God and still another to talk to God. Some have heard of milk, some have seen it and some, again, have tasted it. You feel happy when you see milk; you get nourished and strengthened when you drink it. You will get peace of mind only when you have seen God. You will enjoy bliss and gain strength only when you have talked to Him.[74]

SEEKING

After meeting Swami, Rani Maa decides to live a spiritual life requiring widespread transformation. Life is to be spiritualized with thought, word and deed harmonized with a religious undertone.

> When you come to this path with Baba, it does not mean (we) will become perfect overnight! We have many shortcomings and imperfections, which we must transcend.
>
> For, spiritual life is entirely different from what we (are) used to; our whole life has to be re-oriented and re-organized. Our thoughts, words and deeds everything has to be spiritualized. It isn't easy because we have formed a habit of thinking one way, talking another and doing a third. We have been living like humans, and now, suddenly, we must live a divine life![75]

Nouwen differentiates between living in a state of knowledge about God and a state of being knowledgeable about God and acting on knowledge and experience. He describes the first state as being and the second as becoming. A person in a relationship with God cannot just be or remain passive. A relationship with God necessitates the spiritualization of the person's entire life. This requires making God intertwined with their thoughts, words and deeds so that the ego is lost in the becoming. Becoming is a way for a person to realize their spiritual potential and become like their beloved God.

> Hidden in our minds and hearts lies the treasure we seek. We are not only loved by God, are His reflection, but have the potential to realize that we are the beloved. Living a spiritual life is not about living in this passive awareness of just being but living a life of active understanding of this potential, taking steps to become the beloved. Becoming beloved means making the awareness of our oneness with God, our belovedness, integrated with our entire life. Being the beloved is more than a beautiful thought. Becoming the beloved is blending the revealed truth into whatever a person thinks, talks about and does every minute.[76]

Nouwen mentions that we are verily God Himself. This belief in our potential should manifest in making God a part of everything in our life and seeking and becoming one with God the purpose of our life.

> When our truth is that we are the Beloved and our greatest joy comes by realizing that truth, it follows that this has to be visible and palpable in how we live.[77]

Loving and seeking God is a struggle and a joy. It is a struggle because of the effort needed. It is a joy because of the bliss inherent in engaging with God.

> Becoming is a lifelong effort and a lifelong joy.[78]

James describes the spiritual emotions of a person journeying towards God as moving from a state of being to becoming one with God. People who have traversed the distance describe it as a miracle. It does not occur naturally. After a person accepts and submits to God, God takes control of their life. They begin to believe God's proclamation that they are part of God and God, too.

> Naturally, those who have traversed such an experience should carry away the feeling that it is a miracle rather than a natural process. After surrendering the personal will, it appears like an extraneous higher power had flooded in and taken possession. Moreover, the sense of renovation, safety, cleanness and rightness can also be wonderful and joyful to warrant one's belief in a radically new, substantial nature.[79]

Underhill calls attention to how the desire to seek God intensifies after a spiritual experience. The clarity and vividness of God's experience as truth, perfection and love overwhelm any hesitation, evoking an intense desire for God.

> The first thing that the self observes at that moment of clarity is the pure, sharp radiance of the real. It is the rapture and awe [...] The precursor of that new self must be born [...] a desire: a passionate longing [...] to conform to reality, the perfect which it has seen [...] of goodness, beauty and love—to

> be worthy of it [...] 'This showing is so vehement and strong that the (person) is marvellously moved and shaken' [...] The 'vehemence of this showing': the deep-seated sense of necessity that urges the newly awakened self [...] The transcendental consciousness, exalted by a clear intuition of its goal [...] forces the unwilling mind to thirst for perfection. She entered immediately [...] her efforts towards that self-conquest [...] to the dictates of that pure love which was the aspect of reality she had seen. It is the inner conviction that this transcendence of the unreal is possible.[80]

Nouwen reinforces the influence of the experience of God in motivating a person to aspire to God. The experience of God is very blissful. An aspirant with a spiritual experience strives to establish an enduring relationship with God.

> Every time a person intuits or pays attention to the voice of the beloved within, they want to remain connected with the beloved longer. The experience is akin to a thirsty person digging and finding moist soil, suggesting that water is near. They then want to keep digging. The author highlights his personal experience. He has been exploring and is beginning to connect with God. God is responsive, and he sees water bubbling up. He knows that he is on track; God is near.[81]

Ramana Maharshi explains how to stabilize and evoke permanent feelings in spiritual experiences. He underlines that regular and repeated spiritual practices will enable a devotee to achieve and maintain an unwavering awareness of God. This is in response to a questioner who highlights that his experience of peacefulness, evoked in Ramana Maharshi's presence, ebbs away after he returns home. The devotee articulates a seeker's spiritual desire to sustain the emotions and insights of a spiritual experience by seeking constant engagement with God.

> Devotee: (In the ashram) I was aware of Bhagavan's peace enfolding me for about ten days. While busy at work, there was an undercurrent of that peace, of unity; it was almost like a dual consciousness. Then, it faded entirely, and the old

'stupidities' came in instead. Work leaves no time for separate meditation. Is the constant reminder 'I am', trying to feel it at work, enough?

Maharshi: It will become constant when the mind becomes strengthened. Repeated practice strengthens the mind; such a mind can hold on to the current/present. In that case, engagement in work or no engagement, the current remains unaffected and uninterrupted.[82]

GOD AT WORK

Padma Kasturi relates how Swami engineered a situation for Prof. Kasturi's acceptance of Swami as a personification of God. The incident is symptomatic of how God works to evoke and instil acceptance and firm belief. The belief that St Augustine or Tolstoy derived through their personal experiences and intuitive insights is made more accessible by Swami; He achieved this using dramatic occurrences that force a person to change their thinking. The narrative touches on the tangible nature of the lessons orchestrated by Swami, which serve as powerful spiritual experiences reminiscent of encounters with God throughout history.

Interviewer: What was his first impression of Swami after that first interview? Did he come and tell you anything about how he felt?

Kasturi's daughter: He felt some power but didn't think of divinity then. Swami was too young. He was only 22 years old! He said there was something extraordinary in this young man.

Swami used to go into a trance and give darshan to some in some distant places. He used to come out of the trance. He used to tell us all that happened there. But father was not very satisfied. He was unsure about all Swami had said after coming out of the trance.

Once, when my father was in Swami's room, Swami suddenly fell and went into a trance, and vibhuti came out of

His mouth and hands. After He came out of the trance, He said, 'I had been to Dehradun because one Dr Krishnamurthi—who is coming here to Puttaparthi—his mother had passed away and she was asking for My darshan, and at her last moment, I went and gave her darshan.' Then He started telling him who else was there, and my father got interested and asked Swami if he could take notes. Swami gave him a slip of paper, and my father took notes about who else was there, all that had happened, etc. Then Swami said, 'A letter will come after 3–4 days, and then you can bring your list and tally it!' Then after four days, a letter came, but He didn't open it, however! He sent word to my father.

My father went up and asked him to read both—the letter and the notes—and it was precisely the same!

My father was excited and came running home from the mandir shouting, '*Anandam*! *Anandam*!' (Bliss! Bliss!). I was there but didn't know what had happened to him! He said, 'Oh! We have got Bhagavan! How fortunate we are! Bhagavan! Bhagavan!' He didn't take any food. He was so excited!

He said, 'No! Bhagavan is here! I don't want anything when our Bhagavan is here! We have got Bhagavan! Why do I need anything else?' Swami used to visit people's houses during those days during the evening bhajans. He passed our house and asked my grandmother: 'How is Kasturi? What is he doing?' She cried, 'Oh, Swami! He is not taking any food! All he is saying is, "We have got Bhagavan!" I don't know what has happened to him!' Then Swami said, 'When the Truth is revealed, that's what happens. So don't worry! I will make him alright.' After bhajans, He called him upstairs to His room, joked with him, gave him something to eat and made him normal![83]

ACCEPTANCE AND SURRENDER

James uses a quote to depict a devotee's unquestioning dependence on God.

> My heart bounded in recognition when I heard my Father's cry calling me. I ran, stretched my arms and cried aloud, 'Here I am, my Father.' Oh, happy child, what should I do? 'Love me,' answered my God. 'I do, I do,' I cried passionately. 'Come unto me,' called my Father. 'I will,' my heart panted. Did I stop to ask a single question? Not one. It never occurred to me to ask whether I was good enough, hesitate over my unfitness or wait until I should be satisfied. Satisfied! I was satisfied. Had I not found my God and my Father? Did he not love me? Had he not called me? Since then, I have had direct answers to prayer—so significant as to be like talking with God and hearing his answer. The idea of God's reality has never left me for one moment.[84]

James uses another quote to describe that submission to God results in a person giving up all expectations and accepting whatever God gives. The person loses the fear of pain or loss and gives up hope and expectation of gain. Because of this, they are free and not dependent on anything.

> Where men are enlightened with the true light, they renounce all desire and choice and commit themselves to eternal goodness. Such men are in a state of freedom. They have lost their fear of pain and the hope of reward and live in pure submission to eternal goodness, in fervent love.[85]

Haraldsson quotes the Raja of Venkatagiri,[86] a devotee of Swami, who identifies three mental orientations that form the basis of a person's relationship with God: reverence, respect and surrender motivated by devotion.

> We went, saw and were conquered; He captured us. That is all. By conquered, I mean that we surrendered. It is challenging to explain what caused this, whether it was an attraction for Him or His magnetic personality. He attracted our devotion, and we became his fervent devotees. When we first went to see him, we did not go as devotees; we were reverential, as when we went to any other saint. In Hinduism, it is said that all

> sages should be respected. But personal devotion differs from honouring a sage, paying obeisance or being respectful to a person. Here, we surrendered: it was absolute.[87]

The ensuing experience illustrates the protagonist's adherence to Swami's guidance despite a family-related challenge. She attentively heeds the instructions and promptly takes action. Although her trust in Swami's promise is not explicitly stated, her actions imply a readiness to accept whatever transpires as a manifestation of Swami's blessings.

> Once, Swami told Ratanlal, 'I have given you life.'
>
> This happened in 1971. We were in Parthi for Dussehra. We were staying in the guesthouse on top of the hill. Swami used to talk to Ratanlal daily, 'You have got a car. Use the car. Don't walk up and down the hill.' Ratanlal didn't take Swami's comment seriously; he didn't consider it an instruction to be followed. He did this despite what had happened before he arrived in Parthi. Ratanlal had got a medical done before leaving Bombay. He had a weak constitution and a murmur in his heart. I told him to tell Swami about his medical condition. He was adamant about not telling Swami, asking a rhetorical question, 'Why should I tell Swami?' I played along and said, 'Alright.'
>
> He revisited the doctor after we returned to Bombay. His ECG showed symptoms of a recent heart attack. He refused to get admitted to the hospital. Doctors visited the house every day to check on him. Things were deteriorating, getting from bad to worse. Swami was sending him a letter every third day. In one letter, he wrote, 'How can you have a heart attack when I am in your heart?'
>
> Then a message came asking me to go to Parthi. I was to spend the night in Bangalore. Swami's big station wagon was assigned to take me to Parthi the next day. I quickly got ready and left. I arrived in Bangalore. A person was waiting for me at the airport. I asked him, 'How did you know when I was coming?' He said, 'Swami asked me to go to Bangalore airport and fetch you.' I had not informed Swami about my travel

plans. I reached Brindavan. Swami called me, but he didn't talk to me. He went upstairs. I stepped outside the house. Looking up, I saw Swami framed behind the window grill.

When he came down later, I told him, 'Swami, they (doctors) are saying that Ratanlal had a heart attack and has no chance of survival. And you are saying that it was not a heart attack. I am confused. The doctors are not telling him about his real condition. He continues to lead a normal life. He is not resting...' I did not finish my sentence. Swami said, 'Come on the 21st, attend the birthday on the 23rd and return.'

I returned to Bombay. I telephoned Dr Dastur, the family doctor. I told him, 'I am leaving for Parthi tomorrow. Please take care of Ratanlal in my absence; do home visits with the specialists, like at present, and monitor his condition. Call me if anything is required.'

Dr Dastur was very unhappy. Instead, he was angry. He said, 'Brij, do you understand Ratanlal's condition? I am warning you. We may have to send you word that he is no more. Please reconsider leaving. I suggest that you stay back because it is a Chinese attack. It is not showing on the patient, but the ECG is deteriorating, and we are expecting the end any minute.'

On the morning of the 22nd, I quietly left for Parthi. I never spoke to the doctor. I never spoke to anyone. I packed a small bag, went to the airport, bought a ticket and left. I arrived in Bangalore, took a cab and reached Parthi. As soon as I entered the ashram gate, I saw Prof. Kasturi. He was waiting for me. When he saw me, he said, 'This is my third trip to the gate. Swami frequently asks, "Why has she not come? Why has she not come?"'

I told Kasturi, 'Mr Kasturi, please wait. My condition is terrible. I must pay a penny.' I wanted to visit the washroom. He said, 'No penny, wenny. You come straight to Swami. He is waiting.'

I walked to the end of the small hall. There was a meeting of the volunteers and *Seva dal*. Swami was standing there. Swami looked at me. I immediately said, 'Swami, I have to go for number one.' He said, 'Run and come back.' Swami was still standing there when I returned. He had a plate of food in his hand. I had not eaten all day long. He said, 'You finish this. You go, have a bath and then come to *Shanti Vedika*.[88] I will wait for you.'

I didn't know why Swami wanted me in Shanti Vedika. I was unaware that Raj Mata had given a silver *jhoola*[89] to Swami. When I reached *Shanti Vedika*, I noticed a curtain around it hiding what was inside. Swami was there with the priests and *puja samagri*[90]. I walked up. Kasturi saw me. He called me inside. Swami saw me and asked me, 'Start the puja of the jhoola.' I was a little hesitant. I said, 'Swami, Raj Mata has given the jhoola. She will be unhappy when she comes and sees me doing the puja.' I jocularly added, 'And she will cut my neck.' Swami immediately responded, 'Do the puja. Don't worry. Do the puja because I am telling you. I will save you when Raj Mata sees you and cuts your neck. You don't worry.' Raj Mata walked in when nearly half the puja was over. She saw me and started showering her blessings. She said, 'I was apprehensive about who would do the puja. I have no one from my family here. I don't have my daughter here. You are like my daughter. You are my daughter.'

The puja finished. This was the 22nd. I returned to my room. On the 23rd, I was sitting at the end of the hall. I got a sense that Swami was trying to locate me. Only Prof. Kasturi knew me. No one knew Mrs Ratanlal. Ultimately, Kasturi came and found me. He said, 'Swami is calling you.' I went upstairs. Swami said, 'I have told Java to be near the Ganesh gate. The taxi to take you to Bangalore will be there. Leave at 4:00 am. You will reach the airport at 7:00 am. Catch the 8:30 am flight to Bombay. Take the ticket and return to Bombay with my blessings.'

I reached Bombay airport and took a taxi to the house. I apprehensively rang the bell, not knowing what to expect. As the door opened, I saw five people (doctors) in the place. Dr Dastur looked at me and said, 'Congratulations. The silent heart attack, which had no symptoms or mild symptoms, has passed. It has had no impact on Ratanlal. Now we are happy and relaxed.'[91]

DISCOVERY AND CHANGE

The person who meets Swami experiences a revelation and understanding of the divine truth. They realize that the understanding and awareness evoked within them in their engagement with Swami was orchestrated and masterminded by Him. The engagement with Swami consisted of the encounter, scaffolding of belief, and the induction of a need for a steady spiritual relationship with Him. This need motivates individuals to transform their thoughts and behaviours to establish a lasting and unshakable connection with Swami.

An American developmental psychologist, Prof. Gardner, recognized the characteristics of how people change.

Behavioural change is a fundamental transformation catalysed by multiple influences like changing context and perceptions, new experiences and meeting influential and religious personalities.

> Change is possible when individuals undergo dramatic experiences or encounter luminous personalities or in new surroundings, encircled by peers of a different kind with different mindsets.[92]

Motivation for personal change begins by establishing a meaningful relationship with an important person.

> When a person attempts to craft a change of mind, it is necessary to create a relationship of trust between people.[93]

Hislop interprets Swami's ability to create lasting change in people as an indicator of His divinity.

> The lady had felt a change in her character while with Baba. The 'experience' of difference persisted even after she returned home. Swami, whose being is so subtle, powerful, mysterious and divine that he can change the human heart.[94]

Swami's engagement with a person is always strategic and spiritual. His interventions are based on His acute understanding of human psychology. There are no chance occurrences in what He does with a person. He is never subjective, random or arbitrary. In the following excerpt, Prof. Gokak identifies Swami's incredible capacity to know and understand everyone.

> (He) can read a human being like an open book.[95]

James describes a person's belief-based metamorphosis. He distinguishes between assurance-based confidence in God and belief-based conviction about God. The evocation of confident belief transforms a person. They become sure about God, feel protected by the certainty of God's grace and believe that God will always be by their side in life. As a result, their worries disappear. They become sensitive to their spiritual purpose. Conscious that God permeates everything, they see the world from a new perspective. Love for God becomes the basis of their life. James aptly describes what transpires when a person meets Swami.

> The characteristics of the affective experience (with God), which should be called the state of assurance rather than the faith state, can be easily enumerated. However, it isn't easy to realize their intensity unless one has been through the experience.
>
> The central one is the loss of all the worry, the sense that all is ultimately well with one, the peace, the harmony, the willingness to be, even though the external conditions should remain the same. The certainty of God's grace, justification and salvation is an objective belief that usually accompanies change. A passion for willingness, surrender and admiration is the glowing centre of this state of mind.
>
> The second feature is the sense of perceiving truths not known before. The mysteries of life become lucid; usually, the solution is more or less unutterable in words.
>
> A third peculiarity of the assurance state is the objective change that the world appears to undergo. 'An appearance of newness beautifies every object.'[96]

Underhill conveys that belief is a catalyst for the transformation of a person's way of life. Belief in God, arising from a spiritual experience, can be identified by three distinct attributes:

1. Unshakable conviction and confidence in the reality, nearness and accessibility of God.
2. The emergence of intense love for God is a predominant emotion.
3. A firm determination to lead a spiritual life, driven by this conviction and love.

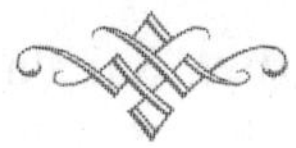

COPYRIGHT ACKNOWLEDGEMENTS

Grateful acknowledgement is made to the following for permission to reprint copyright material:

Penguin Random House for the extracts from *Baba* by Arnold Schulman.

Penguin Random House India for the extracts from *Sri Sathya Sai Baba: A Life* by Bill Aitken.

Sri Ramanasramam for the extracts from *Talks with Sri Ramana Maharshi.*

Abhinav Publications for the extracts from *Bhagavan Sri Sathya Sai Baba* by Dr V.K. Gokak.

Sri Ramakrishna Math, Chennai, for the extracts from *The Gospel of Sri Ramakrishna* by Mahendranath Gupta.

Suzie Parvati Reeves for the extracts from her book *Heaven is This.*

Dr Samuel Sandweiss for the extracts from his book *With Love Man is God.*

Sri Sathya Sai Central Trust, Prasanthi Nilayam, for the extracts from the following books:

- *Prema Dhaara* by Sri Sathya Sai Baba
- *Prema Dhaara 3* by Sri Sathya Sai Baba
- *Bhagavatha Vahini* by Sri Sathya Sai Baba
- *Gita Vahini* by Sri Sathya Sai Baba
- *Ramakatha Rasavahini I and II* by Sri Sathya Sai Baba
- *Discourses on the Bhagavad Gita* by Sri Sathya Sai Baba
- *Sathya Sai Speaks Vols. 1 to 42* by Sri Sathya Sai Baba

- *Jnana Vahini* by Sri Sathya Sai Baba
- *Prema Vahini* by Sri Sathya Sai Baba
- *Summer Roses on the Blue Mountains* by Sri Sathya Sai Baba
- *My Baba and I* by John S. Hislop
- *Sai Baba: The Ultimate Experience* by Phyllis Krystal
- *A Catholic Priest Meets Sai Baba* by Don Mario Mazzoleni
- *My Beloved* by Charles Penn
- *Love is My Form* by B.V. Ramana Rao
- *Sai Baba: The Holy Man and The Psychiatrist* by Samuel H. Sandweiss
- *Spirit and the Mind* by Samuel H. Sandweiss

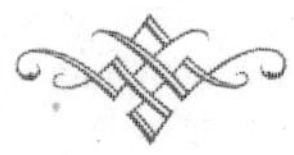

NOTES

BOOK IS A SELF-TEST

1. Sathya Sai Speaks: Discourses by Sri Sathya Sai Baba (translated into English), https://sssbpt.info/english/sss.htm.

PREFACE

1. Swami or Baba are ways of addressing Sathya Sai Baba; appellations are used interchangeably throughout the book. In the literal sense, a swami is a spiritual teacher, guru or master. The term swami can designate a person. It is used either before or after the subject's name. The meaning of the Sanskrit root of the word swami is '[he who is] one with his self' (swa stands for 'self') and is roughly translated as 'he/she who knows and is master of himself/herself'. Baba is a respectful form for addressing an older man or holy man.
2. Brindavan is Swami's residence in Bangalore, Karnataka, India.
3. Ethnography is a research method used in social and behavioural sciences, and studies how people live, behave and interact in their natural environment. Researchers conduct ethnography by becoming a part of the community or organization and immersing themselves in the social grouping they are trying to understand. As members of the community, they can closely observe how people behave and interact, ask questions, make notes, take interviews, seek clarifications to discern the thinking that underlies behaviour, etc. This data and information allow researchers to understand the social, cultural and historical context in which individuals live and interact.
4. A study circle is a gathering of spiritually-oriented people who read excerpts from books. 'Circle, study and circle' sums up what happens in the meeting. One person reads a passage, and then each person examines and talks about what the passage means to them. A study circle looks at different aspects of a spiritual idea.
5. Triangulation refers to using multiple methods or data sources in research to develop a comprehensive understanding of a phenomenon.
6. James, William, *The Varieties of Religious Experience*, Longmans, Green, and Co., New York, 1902. The Project Gutenberg eBook, 2014, https://www.gutenberg.org/files/621/621-h/621-h.html.
7. Underhill, Evelyn, *Mysticism*, Methuen & Co. Ltd., London, 1911, 146, https://ccel.org/ccel/underhill/mysticism.
8. In this book, I use the terms 'spiritual aspirant', 'seeker of God' and 'devotee' interchangeably. A devotee is a person who is extremely loyal to a particular religion, religious figure or God.
9. Aitken, Bill, *Sri Sathya Sai Baba: A Life*, Penguin India, New Delhi, 2006, 1–2.
10. Sathya Sai Speaks: Discourses by Sri Sathya Sai Baba (translated into English), https://sssbpt.info/english/sss.htm.

11. 'Significance of Vibhuti', https://www.saibabaofindia.com/significanceofvibhuti.htm. Vibhuti is sacred ash made of burnt, dried wood. Vibhuti is the most precious object in a spiritual sense. Shiva burnt the God of Desire into a heap of ashes because he agitates the mind and increases existing confusion. When the God of Desire was destroyed, Prema (Love) reigned supreme. Applying this Holy Ash reminds us to achieve our victory over desire. Ash is the ultimate condition; it cannot undergo any further change. Ash cannot fade as flowers do in a day or two. It does not dry and disappear or get soiled and unpotable as water does. It does not lose colour as leaves do in a few hours and does not rot as fruits do in a few days. Ash is ash forever and ever. This state of ash reminds us of our true nature, the Atma, our soul. Our soul never undergoes any change. So burn your vices and bad habits and worship the Lord, rendering yourself pure in thought, word and deed. Reach the state of nothingness and attain liberation by absorbing the essence of the vibhuti.
12. Sagar, B.V.S.S., Personal Interview, 2008.
13. James, William, *The Varieties of Religious Experience*, Longmans, Green, and Co., New York, 1902. The Project Gutenberg eBook, 2014, https://www.gutenberg.org/files/621/621-h/621-h.html.
14. Underhill, Evelyn, *Mysticism*, Methuen & Co. Ltd., London, 1911, 146, https://ccel.org/ccel/underhill/mysticism.
15. Ibid.
16. James, William, *The Varieties of Religious Experience*, Longmans, Green, and Co., New York, 1902. The Project Gutenberg eBook, 2014, https://www.gutenberg.org/files/621/621-h/621-h.html.
17. Ibid.
18. Ibid.

INTRODUCTION

1. James, William, *The Varieties of Religious Experience*, Longmans, Green, and Co., New York, 1902. The Project Gutenberg eBook, 2014, https://www.gutenberg.org/files/621/621-h/621-h.html.
2. Ibid.
3. Sathya Sai Speaks: Discourses by Sri Sathya Sai Baba (translated into English), https://sssbpt.info/english/sss.htm.
4. Living organisms.
5. A sadhaka is someone who follows a particular *sadhana* or way of life designed to realize the goal of one's ultimate ideal, whether it is merging with one's eternal source, brahman, or realizing one's deity.
6. Sathya Sai Baba, *Jnana Vahini: Stream of Spiritual Wisdom*, Sri Sathya Sai Sadhana Trust, Anantapur, 2014, https://www.sssbpt.info/vahinis/Jnana/JnanaVahiniInteractive.pdf.
7. James, William, *The Varieties of Religious Experience*, Longmans, Green, and Co., New York, 1902. The Project Gutenberg eBook, 2014, https://www.gutenberg.org/files/621/621-h/621-h.html.
8. Sri Sathya Sai Baba, *Discourses on the Bhagavad Gita*, Sri Sathya Sai Sadhana Trust, Anantapur, 1988.
9. Manning, Brennan, *Ruthless Trust: The Ragamuffin's Path to God*, HarperCollins Publishers Inc., New York, NY, 2000. Brennan Manning was an American author and laicized priest (lost his legal status as a cleric).

10. Underhill, Evelyn, *Mysticism*, Methuen & Co. Ltd., London, 1911, 152, https://ccel.org/ccel/underhill/mysticism.
11. Trevor, John, *My Quest For God*, Kessinger Publishing, Whitefish, MT, 2007, 32, https://archive.org/details/myquestforgod00trev/page/32/mode/1up.
12. Fowler, James W., *Stages of Faith*, HarperCollins Publishers Inc., New York, NY, 1981, 18.
13. Underhill, Evelyn, *Mysticism*, Methuen & Co. Ltd., London, 1911, https://ccel.org/ccel/underhill/mysticism.
14. James, William, *The Varieties of Religious Experience*, Longmans, Green, and Co., New York, 1902. The Project Gutenberg eBook, 2014, https://www.gutenberg.org/files/621/621-h/621-h.html.
15. Fowler, James W., *Stages of Faith*, HarperCollins Publishers Inc., New York, NY, 1981, 11–16.
16. Sri Sathya Sai Baba, *Gita Vahini*, Sri Sathya Sai Sadhana Trust, Anantapur, 2010, https://www.sssbpt.info/english/vgita.htm.
17. Kempis, Thomas á, *The Imitation of Christ*, William Collins Sons & Co. Ltd., Glasgow, 1963, The Project Gutenberg eBook, 2023, 27–29, https://www.gutenberg.org/ebooks/1653.
18. Sandweiss, Samuel H., *Sai Baba: The Holy Man and the Psychiatrist*, Sri Sathya Sai Sadhana Trust, Anantapur, 1975, 197.
19. James, William, *The Varieties of Religious Experience*, Longmans, Green, and Co., New York, The Project Gutenberg eBook, 1999, 208, https://www.gutenberg.org/files/621/621-h/621-h.html.
20. 'He is My Swami: Part I', *Radio Sai Listeners' Journal*, Vol. 5, No. 5, 2007, https://archive.sssmediacentre.org/journals/Vol_05/01MAY07/14-h2h_special.htm.
21. Manning, Brennan, *Ruthless Trust: The Ragamuffin's Path to God*, HarperCollins Publishers Inc., New York, NY, 2000, 3–7.
22. Dalrymple, Galen C., 'There Are No Bad Days', *DayBreaks Devotions*, 13 January 2021, https://daybreaksdevotions.wordpress.com/2021/01/13/daybreaks-for-1-13-21-there-are-no-bad-days/.
23. Manning, Brennan, *Ruthless Trust: The Ragamuffin's Path to God*, HarperCollins Publishers Inc., New York, NY, 2000, 88.
24. Sri Sathya Sai Baba, *Bhagavatha Vahini*, Sri Sathya Sai Sadhana Trust, Anantapur, 1970, 9–10, http://vahini.org/downloads/vahinispdf/Bhagavatha.pdf.
25. Haraldsson, Erlendur, *Miracles Are My Visiting Cards*, Sai Tower Publishing, Bangalore, 1997, 120.
26. Underhill, Evelyn, *Mysticism*, Methuen & Co. Ltd., London, 1911, 277, https://ccel.org/ccel/underhill/mysticism.
27. Trevor, John, *My Quest For God,* Kessinger Publishing, Whitefish, MT, 2007, 175, https://archive.org/details/myquestforgod00trev/page/32/mode/1up.
28. Gupta, Mahendranath, *The Gospel of Sri Ramakrishna*, Sri Ramakrishna Math, Chennai, 1944, 148.
29. Ibid., 102–103
30. Tzu, Lao, *Tao Te Ching*, http://www.wussu.com/laotzu/laotzu56.html.
31. Aitken, Bill, *Sri Sathya Sai Baba: A Life*, Penguin India, New Delhi, 2006, 77.
32. Sri Sathya Sai Baba, *Discourses on the Bhagavad Gita*, Sri Sathya Sai Sadhana Trust, Anantapur, 1988, 152–153.
33. Menon, Nityananda T., in *Golden Age*, Kingdom of Sathya Sai, Bangalore, 1979, 11.
34. Sathya Sai Speaks: Discourses by Sri Sathya Sai Baba (translated into English), https://sssbpt.info/english/sss.htm.

CHAPTER 1: BELIEF AS AWAKENING

1. Fowler, James W., *Stages of Faith*, HarperCollins Publishers Inc., New York, NY, 1981, 18.
2. Gardner, Howard, *Changing Minds: The Art and Science of Changing Our Own and Other People's Minds*, Harvard Business School Publishing, Boston, MA, 2004, 187, https://archive.org/details/changingmindsart00gard/. Howard Earl Gardner is an American developmental psychologist and Professor of Cognition and Education at Harvard University.
3. Underhill, Evelyn, *Mysticism*, Methuen & Co. Ltd., London, 1911, 152, https://ccel.org/ccel/underhill/mysticism.
4. Ibid. 163
5. Manning, Brennan, *Ruthless Trust: The Ragamuffin's Path to God*, HarperCollins Publishers Inc., New York, NY, 2000, 98.
6. Sandweiss, Samuel H., *Spirit and the Mind*, Sri Sathya Sai Sadhana Trust, Anantapur, 1985, 82.
7. Fowler, James W., *Stages of Faith*, HarperCollins Publishers Inc., New York, NY, 1981, 11.
8. Sri Sathya Sai Baba, *Gita Vahini*, Sri Sathya Sai Sadhana Trust, Anantapur, 2010, 228–229, https://www.sssbpt.info/vahinis/Gita/GitaVahiniInteractive.pdf.

CHAPTER 2: SPIRITUAL QUEST

1. Sathya Sai Speaks: Discourses by Sri Sathya Sai Baba (translated into English), https://sssbpt.info/english/sss.htm.
2. Kumar, Anil, Personal Interview, 2008.
3. Sri Sathya Sai Baba, *Prema Dhaara: A Collection of Letters from Bhagavan Sri Sathya Sai Baba to His Students*, Sri Sathya Sai Sadhana Trust, Anantapur, 1999, 24.
4. Merton, Thomas, *The Seven Storey Mountain*, Harcourt, Inc., Orlando, FL, 1999, 31.
5. Tolstoy, Leo, *A Confession*, 1882, 3, https://archive.org/details/leo-tolstoy_a-confession_aylmer-maude/page/n1/mode/2up.
6. Ibid. 8
7. Ibid. 8
8. Ibid. 4
9. Ibid. 6
10. Ibid. 8
11. Ibid. 2, 8
12. Ibid. 12
13. Ibid. 14–15
14. Ibid. 16–17
15. Fowler, James W., *Stages of Faith*, HarperCollins Publishers Inc., New York, NY, 1981, xii.
16. Pagels, Elaine, *Beyond Belief*, Random House, New York, NY, 2003, 4–6.
17. Christian doctrinal beliefs are inviolable. First, Christians believe there's only one God, and He created the Heaven and the Earth. The Divine Godhead consists of the trinity: the Father (God himself), the Son (Jesus Christ) and the Holy Spirit. Second, the essence of Christianity revolves around the life, death and resurrection of Jesus. Christians believe that God sent his son Jesus, the Messiah, to save the world. They believe Jesus was crucified on the cross to offer the forgiveness of sins and was resurrected three days after his death before ascending to Heaven. Third, Christians contend that Jesus will return to

earth again in the Second Coming. Fourth, the Holy Bible includes essential scriptures that outline Jesus' teachings and offer instructions for how Christians should live.

18. A deeper connection with God involves developing a direct connection with God, allowing them to talk to and spend time with Him. They can pray/talk to God about the things in their life and receive guidance from Him.
19. Pagels, Elaine, *Beyond Belief*, Random House, New York, NY, 2003, 26–27.
20. Mazzoleni, Mario, *A Catholic Priest Meet Sai Baba*, Sri Sathya Sai Sadhana Trust, Anantapur, 2002, 10, 16.
21. Salzberg, Sharon, *Faith*, Riverhead Books, New York, NY, 2002, 118.
22. Mazzoleni, Mario, *A Catholic Priest Meet Sai Baba*, Sri Sathya Sai Sadhana Trust, Anantapur, 2002, 12.
23. Sri Sathya Sai Baba, *Sanathana Sarathi*, https://sathyasaibaba.wordpress.com/2009/05/29/aconversation-with-sri-sathya-sai-baba/.
24. *Talks with Sri Ramana Maharshi*, Sri Ramanasramam, Tiruvannamalai, 1955, 547.
25. Fowler, James W., *Stages of Faith*, HarperCollins Publishers Inc., New York, NY, 1981, xi–xii.
26. Mazzoleni, Mario, *A Catholic Priest Meet Sai Baba*, Sri Sathya Sai Sadhana Trust, Anantapur, 2002, 21.
27. Tolstoy, Leo, *A Confession*, 1882, 46–47, https://archive.org/details/leo-tolstoy_a-confession_aylmer-maude/page/n1/mode/2up.
28. Ibid. 48–49
29. Ibid. 66–67
30. Merton, Thomas, *The Seven Storey Mountain*, Harcourt, Inc., Orlando, FL, 1999, 125.
31. Tolstoy, Leo, *A Confession*, 1882, 20–21, https://archive.org/details/leo-tolstoy_a-confession_aylmer-maude/page/n1/mode/2up.
32. Ibid. 49–50
33. Ibid. 50–51
34. Sathya Sai Speaks: Discourses by Sri Sathya Sai Baba (translated into English), https://sssbpt.info/english/sss.htm.
35. Sri Sathya Sai Baba, *Discourses on the Bhagavad Gita*, Sri Sathya Sai Sadhana Trust, Anantapur, 1988, 101.

CHAPTER 3: BEING READY FOR GOD

1. Schulman, Arnold, *Baba*, The Viking Press, New York, NY, 1971, 168.
2. Baskin, Diana, *Divine Memories of Sathya Sai Baba*, Sri Sathya Sai Sadhana Trust, Anantapur, 1990, 15.
3. Schulman, Arnold, *Baba*, The Viking Press, New York, NY, 1971, 103.
4. Mazzoleni, Mario, *A Catholic Priest Meet Sai Baba*, Sri Sathya Sai Sadhana Trust, Anantapur, 2002, 11.
5. Iyer, Sunder, Speech at the Cleveland Sai Center, 2003.
6. *Talks with Sri Ramana Maharshi*, Sri Ramanasramam, Tiruvannamalai, 1955, 138.
7. Iyer, Sunder, Speech at the Cleveland Sai Center, 2003.
8. Penn, Charles, *My Beloved*, Sri Sathya Sai Foundation of Trinidad and Tobago, Port of Spain, 1981, 10.
9. *Nine Gems: Part 2*, Sri Sathya Sai Scriptural Studies Committee, Anantapur, https://www.sathyasai.org/birthday/2021/study-guides.
10. Sathya Sai Speaks: Discourses by Sri Sathya Sai Baba (translated into English), https://sssbpt.info/english/sss.htm.
11. Ibid.

12. Sandweiss, Samuel H., *With Love: Man is God*, Birthday Publishing Co., San Diego, CA, 2004, 184.
13. Sathya Sai Speaks: Discourses by Sri Sathya Sai Baba (translated into English), https://saispeaks.sathyasai.org/discourse/sweeten-and-lighten-life.
14. Aitken, Bill, *Sri Sathya Sai Baba: A Life*, Penguin India, New Delhi, 2006, 221–222.
15. Kelman, John, *Among Famous Books*, Hodder and Stoughton, New York, NY, 1912, https://archive.org/details/amongfamousbook00kelmgoog/page/n6/mode/2up.
16. Thompson, Francis, *The Hound of Heaven*, 1890, http://www.houndofheaven.com/poem.
17. Kelman, John, *Among Famous Books*, Hodder and Stoughton, New York, NY, 1912, 309, 311–312, https://archive.org/details/amongfamousbook00kelmgoog/page/n6/mode/2up.
18. Ibid.
19. Mazzoleni, Mario, *A Catholic Priest Meet Sai Baba*, Sri Sathya Sai Sadhana Trust, Anantapur, 2002, 63.
20. Schulman, Arnold, *Baba*, The Viking Press, New York, NY, 1971, 16.
21. Mazzoleni, Mario, *A Catholic Priest Meet Sai Baba*, Sri Sathya Sai Sadhana Trust, Anantapur, 2002, 54–56.
22. Ibid. 8
23. Tolstoy, Leo, *A Confession*, 1882, 64, https://archive.org/details/leo-tolstoy_a-confession_aylmer-maude/page/n1/mode/2up.
24. Ibid. 64
25. Ibid. 64
26. Sandweiss, Samuel H., *Sai Baba: The Holy Man and the Psychiatrist*, Sri Sathya Sai Sadhana Trust, Anantapur, 1975, 68.
27. Tillich, Paul, *The Courage To Be*, Yale University Press, New Haven and London, 1952, xxi–xxii. Paul Johannes Tillich was a Christian philosopher and theologian who is regarded as one of the most influential theologians of the 20th century.
28. Aitken, Bill, *Sri Sathya Sai Baba: A Life*, Penguin India, New Delhi, 2006, 12–13.
29. Sandweiss, Samuel H., *Sai Baba: The Holy Man and the Psychiatrist*, Sri Sathya Sai Sadhana Trust, Anantapur, 1975, 45.
30. Kumar, Anil, Personal Interview, 2008.
31. Reddy, N., 'The Source, Sweetness and Sustenance of My Life: My Sai', *Radio Sai Listeners' Journal*, Vol. 5, No. 6, 2007, https://archive.sssmediacentre.org/journals/Vol_05/01JUN07/07-nreddy.html.
32. Gupta, Mahendranath, *The Gospel of Sri Ramakrishna*, Sri Ramakrishna Math, Chennai, 1944, 270.
33. Sri Sathya Sai Baba, *Gita Vahini*, Sri Sathya Sai Sadhana Trust, Anantapur, 2010, 13, https://www.sssbpt.info/vahinis/Gita/GitaVahiniInteractive.pdf.
34. Sri Sathya Sai Baba, *Discourses on the Bhagavad Gita*, Sri Sathya Sai Sadhana Trust, Anantapur, 1988, 99.
35. Ramana Rao, B.V., *Love Is My Form*, Sri Sathya Sai Sadhana Trust, Anantapur, 2000, 3, 21. Ramana Rao was one of the first Seva Dal coordinators when the Sri Sathya Sai Organization was in its infancy. He was the editor of the *Sanathan Sarathi* magazine for many years.
36. Sri Sathya Sai Baba, *Prema Dhaara 3*, Sri Sathya Sai Sadhana Trust, Anantapur, 2009, 74.
37. Bhagvantham, S, 'The Myriad Facets of Sri Sathya Sai Baba', *Hridya Brindavan: A Garland of Gratitude*, Sri Sathya Sai Hostel, Bangalore, 1977, 24–25.
38. Underhill, Evelyn, *Mysticism*, Methuen & Co. Ltd., London, 1911, https://ccel.org/ccel/underhill/mysticism.
39. Mazzoleni, Mario, *A Catholic Priest Meet Sai Baba*, Sri Sathya Sai Sadhana Trust, Anantapur, 2002, 46.

40. Changkakoti, Rupak, Personal Interview, 2009.
41. Sheen, Fulton J., *Life of Christ*, Image Books/Doubleday, New York, NY, 1977, 45, https://sacredheartshrine.org/wp-content/uploads/2018/08/Life-of-Christ-Fulton-J.-Sheen.pdf.
42. Sathya Sai Speaks: Discourses by Sri Sathya Sai Baba (translated into English), https://sssbpt.info/english/sss.htm.
43. *Sayings of Ramakrishna*, https://sriramakrishna.in/2018/01/19/the-master-in-various-moods/. Ramakrishna Paramahansa is regarded as an avatar, the manifestation of God on earth.
44. 'The Master in Various Moods', http://ramakrishnateachings.blogspot.com/2010/04/sri-ramakrishna-god-cannot-be-realized.html.
45. Sheen, Fulton J., *Life of Christ*, Image Books/Doubleday, New York, NY, 1977, 30, https://sacredheartshrine.org/wp-content/uploads/2018/08/Life-of-Christ-Fulton-J.-Sheen.pdf.
46. *Talks with Sri Ramana Maharshi*, Sri Ramanasramam, Tiruvannamalai, 1955, 535.
47. Sheen, Fulton J., *Life of Christ*, Image Books/Doubleday, New York, NY, 1977, 28–29, https://sacredheartshrine.org/wp-content/uploads/2018/08/Life-of-Christ-Fulton-J.-Sheen.pdf.
48. Merton, Thomas, *The Seven Storey Mountain*, Harcourt, Inc., Orlando, FL, 1999, 125.
49. Sri Sathya Sai Baba, *Ramakatha Rasavahini II*, Sri Sathya Sai Sadhana Trust, Anantapur, 2002, 43–44.
50. Sandweiss, Samuel H., *Sai Baba: The Holy Man and The Psychiatrist*, Sri Sathya Sai Sadhana Trust, Anantapur, 1975, 29–30.
51. Krystal, Phyllis, *Sai Baba: The Ultimate Experience*, Sri Sathya Sai Sadhana Trust, Anantapur, 1998, 11–12.
52. Reeves, Suzie P., *Heaven is This*, Sai Tower Publishing, Bangalore, 2001, 20–23. Suzie Parvati Reeves was a Canadian fashion designer and boutique owner. From 1976 to 2000, she lived in Prasanthi Nilayam and Brindavan ashram (religious community).
53. Krystal, Phyllis, *Sai Baba: The Ultimate Experience*, Sri Sathya Sai Sadhana Trust, Anantapur, 1998, 21–23.
54. Reeves, Suzie P., *Heaven is This*, Sai Tower Publishing, Bangalore, 2001, 28.
55. Ibid. 27–28
56. Schulman, Arnold, *Baba*. The Viking Press, New York, NY, 1971, 16.
57. Reeves, Suzie P., *Heaven is This*, Sai Tower Publishing, Bangalore, 2001, 94–95.
58. Mazzoleni, Mario, *A Catholic Priest Meet Sai Baba*, Sri Sathya Sai Sadhana Trust, Anantapur, 2002, 53–56.
59. Ibid. 39–40
60. Ibid. 58
61. Baskin, Diana, *Divine Memories of Sathya Sai Baba*, Sri Sathya Sai Sadhana Trust, Anantapur, 1990, 13–14. Diana Baskin has authored three books about her experiences with Swami. She met Swami in 1969 and visited India many times each year to spend time with Swami.
62. 'Mesmerizing Moments with the Divine Master', *Radio Sai Listeners' Journal*, Vol. 6, No. 4, 2008, http://media.radiosai.org/Journals/Vol_06/01APR08/14-h2h_special.htm.
63. Ramana Rao, B.V., *Love Is My Form*, Sri Sathya Sai Sadhana Trust, Anantapur, 2000, 5–16.
64. Samarpan and Practical Spirituality: Talks by Sathyajit Salian, YouTube, https://www.youtube.com/watch?v=CurEidEPOx0; https://www.youtube.com/watch?v=AHt_-yvKBDA. Salian served Swami for many years.
65. Ibid.
66. Ibid.
67. Ibid.
68. Reeves, Suzie P., *Heaven is This*, Sai Tower Publishing, Bangalore, 2001, 95–96.

69. Manning, Brennan, *Ruthless Trust: The Ragamuffin's Path to God*, HarperCollins Publishers Inc., New York, NY, 2000, 64.
70. Schulman, Arnold, *Baba*, The Viking Press, New York, NY, 1971, 21.
71. Ibid. 23
72. Ibid. 76
73. Mazzoleni, Mario, *A Catholic Priest Meet Sai Baba*, Sri Sathya Sai Sadhana Trust, Anantapur, 2002, 63.
74. Iyer, Sunder, Speech at the Cleveland Sai Center, 2003.
75. Sandweiss, Samuel H., *Sai Baba The Holy Man and The Psychiatrist*, Sri Sathya Sai Sadhana Trust, Anantapur, 1975, 19–21.
76. Schulman, Arnold, *Baba*, The Viking Press, New York, NY, 1971, 26.
77. 'Marks of True Devotion (Part 1)', Ramakrishna-Vivekananda Center of New York, https://ramakrishna.org/marksoftruedevotion1.html.
78. Photographic plates preceded photographic film as a capture medium in photography. The light-sensitive emulsion of silver salts was coated on a glass plate.
79. Gupta, Mahendranath, *The Gospel of Sri Ramakrishna*, Sri Ramakrishna Math, Chennai, 1944, 142, 276. https://estudantedavedanta.net/THE%20GOSPEL%20OF%20SRI%20RAMAKRISHNA.pdf.

CHAPTER 4: FACE TO FACE WITH GOD

1. Underhill, Evelyn, *Mysticism*, Methuen & Co. Ltd., London, 1911, https://ccel.org/ccel/underhill/mysticism.
2. James, William, *The Varieties of Religious Experience*, Longmans, Green, and Co., New York, 1902. The Project Gutenberg eBook, 2014, https://www.gutenberg.org/files/621/621-h/621-h.html.
3. Merton, Thomas, *The Seven Storey Mountain*, Harcourt, Inc., Orlando, FL, 1999, 311–312.
4. Souljourns | Christian Moevs | Sai Baba, YouTube, https://youtu.be/fJgIdbzY-1k?si=QOOz49-Stm3DlPI. Christian Moevs is professor emeritus of Italian at the University of Notre Dame.
5. Underhill, Evelyn, *Mysticism*, Methuen & Co. Ltd., London, 1911, https://ccel.org/ccel/underhill/mysticism.
6. Ibid. 165
7. Ibid. 307
8. Manning, Brennan, *Ruthless Trust: The Ragamuffin's Path to God*, HarperCollins Publishers Inc., New York, NY, 2000, 52.
9. Sandweiss, Samuel H., *Sai Baba The Holy Man and The Psychiatrist*, Sri Sathya Sai Sadhana Trust, Anantapur, 1975, 49.
10. Gupta, Mahendranath, *The Gospel of Sri Ramakrishna*, Sri Ramakrishna Math, Chennai, 1944, 734.
11. James, William, *The Varieties of Religious Experience*, Longmans, Green, and Co., New York, 1902. The Project Gutenberg eBook, 2014, https://www.gutenberg.org/files/621/621-h/621-h.html.
12. Ibid.
13. Brainerd, David, 'Oh, That I May Never Loiter on My Heavenly Journey', Desiring God, 31 January 1990, https://www.desiringgod.org/messages/oh-that-i-may-never-loiter-on-my-heavenly-journey.
14. James, William, *The Varieties of Religious Experience*, Longmans, Green, and Co., New York, 1902. The Project Gutenberg eBook, 2014, https://www.gutenberg.org/files/621/621-h/621-h.html.

15. 'An Introduction to Sri Ramana's Life and Teachings', DavidGodman.org, https://www.davidgodman.org/an-introduction-to-sri-ramanas-life-and-teachings/.
16. James, William, *The Varieties of Religious Experience*, Longmans, Green, and Co., New York, 1902. The Project Gutenberg eBook, 2014, https://www.gutenberg.org/files/621/621-h/621-h.html.
17. Ibid.
18. Ibid.
19. Coe, George A., *The Spiritual Life: Studies in the Science of Religion*, Eaton & Mains, New York, 1900, https://archive.org/details/spirituallifest02coegoog.
20. Sri Sathya Sai Baba, *Bhagavatha Vahini*, Sri Sathya Sai Sadhana Trust, Anantapur, 1970, 85.
21. Sheen, Fulton J., *Life of Christ*, Image Books/Doubleday, New York, NY, 1977, 28, https://sacredheartshrine.org/wp-content/uploads/2018/08/Life-of-Christ-Fulton-J.-Sheen.pdf.
22. Ibid. 29
23. Kasturi, N., 'Resume (1926–1961)', Sathyam Sivam Sundaram: The Life of Bhagavan Sri Sathya Sai Baba, http://vahini.org/sss/ii/resume.html.
24. Vijay Sai, B.S., 'My Sweet Sai', *Trayee Saptamayee*, Sri Sathya Sai Institute of Higher Learning, Bangalore, 1995, 9.
25. Aitken, Bill, *Sri Sathya Sai Baba: A Life*, Penguin India, New Delhi, 2006, 141–142.
26. Schulman, Arnold, *Baba*, The Viking Press, New York, NY, 1971, 107.
27. Aitken, Bill, *Sri Sathya Sai Baba: A Life*, Penguin India, New Delhi, 2006, 247.
28. Ibid. 27–28
29. Sheen, Fulton J., *Life of Christ*, Image Books/Doubleday, New York, NY, 1977, 41–42.
30. Gokak, V.K., *Bhagavan Sri Sathya Sai Baba*, Abhinav Publications, New Delhi, 1975, 7–8.
31. Gupta, Mahendranath, *The Gospel of Sri Ramakrishna*, Sri Ramakrishna Math, Chennai, 1944, 77.
32. Schulman, Arnold, *Baba*, The Viking Press, New York, NY, 1971, 108.
33. Mazzoleni, Mario, *A Catholic Priest Meet Sai Baba*, Sri Sathya Sai Sadhana Trust, Anantapur, 2002, 65–66.
34. Roberts, Paul W., *Empire of the Soul: Some Journeys in India*, Riverhead Books, New York, NY, 1996, 24–44. Paul Roberts was a Canadian writer. His first-hand account of his six-month experience with Sri Sathya Sai Baba at Puttaparthi in 1975 was published in a fashion magazine, Vogue Canada (December 1975), https://www.sathyasai.org/inspiring-stories/sathya-sai-baba-vogue-magazine. Paul Roberts has written about his visit in his book as well.
35. Aitken, Bill, *Sri Sathya Sai Baba: A Life*, Penguin India, New Delhi, 2006, 148–149.
36. Iyer, Sunder, Speech at the Cleveland Sai Center, 2004.
37. Ratanlal, B., Personal Interview, 2011. Mrs Ratanlal cooked for Swami for nearly five decades.
38. Aitken, Bill, *Sri Sathya Sai Baba: A Life*, Penguin India, New Delhi, 2006, 31.
39. Edwards, Jonathan, *The Life of Rev. David Brainerd, Chiefly Extracted from His Diary*, American Tract Society, New York. The Project Gutenberg eBook, 2021, https://www.gutenberg.org/files/65066/65066-h/65066-h.htm.
40. Sri Sathya Sai Baba, *Ramakatha Rasavahini I*, Sri Sathya Sai Sadhana Trust, Anantapur, 2002, 158.
41. Merton, Thomas, *The Seven Storey Mountain*, Harcourt, Inc., Orlando, FL, 1999, 41.
42. Phani Kumar, N., 'Sai: My Soul, and My Goal', *Sai Nandana*, Sri Sathya Sai Senior Boys Hostel, Anantapur, 2000, 53.
43. Schulman, Arnold, *Baba*, The Viking Press, New York, NY, 1971, 84.
44. Reeves, Suzie P., *Heaven is This*, Sai Tower Publishing, Bangalore, 2001, 112–113.
45. Ibid. 107

46. Ibid. 125
47. Krystal, Phyllis, *Sai Baba: The Ultimate Experience*, Sri Sathya Sai Sadhana Trust, Anantapur, 1998, 225.
48. Aitken, Bill, *Sri Sathya Sai Baba: A Life*, Penguin India, New Delhi, 2006, 252.
49. Hislop, John S, *My Baba and I*, Sri Sathya Sai Sadhana Trust, Anantapur, 1999, 3.
50. Sandweiss, Samuel H., *Spirit and the Mind*, Sri Sathya Sai Sadhana Trust, Anantapur, 1985, 147.
51. Reeves, Suzie P., *Heaven is This*, Sai Tower Publishing, Bangalore, 2001, 127.
52. Sandweiss, Samuel H., *Sai Baba: The Holy Man and The Psychiatrist*, Sri Sathya Sai Sadhana Trust, Anantapur, 1975, 19–21.
53. Sandweiss, Samuel H., *With Love, Man is God*, Birthday Publishing Co., San Diego, CA, 2004, 67–69.
54. Krystal, Phyllis, *Sai Baba: The Ultimate Experience*, Sri Sathya Sai Sadhana Trust, Anantapur, 1998, 40–42.
55. Ramana, Rao, B.V., *Love Is My Form*, Sri Sathya Sai Sadhana Trust, Anantapur, 2000, 24–25.
56. Goldstein, Michael, 'A Discourse for Devotees', Sri Sathya Sai Baba Website, http://www.saibaba.ws/articles1/discoursegoldstein.htm.
57. Haraldsson, Erlendur, *Miracles Are My Visiting Cards*, Sai Tower Publishing, Bangalore, 1997, 153.
58. Baskin, Diana, *Divine Memories of Sathya Sai Baba*, Sri Sathya Sai Sadhana Trust, Anantapur, 1990, 16–19.
59. Ibid. 21–23
60. Schulman, Arnold, *Baba*, The Viking Press, New York, NY, 1971, 108.
61. Ramana Rao, B.V., *Love Is My Form*, Sri Sathya Sai Sadhana Trust, Anantapur, 2000, 23.
62. Gupta, Mahendranath, *The Gospel of Sri Ramakrishna*, Sri Ramakrishna Math, Chennai, 1944, 79–81.
63. 'Enthralling Encounters with Eternity', *Radio Sai Listeners' Journal*, Vol. 5, No. 10, 2007, https://archive.sssmediacentre.org/journals/Vol_05/01OCT07/14-h2h_special.htm.
64. Ibid.
65. Roberts, Paul W., *Empire of the Soul: Some Journeys in India*, Riverhead Books, New York, NY, 1996, 24–44.
66. Sathyajit Speaks in Sundaram; Samarpan: Talk by Sathyajit Salian, YouTube, https://www.youtube.com/watch?v=n1EkDctaCPg; https://www.youtube.com/watch?v=CurEidEPOx0.
67. Reeves, Suzie P., *Heaven is This*, Sai Tower Publishing, Bangalore, 2001, 160.
68. Iyer, Sunder, Speech at the Cleveland Sai Center, 2004.
69. Ramana Rao, B.V., *Love Is My Form*, Sri Sathya Sai Sadhana Trust, Anantapur, 2000,17–21.
70. Ibid. 22–23
71. Sheen, Fulton J., *Life of Christ*, Image Books/Doubleday, New York, NY, 1977, 95–99.
72. Ibid. 118
73. Ibid. 221
74. Ibid. 281
75. Iyer, Sunder, Speech at the Cleveland Sai Center, 2004.
76. Schulman, Arnold, *Baba*, The Viking Press, New York, NY, 1971, 166.
77. James, William, *The Varieties of Religious Experience*, Longmans, Green, and Co., New York, 1902. The Project Gutenberg eBook, 2014, https://www.gutenberg.org/files/621/621-h/621-h.html.
78. Souljourns | Christian Moevs | Sai Baba, YouTube, https://youtu.be/fJgIdbzY-1k?si=QOOz49-Stm3DlPI.

CHAPTER 5: LOVE BEYOND MEASURE

1. Aitken, Bill, *Sri Sathya Sai Baba: A Life*, Penguin India, New Delhi, 2006, 24–25.
2. Gupta, Mahendranath, *The Gospel of Sri Ramakrishna*, Sri Ramakrishna Math, Chennai, 1944, 725.
3. Ibid. 725–726
4. Manning, Brennan, *Ruthless Trust: The Ragamuffin's Path to God*, HarperCollins Publishers Inc., New York, NY, 2000, 65.
5. 'Mesmerizing Moments with the Divine Master', *Radio Sai Listeners' Journal*, Vol. 6, No. 4, 2008, https://archive.sssmediacentre.org/journals/Vol_06/01MAY08/14-h2h_special.htm.
6. Manning, Brennan, *Ruthless Trust: The Ragamuffin's Path to God*, Harper Collins Publishers Inc., New York, NY, 2000, 59.
7. St John of the Cross, *Dark Night of the Soul*, Christian Classics Ethereal Library, Grand Rapids, MI, 2009, 94, https://ccel.org/ccel/j/john_cross/dark_night/cache/dark_night.pdf.
8. Underhill, Evelyn, *Mysticism*, Methuen & Co. Ltd., London, 1911, https://ccel.org/ccel/underhill/mysticism.
9. James, William, *The Varieties of Religious Experience*, Longmans, Green, and Co., New York, 1902. The Project Gutenberg eBook, 2014, https://www.gutenberg.org/files/621/621-h/621-h.html.
10. Ibid.
11. Hislop, John S., in *Golden Age*, Kingdom of Sathya Sai, Bangalore, 1979, 35.
12. Manning, Brennan, *Ruthless Trust: The Ragamuffin's Path to God*, Harper Collins Publishers Inc., New Yorhk, NY, 2000, 62–63.
13. Sandweiss, Samuel H., *Spirit and the Mind*, Sri Sathya Sai Sadhana Trust, Anantapur, 1985, 209.
14. Aitken, Bill, *Sri Sathya Sai Baba: A Life*, Penguin India, New Delhi, 2006, 169–170.
15. Mazzoleni, Mario, *A Catholic Priest Meet Sai Baba*, Sri Sathya Sai Sadhana Trust, Anantapur, 2002, 119.
16. Gupta, Mahendranath, *The Gospel of Sri Ramakrishna*, Sri Ramakrishna Math, Chennai, 1944, 277.
17. Mazzoleni, Mario, *A Catholic Priest Meet Sai Baba*, Sri Sathya Sai Sadhana Trust, Anantapur, 2002, 57.
18. Ibid. 57–58
19. Sri Sathya Sai Baba, *Bhagavatha Vahini*, Sri Sathya Sai Sadhana Trust, Anantapur, 1970, 216.
20. Sri Sathya Sai Baba, *Ramakatha Rasavahini II*, Sri Sathya Sai Sadhana Trust, Anantapur, 2002, 41–42.
21. Sri Sathya Sai Baba, *Ramakatha Rasavahini I*, Sri Sathya Sai Sadhana Trust, Anantapur, 2002, 161–162.
22. Mazzoleni, Mario, *A Catholic Priest Meet Sai Baba*, Sri Sathya Sai Sadhana Trust, Anantapur, 2002, 120.
23. Shroff, Ravindra, 'The Metamorphosis', *Hridya Brindavan A Garland of Gratitude*, Sri Sathya Sai Hostel, Bangalore, 1977, 38.
24. Prakash, C.M., 'The Joy of God's Presence', *Hridya Brindavan A Garland of Gratitude*, Sri Sathya Sai Hostel, Bangalore, 1977, 72–77.
25. Aitken, Bill, *Sri Sathya Sai Baba: A Life*, Penguin India, New Delhi, 2006, 2.
26. Ibid. 250
27. Ibid. 242
28. Ray, Abhijit, 'The Human in the Divine', *Hridya Brindavan A Garland of Gratitude*, Sri Sathya Sai Hostel, Bangalore, 1977, 18.

29. 'Mesmerizing Moments with the Divine Master', *Radio Sai Listeners' Journal*, Vol. 6, No. 5, 2008, https://archive.sssmediacentre.org/journals/Vol_06/01MAY08/14-h2h_special.htm.
30. Ramana Rao, B.V., *Love is My Form*, Sri Sathya Sai Sadhana Trust, Anantapur, 2000, 21–22.
31. Sandweiss, Samuel H., *With Love Man is God*, Birthday Publishing Co., San Diego, CA, 2004, 83.
32. Baskin, Diana, *Divine Memories of Sathya Sai Baba*, Sri Sathya Sai Sadhana Trust, Anantapur, 1990, 6.
33. Ibid. 35
34. Mazzoleni, Mario, *A Catholic Priest Meet Sai Baba*, Sri Sathya Sai Sadhana Trust, Anantapur, 2002, 68.
35. Gupta, Mahendranath, *The Gospel of Sri Ramakrishna*, Sri Ramakrishna Math, Chennai, 1944, 78.
36. Ibid. 89–90
37. Tillich, Paul, *The Courage To Be*, Yale University Press, New Haven & London, 1952, xxi–xxii.
38. Sandweiss, Samuel H., *Sai Baba: The Holy Man and The Psychiatrist*, Sri Sathya Sai Sadhana Trust, Anantapur, 1975, 43.
39. Iyer, Sunder, Speech delivered at Cleveland Sai Center, 2004.
40. Sri Sathya Sai Baba, *Prema Vahini*, Sri Sathya Sai Sadhana Trust, Anantapur, 1970.
41. Aitken, Bill, *Sri Sathya Sai Baba: A Life*, Penguin India, New Delhi, 2006, 103–104.
42. Sri Sathya Sai Baba, *Sanathana Sarathi, 2016*, https://www.sssbpt.info/ssspeaks/volume26/d930412.pdf.
43. Ibid.
44. Ibid.
45. Ibid.
46. Ibid.
47. Ibid.
48. Levin, Howard, *Good Chances*, Sri Sathya Sai Towers Hotels Pvt. Ltd., Anantapur, 1996.

CHAPTER 6: ACCEPTANCE AND ACTION

1. Tolstoy, Leo, *A Confession*, 1882, 65–67, https://archive.org/details/leo-tolstoy_a-confession_aylmer-maude/page/n65/mode/2up?q=%22belief+in+that+Will%22.
2. Underhill, Evelyn, *Mysticism*, Methuen & Co. Ltd., London, 1911, https://ccel.org/ccel/underhill/mysticism.
3. Ibid.
4. Sheen, Fulton J., *Life of Christ*, Image Books/Doubleday, New York, NY, 1977, 46, https://sacredheartshrine.org/wp-content/uploads/2018/08/Life-of-Christ-Fulton-J.-Sheen.pdf.
5. Ibid. 87
6. Sathya Sai Speaks: Discourses by Sri Sathya Sai Baba (translated into English), https://sssbpt.info/english/sss.htm.
7. Jhalani, Anoop, 'The Search for God', *Hridya Brindavan A Garland of Gratitude*, Sri Sathya Sai Hostel, Bangalore, 1977, 1.
8. Nouwen, Henri J.M., *Life of the Beloved*, The Crossroad Publishing Co., New York, NY, 1992, 43–44.
9. Gardner, Howard, *Changing Minds: The Art and Science of Changing Our Own and Other People's Minds*, Harvard Business School Publishing, Boston, MA, 2004, 5, https://archive.org/details/changingmindsart00gard/.

10. James, William, *The Varieties of Religious Experience*, Longmans, Green, and Co., New York, 1902. The Project Gutenberg eBook, 2014, https://www.gutenberg.org/files/621/621-h/621-h.html.
11. Sathyajit Speaks in Sundaram; Samarpan: Talk by Sathyajit Salian, YouTube, https://www.youtube.com/watch?v=n1EkDctaCPg; https://www.youtube.com/watch?v=CurEidEPOx0.
12. Bhagvantham, S., 'The Myriad Facets of Sri Sathya Sai Baba', *Hridya Brindavan A Garland of Gratitude*, Sri Sathya Sai Hostel, Bangalore, 1977, 23.
13. Gokak, V.K., *Bhagavan Sri Sathya Sai Baba*, Abhinav Publications, New Delhi, 1975, 21.
14. Changkakoti, Rupak, Personal Interview, 2009.
15. Sandweiss, Samuel H., *Sai Baba The Holy Man and The Psychiatrist*, Sri Sathya Sai Sadhana Trust, Anantapur, 1975, 50.
16. Hislop, John S., *My Baba and I*, Sri Sathya Sai Sadhana Trust, Anantapur, 1999, vii.
17. Ibid. 15–16
18. Sandweiss, Samuel H., *Sai Baba The Holy Man and The Psychiatrist*, Sri Sathya Sai Sadhana Trust, Anantapur, 1975, 25–26.
19. Krystal, Phyllis, *Sai Baba: The Ultimate Experience*, Sri Sathya Sai Sadhana Trust, Anantapur, 1998, 77.
20. Schulman, Arnold, *Baba*, The Viking Press, New York, NY, 1971, 68.
21. Ibid. 168
22. Gupta, Mahendranath, *The Gospel of Sri Ramakrishna*, Sri Ramakrishna Math, Chennai, 1944, 625.
23. Sri Sathya Sai Baba, *Summer Roses on The Blue Mountains*, Sri Sathya Sai Sadhana Trust, Anantapur, 1977, 236.
24. Aitken, Bill, *Sri Sathya Sai Baba: A Life*, Penguin India, New Delhi, 2006, 33.
25. Gupta, Mahendranath, *The Gospel of Sri Ramakrishna*, Sri Ramakrishna Math, Chennai, 1944, 568.
26. Aitken, Bill, *Sri Sathya Sai Baba: A Life*, Penguin India, New Delhi, 2006, 140.
27. James, William, *The Varieties of Religious Experience*, Longmans, Green, and Co., New York, 1902. The Project Gutenberg eBook, 2014, https://www.gutenberg.org/files/621/621-h/621-h.html.
28. Sandweiss, Samuel H., *Sai Baba The Holy Man and The Psychiatrist*, Sri Sathya Sai Sadhana Trust, Anantapur, 1975, 84.
29. Mazzoleni, Mario, *A Catholic Priest Meets Sai Baba*, Sri Sathya Sai Sadhana Trust, Anantapur, 2002, 58.
30. Gupta, Mahendranath, *The Gospel of Sri Ramakrishna*, Sri Ramakrishna Math, Chennai, 1944, 173–174.
31. Ibid. 836
32. Chandra, Y. Satish, 'The Eternal Benefactor', *Golden Age*, Kingdom of Sathya Sai, Bangalore, 1979, 22.
33. St Augustine, *The Confessions of Saint Augustine*, Christian Classics Ethereal Library, Grand Rapids, MI, 1999, 230, https://ccel.org/ccel/a/augustine/confess/cache/confess.pdf.
34. James, William, *The Varieties of Religious Experience*, Longmans, Green, and Co., New York, 1902. The Project Gutenberg eBook, 2014, https://www.gutenberg.org/files/621/621-h/621-h.html.
35. Hislop, John S., *My Baba and I*, Sri Sathya Sai Sadhana Trust, Anantapur, 1999, 15–16.
36. Nouwen, Henri J.M., *Life of the Beloved*, The Crossroad Publishing Co., New York, NY, 1992, 36–37.
37. Sandweiss, Samuel H., *With Love Man is God*, Birthday Publishing Co., San Diego, CA, 2004, 39.

38. Nouwen, Henri J. M, *Life of the Beloved*, The Crossroad Publishing Co., New York, NY, 1992, 53–54.
39. Sri Sathya Sai Baba, *Prema Dhaara 3*, Sri Sathya Sai Sadhana Trust, Anantapur, 2009, 138.
40. Tillich, Paul, *The Courage To Be*, Yale University Press, New Haven & London, 1952, 160.
41. Navaratri, in Hinduism, is a major festival honouring the divine feminine. It occurs over nine days during the month of Ashvin or Ashvina (in the Gregorian calendar, usually September–October). It often ends with Dussehra (also called Vijayadashami) celebrations on the 10th day.
42. Gopal or Gopala is a name for the child Krishna. Govardhan is the mountain that Lord Krishna lifted to save the residents of Gokul. This act earned Sri Krishna the name Giridhar.
43. Pratima (Sanskrit: image or likeness of a deity), also called murti (Sanskrit: form or manifestation) or vigraha (Sanskrit: form), in Hinduism, is a sacred image or depiction of a deity.
44. Ratanlal, B., Personal Interview, 2011.
45. Sandweiss, Samuel H., *Sai Baba: The Holy Man and The Psychiatrist*, Sri Sathya Sai Sadhana Trust, Anantapur, 1975, 47–48.
46. Ibid. 184–185
47. Haraldsson, Erlendur, *Miracles Are My Visiting Cards*. Sai Tower Publishing, Bangalore, 1997, 124.
48. Vahana means 'that which carries, that which pulls' and denotes the being, typically an animal, a particular Hindu God uses as a vehicle. The vahana is often called the deity's mount in this capacity. Brahma's vahana is a hamsa or swan. Garuda, an eagle, is the vahana of Vishnu. Nandi, a bull, is the vahana of Shiva.
49. Ramana Rao, B.V., *Love is My Form*, Sri Sathya Sai Sadhana Trust, Anantapur, 2000, 25.
50. Schulman, Arnold, *Baba*, The Viking Press, New York, NY, 1971, 14.
51. Ibid. 15
52. Mazzoleni, Mario, *A Catholic Priest Meet Sai Baba*, Sri Sathya Sai Sadhana Trust, Anantapur, 2002, 67–68.
53. 'Mesmerizing Moments with the Divine Master', *Radio Sai Listeners' Journal*, Vol. 6, No. 4, 2008, https://archive.sssmediacentre.org/journals/Vol_06/01APR08/14-h2h_special.htm.
54. Schulman, Arnold, *Baba*, The Viking Press, New York, NY, 1971, 169.
55. St Augustine, *The Confessions of Saint Augustine*, Christian Classics Ethereal Library, Grand Rapids, MI, 1999, 159, https://ccel.org/ccel/a/augustine/confess/cache/confess.pdf.
56. Narain, Govind, 'Follow the Master', *Golden Age*, Kingdom of Sathya Sai, Bangalore, 1979, 18–19.
57. Hislop, John S., *My Baba and I*. Sri Sathya Sai Sadhana Trust, Anantapur, 1999, vi–vii.
58. Aitken, Bill, *Sri Sathya Sai Baba: A Life*, Penguin India, New Delhi, 2006, 154.
59. The ashram dairy.
60. The ashram elephant who was attached to Swami.
61. Reeves, Suzie P., *Heaven is This*, Sai Tower Publishing, Bangalore, 2001, 161–162.
62. Ibid. 165–169
63. Ibid. 175–177
64. Ibid. 221
65. Sandweiss, Samuel H., *With Love, Man is God*. Birthday Publishing Co., San Diego, CA, 2004, 186–191.
66. St Augustine, *The Confessions of Saint Augustine*, Christian Classics Ethereal Library, Grand Rapids, MI, 1999, 217, https://ccel.org/ccel/a/augustine/confess/cache/confess.pdf.

67. *Talks with Sri Ramana Maharshi*, Sri Ramanasramam, Tiruvannamalai, 1955, 267.
68. Mazzoleni, Mario, *A Catholic Priest Meet Sai Baba*, Sri Sathya Sai Sadhana Trust, Anantapur, 2002, 58.
69. Tillich, Paul, *The Courage To Be*, Yale University Press, New Haven & London, 1952, 188.
70. Tolstoy, Leo, *A Confession*, 1882, 64–65, https://archive.org/details/leo-tolstoy_a-confession_aylmer-maude/page/n65/mode/2up?q=%22belief+in+that+Will%22.
71. Iyer, V.R. Krishna, 'Lead Kindly Light', *Golden Age*, Kingdom of Sathya Sai, Bangalore, 1979, 26.
72. Sandweiss, Samuel H., *Sai Baba The Holy Man and The Psychiatrist*, Sri Sathya Sai Sadhana Trust, Anantapur, 1975, 80–81.
73. Samarpan and Practical Spirituality: Talks by Sathyajit Salian, YouTube, https://www.youtube.com/watch?v=CurEidEPOx0; https://www.youtube.com/watch?v=AHt_-yvKBDA.
74. Gupta, Mahendranath, *The Gospel of Sri Ramakrishna*, Sri Ramakrishna Math, Chennai, 1944, 368.
75. 'Mesmerizing Moments with the Divine Master', *Radio Sai Listeners' Journal*, Vol. 6, No. 5, 2008, https://archive.sssmediacentre.org/journals/Vol_06/01MAY08/14-h2h_special.htm.
76. Nouwen, Henri J.M., *Life of the Beloved*, The Crossroad Publishing Co., New York, NY, 1992, 44–46.
77. Ibid. 46–47
78. Ibid. 66
79. James, William, *The Varieties of Religious Experience*, Longmans, Green, and Co., New York, 1902. The Project Gutenberg eBook, 2014, https://www.gutenberg.org/files/621/621-h/621-h.html.
80. Underhill, Evelyn, *Mysticism*, Methuen & Co. Ltd., London, 1911, https://ccel.org/ccel/underhill/mysticism.
81. Nouwen, Henri J.M., *Life of the Beloved*, The Crossroad Publishing Co., New York, NY, 1992, 36–37.
82. *Talks with Sri Ramana Maharshi*, Sri Ramanasramam, Tiruvannamalai, 1955, 280–281.
83. 'He is My Swami: Part I', *Radio Sai Listeners' Journal*, Vol. 5, No. 5, 2007, https://archive.sssmediacentre.org/journals/Vol_05/01MAY07/14-h2h_special.htm. Padma Kasturi is the daughter of Prof. N. Kasturi, who lived with Swami for many decades and wrote his biography.
84. James, William, *The Varieties of Religious Experience*, Longmans, Green, and Co., New York, 1902. The Project Gutenberg eBook, 2014, https://www.gutenberg.org/files/621/621-h/621-h.html.
85. Ibid. 43
86. Venkatagiri was a princely state about a hundred kilometres north of Chennai. The Raja of Venkatagiri was one of the early devotees of Baba.
87. Haraldsson, Erlendur, *Miracles Are My Visiting Cards*, Sai Tower Publishing, Bangalore, 1997, 80.
88. Shanti Vedika was a raised octagonal platform in the temple (mandir) compound about 50 yards from the mandir where functions used to take place.
89. Jhoola is a swing hanging by two chains from a frame.
90. Puja samagri are items required for worship like basil leaves, holy water, rose water, betel leaves, areca nut, etc.
91. Ratanlal, B., Personal Interview, 2011.
92. Gardner, Howard, *Changing Minds: The Art and Science of Changing Our Own and Other People's Minds*, Harvard Business School Publishing, Boston, MA, 2004, 62, https://archive.org/details/changingmindsart00gard/.

93. Ibid. 159
94. Hislop, John S., *My Baba and I*, Sri Sathya Sai Sadhana Trust, Anantapur, 1999, 3.
95. Gokak, V.K., *Bhagavan Sri Sathya Sai Baba*, Abhinav Publications, New Delhi, 1975, 80.
96. James, William, *The Varieties of Religious Experience*, Longmans, Green, and Co., New York, 1902. The Project Gutenberg eBook, 2014, https://www.gutenberg.org/files/621/621-h/621-h.html.

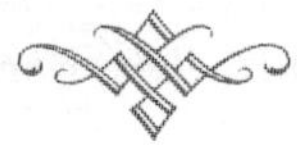

BIBLIOGRAPHY

Aitken, Bill, *Sri Sathya Sai Baba: A Life*, Penguin India, 2006.

Anonymous, *Talks with Sri Ramana Maharshi*, Sri Ramanasramam, 1955.

Baskin, Diana, *Divine Memories of Sathya Sai Baba*, Sri Sathya Sai Sadhana Trust, 1990.

Coe, George A., *The Spiritual Life: Studies in the Science of Religion*, Eaton & Mains, 1900. Internet Archive, 2009.

Edwards, Jonathan, *The Life of Rev. David Brainerd, Chiefly Extracted from His Diary*, American Tract Society. The Project Gutenberg eBook, 2021.

Fowler, James W., *Stages of Faith*, HarperCollins Publishers Inc., 1981.

Gardner, Howard, *Changing Minds: The Art and Science of Changing Our Own and Other People's Minds*, Harvard Business School Publishing, 2004. Internet Archive, 2012.

Gokak, V.K., *Bhagavan Sri Sathya Sai Baba*, Abhinav Publications, 1975.

Gupta, Mahendranath, *The Gospel of Sri Ramakrishna*, Ramakrishna Math and Ramakrishna Mission, 1944. Internet Archive, 2008.

Haraldsson, Erlendur, *Miracles Are My Visiting Cards*, Sai Tower Publishing, 1997.

Hislop, John S., *My Baba and I*, Sri Sathya Sai Sadhana Trust, 1999.

James, William, *The Varieties of Religious Experience*, Longmans, Green, and Co., 1902. The Project Gutenberg eBook, 2014.

Kelman, John, *Among Famous Books*, Hodder and Stoughton, 1912. Internet Archive, 2008.

Kempis, Thomas á, *The Imitation of Christ*, William Collins Sons & Co. Ltd., 1963. The Project Gutenberg eBook, 2023.

Krystal, Phyllis, *Sai Baba: The Ultimate Experience*, Sri Sathya Sai Sadhana Trust, 1998.

Manning, Brennan, *Ruthless Trust: The Ragamuffin's Path to God*, Harper Collins Publishers Inc., 2000.

Mazzoleni, Mario, *A Catholic Priest Meet Sai Baba*, Sri Sathya Sai Sadhana Trust, 2002.

Merton, Thomas, *The Seven Storey Mountain*, Harcourt, Inc., 1999.

Nouwen, Henri J.M., *Life of the Beloved*, The Crossroad Publishing Co., 1992.

Pagels, Elaine, *Beyond Belief*, Random House, 2003.

Penn, Charles, *My Beloved*, Sri Sathya Sai Foundation of Trinidad and Tobago, 1981.

Ramana Rao, B.V., *Love Is My Form*, Sri Sathya Sai Sadhana Trust, 2000.

Reeves, Suzie P., *Heaven is This*, Sai Tower Publishing, 2001.

Roberts, Paul W., *Empire of the Soul: Some Journeys in India*, Riverhead Books, 1996.

Saint Augustine, *Confessions*, Henry Chadwick (trans.), Oxford University Press, 2009.

Salzberg, Sharon, *Faith*, Riverhead Books, 2002.

Sandweiss, Samuel H., *Sai Baba: The Holy Man and the Psychiatrist*, Sri Sathya Sai Sadhana Trust, 1975.

Sandweiss, Samuel H., *Spirit and the Mind*, Sri Sathya Sai Sadhana Trust, 1985.

Sandweiss, Samuel H., *With Love, Man is God*, Birthday Publishing Co., 2004.

Schulman, Arnold, *Baba*, The Viking Press, 1971.

Sheen, Fulton J., *Life of Christ*, Image Books/Doubleday, 1977.

Sri Sathya Sai Baba, *Bhagavatha Vahini*, Sri Sathya Sai Sadhana Trust, 1970.

Sri Sathya Sai Baba, *Discourses on the Bhagavad Gita*, Sri Sathya Sai Sadhana Trust, 1988.

Sri Sathya Sai Baba, *Gita Vahini*, Sri Sathya Sai Sadhana Trust, 2010.

Sathya Sai Baba, *Jnana Vahini: Stream of Spiritual Wisdom*, Sri Sathya Sai Sadhana Trust, 2002.

Sri Sathya Sai Baba, *Prema Dhaara: A Collection of Letters from Bhagavan Sri Sathya Sai Baba to His Students*, Sri Sathya Sai Sadhana Trust, 1999.

Sri Sathya Sai Baba, *Prema Dhaara 3*, Sri Sathya Sai Sadhana Trust, 2009.

Sri Sathya Sai Baba, *Prema Vahini*, Sri Sathya Sai Sadhana Trust, 1970.

Sri Sathya Sai Baba, *Ramakatha Rasavahini I and II*, Sri Sathya Sai Sadhana Trust, 2002.

Sri Sathya Sai Baba, *Sathya Sai Speaks Vol. 1 to 42: Discourses by Sri Sathya Sai Baba*, Sri Sathya Sai Sadhana Trust, 1953–2009.

Sri Sathya Sai Baba, *Summer Roses on The Blue Mountains*, Sri Sathya Sai Sadhana Trust, 1977.

St Augustine, *The Confessions of Saint Augustine*, Edward B. Pusey, D.D. (trans.), Christian Classics Ethereal Library, 2018.

St John of the Cross, *Dark Night of the Soul*, E. Allison Peers (trans.), Christian Classics Ethereal Library, 2009.

Tillich, Paul, *The Courage To Be*, Yale University Press, 1952.

Tolstoy, Leo, *A Confession*, Aegypan Press, 1887, Aylmer and Louise Maude (trans.), 1921. Internet Archive, 2021.

Trevor, John, *My Quest For God*, Labour Prophet Office, 1897. Internet Archive, 2008.

Underhill, Evelyn, *Mysticism: A Study in the Nature and Development of Man's Spiritual Consciousness*, Methuen & Co. Ltd., London, 1911. Christian Classics Ethereal Library.